Advance Praise ... ING CULTURE

"Kembrew McLeod's lively and accessible book makes a persuasive case for the centrality of intellectual property law in shaping popular cultural practices. Rich in contemporary and historical examples that range from hip-hop sampling practices to appropriations of indigenous knowledge, *Owning Culture* will serve as a great introductory text for students in communication, anthropology, and cultural studies."

Rosemary Coombe, Canada Research Chair in Law,
Communication, and Cultural Studies, York University;
author of The Cultural Life of Intellectual Properties:
Authorship, Appropriation, and the Law

"This is the most accessible, entertaining, and compelling book on intellectual property law I have encountered. Kembrew McLeod uses an array of fascinating cases to show how intellectual property law impacts our culture. The results are a sobering demonstration of corporate power and the triumph of property rights over other freedoms."

Professor Justin Lewis, Department of Journalism,
Media and Cultural Studies, Cardiff University, United Kingdom;
author of Constructing Public Opinion

OWNING CULTURE

Toby Miller
General Editor

Vol. 1

PETER LANG
New York • Washington, D.C./Baltimore • Bern
Frankfurt am Main • Berlin • Brussels • Vienna • Oxford

Kembrew McLeod

OWNING CULTURE

Authorship, Ownership, and Intellectual Property Law

PETER LANG
New York • Washington, D.C./Baltimore • Bern
Frankfurt am Main • Berlin • Brussels • Vienna • Oxford

LIBRARY OF CONGRESS CATALOGING-IN-PUBLICATION DATA

McLeod, Kembrew.
Owning culture: authorship, ownership,
and intellectual property law / Kembrew McLeod.
p. cm. — (Popular culture and everyday life; vol. 1)
Includes bibliographical references and index.
1. Intellectual property—Social aspects—United States.
2. United States—Social life and customs. I. Title. II. Series.
KF2979 .M35   346.7304'8—dc21   00-049734
ISBN 0-8204-5157-6
ISSN 1529-2428

DIE DEUTSCHE BIBLIOTHEK-CIP-EINHEITSAUFNAHME

McLeod, Kembrew:
Owning culture: authorship, ownership,
and intellectual property law / Kembrew McLeod
.—New York; Washington, D.C./Baltimore; Bern;
Frankfurt am Main; Berlin; Brussels; Vienna; Oxford: Lang.
(Popular culture and everyday life; Vol. 1)
ISBN 0-8204-5157-6

Cover design by Lisa Dillon

The paper in this book meets the guidelines for permanence and durability
of the Committee on Production Guidelines for Book Longevity
of the Council of Library Resources.

Printed in the United States of America

Table of Contents

Acknowledgments

First, I want to thank Sophy Craze and Toby Miller for caring about this project and giving me the opportunity to bring it to fruition. Sophy was one of the only editors who had a full understanding of what I was trying to convey in this book, and her support and guidance was essential.

For pushing me to go to college even when I didn't want to (and making all of this possible), I thank my mom, and I also thank my dad for teaching me early on to think outside the box, which is what I had to do for this project.

Bruce Busching helped inspire me to pursue an advanced degree, and once I entered grad school David Bromley took me under his wing and provided me with lots of support (and many muffins!). Melissa Click heard about this idea before nearly anyone, and over the course of the five years we lived together (and beyond), she continued to give me encouragement.

A special thank you to Sut Jhally, Briankle Chang, David Lenson, Justin Lewis and Rosemary Coombe, all of whom provided me with sound guidance during the early stages of writing this book. And near the end, Michael England's assistance with formatting my references and endnotes kept everything on schedule.

The idea for the epilogue of this book came from a particularly memorable camping trip with Susan Ericsson, Eric Morgan and Lisa Rudnick, all of whom have heard more than their fair share of talk about intellectual property law. Furthermore, Lisa Rudnick's input when I wrote the first draft of this book was crucial in helping to develop some of the key ideas contained here, more so than she probably realizes.

Thanks to Negativland for getting sued in 1991 and sparking my interest in the topic of intellectual property, and special thanks to Mark Hosler for taking my phone calls about this suit over the course of the 1990s. Also, I appreciate Steve Jones's willingness to look over parts of this manuscript and give his feedback.

Last, but certainly not least, for enduring my endless talk about this project, the following friends and colleagues also deserve a major shout-out: Alpha Anderson, Lee Blackstone, Lynn Comella, Andres Correra, Amanda Cuevas, Bryan Cuevas, Melissa Deem, Esteban Del Rio, Melanie DeSilva, Stuart Downs, Vincent Doyle, Greg Elmer, Kennan Gudjonson, Angie Hauser, Janice Haynes, Lisa Henderson, Nina Huntmann, Nancy Inouye, Ann Johnson, Alicia Kemmitt, Katie Lebesco, Carmen McClish, Michael Morgan, Chris Nelson, Saila Poutianen, Kirk Robinson, Tim Shary, Rob Sloan, Matt Soar, John Sorensen, Allison Speights, Cindy Suopis and Amy Wan.

Collectively, all of you turn on my heart light, especially when I'm caught between the moon and New York City. You are the wind beneath my wings; you're the meaning in my life (you're the inspiration) and nothing compares to you.

In all sincerity, thank you.

Preface

Because I'm writing a book about intellectual property law, there is some relevant information I should divulge before I begin in earnest. I trademarked the phrase "freedom of expression." No, I'm not joking and, yes, I have proof. In my possession I have trademark number 2,127,381 and a certificate from the U.S. government that reads, "The application was examined and determined to be in compliance with the requirements of the law and with the regulations prescribed by the Commissioner of Patents and Trademarks, and that the Applicant is entitled to registration of the Mark . . . Freedom of Expression."

Does this mean I can sue anyone in the United States for using the term without my permission? No, not really. My self-produced publication, *Freedom of Expression*®, was registered only under Class 16 of the international schedule of classes of goods and services, which covers, generally, "printed matter" and the like. But even though I can't prevent someone from using the term in *all* situations, I can still sue for the unauthorized use of "freedom of expression" in *some* contexts.

I first started thinking about issues surrounding intellectual property law, culture and power nearly 10 years ago, when I was an undergraduate working under Professor Bruce Busching. In his office one day, discussing a presentation about intellectual property law I was to do as a teaching assistant for his class in advanced critical social theory, we joked about trademarking "freedom of expression" and, after some thought, I decided to try it. It took me a while to trademark the phrase because, unlike corporations that have the deep pockets to shell out the money for the numerous trademarks they register, I simply did not have the $245 it would cost to immediately register it.

Three years later I underwent the process of registering the mark, starting with searching a database to make sure no one else had beaten

me to the proverbial punch, after which I carefully filled out the application form and dropped a check in an envelope. Because that fee was
nonrefundable, it was an unnerving process because the U.S. Patent and
Trademark Office (PTO) might, as one person told me, "laugh my application out of the office." I had an uneasy feeling that someone in the
government would see that my application was nothing more than a satirical joke, a comment on what I have labeled "the private ownership of
culture." This phrase refers to the increasing expansion of what intellectual property law can protect, including human genes, scents, the term
"white meat" and particular shades of green. (When the Starbucks Coffee
chain moved into Amherst, Massachusetts, where I worked on my doctor-
ate, an independently owned coffee shop received a letter threatening
legal action for daring to serve coffee in plain green cups—apparently,
Starbucks trademarked that shade of green in conjunction with food and
drink service items.)

Despite the eyebrow-raising examples mentioned above, I thought that
the PTO would draw the line with my idea. In fact, my application did hit
a snag early on when the PTO sent a letter informing me that aspects of
it were "not acceptable." Fortunately, it wasn't that the PTO found the
idea of someone owning "freedom of expression" morally, socially and
politically unsettling; I had simply filled out the application incorrectly.
Because, in part, "the mark is not typed entirely in capital letters," as a
PTO lawyer wrote, I had to amend my application, after which I waited
approximately six months to receive in the mail a certificate designating
me as the owner of freedom of expression®.

I felt like a proud father and wanted to share the news with the rest of
the world. To do so, I came up with the idea of executing a media prank
in which I would threaten to sue someone who used freedom of expres-
sion® without my permission. Regardless of how one feels about the ethics of manipulating the media, I have found media pranks to be an effective, interesting and unconventional way of engaging in cultural criticism
beyond the limited scope of academia. Employing the services of my old
high school prankster friend Brendan Love, who posed as the publisher
of a fictional punk rock magazine also titled *Freedom of Expression*, I
started to lay the groundwork for my plan. To add legitimacy to this potential news story, I hired Attorney at Law Joan R. Golowich (who did not
know this was a joke) to send a letter ordering Brendan to cease and
desist his use of the phrase.

Before I had my first meeting with Ms. Golowich, my boss at Amherst
College Library, Margaret Groesbeck, declared, in the same words some-

one else used a few years earlier, that this lawyer would "laugh me out of her office." Thankfully, I learned that intellectual property law is entirely humorless, and after informing Ms. Golowich of my intention to sue someone for using freedom of expression® without permission and after she examined my documents, she confidently told me that we had a case and that she would draft a letter to Mr. Love immediately. Here are some unintentionally hilarious excerpts from my lawyer's letter:

> We represent Kembrew McLeod of Sunderland, Massachusetts, the owner of the federally registered trademark, FREEDOM OF EXPRESSION . . . Your company has been using the mark Freedom of Expression . . . Such use creates a likelihood of confusion in the market and also creates a substantial risk of harm to the reputation and goodwill of our client. This letter, therefore, constitutes formal notice of your infringement of our client's trademark rights and a demand that you refrain from all further use of Freedom of Expression.

I made copies of the letter and my trademark certificate and sent them, along with a press release, to local media. The point of this particular media prank was to "play it straight" and never let on to a reporter my intention to engage in social commentary—I would let the news story itself be the social commentary. That is, rather than someone reading a quote from me stating "I'm concerned with the way intellectual property law facilitates the appropriation of significant aspects of our culture by corporations . . . blah blah blah," I wanted to orchestrate the story in a way that newspaper readers would come to that conclusion on their own. I did my best to sound serious when a woman with a wonderfully rhyming name that reminded me of a certain suicide ritual, Mary Carey, interviewed me on behalf of the regional paper, the *Daily Hampshire Gazette*.

The story, which fittingly appeared in the Fourth of July weekend edition on the local section's front page, was cleverly titled "Freedom, an expression of speech."[1] Carey did a good job of writing a balanced, "objective" story by interviewing both Brendan and myself, but it was nonetheless slanted in the direction of highlighting the absurdity of someone being able to own freedom of expression®. The article closed with the following poker-faced quote from myself: "I didn't go to the trouble, the expense and the time of trademarking Freedom of Expression just to have someone else come along and think they can use it whenever they want."[2]

Unfortunately, the *Daily Hampshire Gazette* refused to give me permission to reprint the article in this book. After I filled out the paper's copyright notice form, informing them that the article was a prank, the paper returned my request to reprint it with a handwritten note that stated simply, "Permission *denied*. [signed] Jim Hardy, Editor 3/18/99."[3] (The *Gazette* did not want me to reprint it, obviously, because the paper had no desire to be embarrassed by having it used in an unfavorable context.) I was especially struck by the fact the editor emphasized his disapproval by underlining "denied," and I wondered if he was at all aware of the irony that he was using copyright law to attempt to prevent the reprinting of an article that was itself *about intellectual property law being employed to restrict freedom of expression!*

Even if I did reprint the article in full, it ought to fall within the domain of "fair use" as outlined the 1976 U.S. copyright statute. "Fair use" evolved from court decisions that recognized the fact that absolute control of copyrighted works would circumscribe creativity and, perhaps more importantly, limit commerce.[4] The "fair use" statute recognizes that, in certain contexts, aspects of copyrighted works can be legally reproduced, and it allows for the appropriation of copyrighted works for use in, for instance, "criticism, comment, news reporting, teaching . . . scholarship, or research," according to the 1976 U.S. copyright statute.[5] Fair use may apply to a variety of other situations not listed above, and in determining whether a work is fair use, the U.S. Congress outlined the following four factors:

(1)   The purpose and character of the use, including whether such use is of a commercial nature or is for nonprofit educational purposes

(2)   The nature of the copyrighted work

(3)   The amount and substantiality of the portion used in relation to the copyrighted work as a whole

(4)   The effect of the use upon the potential market for or value of the copyrighted work[6]

Nevertheless, the *Daily Hampshire Gazette* could still bring a copyright infringement lawsuit against Peter Lang Publishing and myself, and the paper could get an injunction to keep the book from being distributed until a ruling. Although it is true that such a reprint might be considered "fair use" in a court of law, it is possible that it wouldn't; this uncertainty is fueled by the inconsistency and contradictions surrounding intellectual property case law. Even the 1994 2 Live Crew Supreme Court ruling (*Campbell v. Acuff-Rose Music, Inc.*)—which expanded the criteria for judging "fair use"—was ambiguous, particularly (but not only) because it referred to "fair use" only within the context of parody.[7]

In the end, there is no certainty that a court would rule that the reprinting of the *Daily Hampshire Gazette* article was "fair use," and if a court did, the newspaper could still engage in a long, costly appeals process. Because of this very real scenario, my publisher won't allow me to reprint it in the first place, the result of what the Supreme Court has called a "chilling effect." In "'The Sound of Silence': Academic Freedom and Copyright," Whitely discusses the ways in which copyright works to restrict what can be reprinted in academic books and journals, to make it more difficult to engage with certain cultural texts in order to critique or discuss them.[8] (I use "cultural text" as a broad term that refers to songs, television shows, motion pictures, web sites and a variety of other forms of cultural expression.)

Responding to Whitely's essay, Timothy Taylor supported her assertions, giving personal examples of the way in which copyright law, to a certain extent, shaped and limited the content of his book, *Global Pop* (examples that, after speaking to numerous colleagues, he said were fairly commonplace).[9] Taylor stated,

> My editor at Routledge tended to be extremely cautious about such matters; if we had a refusal from anyone, no matter how unconsidered, he wouldn't allow anything to be reprinted save the usual four or five lines of lyrics. I don't think this is an unusual practice on his part, but simply cautious; no editor wants to be the person of whom an example is made in a lawsuit. And this, of course, is the way the "industry" operates: they can't go after everyone, but they can go after someone in enforcing their extremely narrow (and, to them, profitable) notion of what "fair use" means.[10]

In 1991, Sut Jhally, professor of communication at the University of Massachusetts, Amherst, received a letter from MTV's lawyers for his use of the trademarked MTV logo and copyrighted broadcasts in his *Dreamworlds* video, which critiqued the sexist images contained in many of the videos MTV aired. In a letter to Jhally and to the university, MTV threatened legal action if Jhally did not cease his distribution of the *Dreamworlds* video. This is a clear example of how intellectual property law is used ideologically, because it is obvious that this educational video, which featured a sober British voice lecturing over the video images, without music, did not threaten MTV's market.

In other words, no one was going to purchase a copy of *Dreamworlds* in place of watching the network's programming; quite simply, MTV did not like the opinion that Jhally was espousing. Despite the fact that Jhally's appropriations of the music network's intellectual property fit the very definition of "fair use," as well as the fact that University of Massachusetts lawyers acknowledged this, the lawyers advised Jhally to not make a public issue of MTV's actions.

When Jhally insisted on continuing his distribution of *Dreamworlds*, the university lawyers backed away and told him he was on his own because—like most organizations or businesses—they did not want to deal with a potentially costly lawsuit. In response, Jhally set up the Media Education Foundation (MEF) to distribute the video and to take the brunt of any lawsuit, then proceeded to play a game of legal chicken with MTV, sending out press releases to major news outlets, many of which picked up the story.[11]

MTV officials never publicly responded to Jhally's critique in *Dreamworlds*, nor did it pursue further legal action, presumably because they knew the video genuinely did constitute "fair use" and because they had suffered the public embarrassment of Jhally calling their legal bluff. Since 1991, MEF has employed the most liberal notions of "fair use," producing numerous videos that use privately owned media texts to engage in cultural criticism.

Returning to the issue of academic book publishing, there are numerous other examples of authors engaging in criticisms of media texts who are being denied copyright permission to reprint the very thing they are critiquing. Em Griffin, in his introductory book for communication undergraduates, reprinted an analysis of a Diet Coke television commercial that a former student gave, and then wrote:

> Although Marty's reading of the Diet Coke commercial may not appear particularly radical, it includes a significant—if implicit—social critique. Highlighting our culture's obsession with thinness, he suggests that the ad plays to viewer anxiety over excess pounds through association with the rotund pachyderm. In fact, Marty's claim that the ad targeted weight-conscious viewers was sufficiently subversive to incur the disapproval of Coca-Cola. The company expressed its displeasure with his analysis by denying me permission to run photos from the ad in this book.[12]

Em Griffin told me that, like most book deals, his contract with McGraw-Hill required him to secure permission to reprint copyrighted materials. Because Coca-Cola was "so adamant that under no circumstances would they let this be used in connection with Marty's critique," Griffin said, "I didn't pursue the issue when they said [his critique] would have to be dropped before they gave permission. . . . Put another way, I was scared off."[13]

When Sut Jhally was finalizing a contract with Routledge for a book that would be much like *Dreamworlds* but critiqued sexist images in media texts more broadly, he hit a major snag when he insisted on using numerous advertisements and images without asking permission, claiming "fair use." The Routledge editor checked with the legal department of Thompson International, the parent company, but the lawyers refused to allow these unauthorized reprintings despite the fact that it was exactly this type of appropriation for which the "fair use" statute was written. Many businesses, institutions and universities are reluctant to sanction critiques and other intellectual endeavors that fit the definition of fair use because of the extremely high expense of litigating an intellectual property case.

Therefore, letters from corporate lawyers act as *de facto* cease-and-desist court orders, and the proliferation of these letters gives way to self-censorship. In this environment, the obvious question to ask is how in the world are people supposed to critique the ubiquitous, privately owned texts that help shape our consciousness without being able to reproduce them? ("Okay, close your eyes and imagine a scantily clad woman and a Diet Dr. Pepper bottle, now. . . .") People still do engage in such activities within more independent organizations like Jhally's Media Education Foundation. Businesses that must make more conservative interpretations of "fair use" as a protection from costly litigation, however, are far more constrained.

Notes

1   Carey, M. (1998, July 4–5). Freedom, an expression of speech. *Daily Hampshire Gazette,* p. 9.

2   Ibid., p. 9.

3   Jim Hardy, personal communication, March 18, 1999.

4   Buskirk, M. (1992). Commodification as censor: copyrights and fair use. *October, 60,* pp. 82–109.

5   Ibid., p. 91.

6   Elias, S. (1996). *Patent, copyright & trademark: A desk reference to intellectual property law.* Berkeley: Nolo Press, p. 169.

7   (1994). *Campbell v. Acuff-Rose Music, Inc.*, 114 S. Ct. 1164 (U.S.S.C.).

8   Whitely, S. (1997). "The sound of silence": Academic freedom and copyright. *Popular Music, 16, 2,* pp. 220–222.

9   Taylor, T. D. (1998). "Fair use isn't fair": A response to Sheila Whitely. *Popular Music, 17, 1,* pp. 129–132.

10   Ibid., pp. 129–130.

11   Sut Jhally, personal communication, July 29, 1999.

12   Griffin, E. (1997). *A first look at communication.* New York: McGraw-Hill, p. 17.

13   Em Griffin, personal communication, September 7, 1999.

Chapter 1

The Private Ownership of Culture

This book demonstrates how the fabric of social life in most Western countries—and increasingly, the world—is becoming more deeply immersed in the domain of intellectual property law. Intellectual property law has expanded to allow for a number of bemusing and sometimes disturbing scenarios. For instance, Mrs. Smith's (the multimillion dollar food corporation) threatened to sue Mrs. Bacon (the owner of a small St. Petersburg, Florida bakery) for her unauthorized use of the phrase "old fashioned," which Mrs. Smith's had trademarked.[1] In another example, Human Genome Sciences has patented over 100 human genes or gene fragments that are connected to various diseases,[2] and AOL/Time-Warner owns the song "Happy Birthday to You" and polices its public use.[3] And, in the most wacky and postmodern of ironies, Kraft Foods Inc. owns the trademark to "real" in conjunction with cheese, even though the vegetable oil laden, individually wrapped foodstuff slices they market certainly do not fit the definition of real cheese. Furthermore, Kraft Foods Inc. can use intellectual property law to prevent other food companies that make cheese that is *genuinely real* from using that marker of authenticity!

I hope that my narrative about trademarking freedom of expression® in the preface to this book was not *simply* an exercise in self-indulgence; it touched on many of the central points here. First, like all property law, intellectual property law reinforces a condition whereby individuals and corporations with greater access to capital can maintain and increase unequal social relations. Corporations stake their claims on many areas of culture because they can easily afford to pay for numerous $245 application fees, something ordinary people like myself most certainly cannot do. While $245 may not seem to be a huge amount of money that is out of reach for many people, the cost of registering hundreds of thousands of trademarks is. This makes the privatization of culture an activity that only large corporations can engage in. Perhaps more important than the actual *capital* required to register trademarks is the *cultural capital* needed to do such a thing; that is, it would not even occur to the vast majority of people to trademark something.

Further, having access to vast amounts of capital allows corporations to purchase already existing "warehouses" of cultural software (i.e., the copyrights and trademarks for television shows, motion pictures, etc.). Because the ownership of cultural software represents one of the most lucrative contemporary markets, intellectual property law helps facilitate the increasing consolidation of ownership that is taking place in communication industries by giving intellectual property-owning companies more leverage to buy others out.

Speaking of corporate consolidation, gone are the "good old days" when self-censorship was the result primarily of centralized ownership—back when a news story or program would be pulled because it might offend the parent company (of course, this is still the case). Now, intellectual property-holding companies can exercise their influence on companies to which they are not connected by refusing to grant permission for the use of a sound sample, photograph, movie clip, newspaper article and whatnot. Even the mere threat of a lawsuit may prevent a work that appropriates from an intellectual property holder from being distributed, as is the case with the viable scenario I discussed earlier concerning the *Daily Hampshire Gazette*. Coombe states:

> Faced with the threat of litigation, most local parodists, political activists, and satirical bootleggers will cease their activities. Lawyers advising their clients as to whether to threaten an injunction when they find their copyright or trademarks used in an unwelcome fashion will not be considering the most liberal readings of Lockean natural rights theory, but the most conservative of judicial opinions.[4]

Coombe documents that an increasingly diminishing number of defenses are available in intellectual property cases, and that "free speech defenses are inconsistently interpreted and often dismissed without due consideration."[5] Just as the *Daily Hampshire Gazette* employed copyright law to attempt to prevent the reprinting of their article (ostensibly to save them from embarrassment), intellectual property law is often used ideologically to prevent the use of a property from being used in unfavorable contexts.

When my lawyer stated that Brendan's unauthorized use of freedom of expression® "creates a substantial risk of harm to the reputation and goodwill of our client," it may have sounded silly. But the language she used is common to trademark litigation, especially because "harm to the reputation" of a trademark holder is often cited when a trademark is used in a manner that is subversive or unflattering to the owner. It is important to note that because so much of our communicative and social practices take place in domains in which some form of commercial activity is engaged, it becomes easier to justify (and win) intellectual property lawsuits on the theory that somewhere profit is directly or indirectly made.

All this is not to say that the effects of centralized ownership is no longer a concern. It is just that intellectual property law creates an additional variable to consider when looking at the limitations placed on freedom of expression®. In fact, centralized ownership and intellectual property law often work together in disturbing ways, especially in the area of biotechnology, a field that is dominated by a shrinking number of firms that have been infused with a massive amount of capital following the expansion of what patent law can protect. At the turn of the century, hundreds of human genes that are connected to AIDS, breast cancer and many other diseases are being patented by biotech and pharmaceutical companies, giving those firms a government-sanctioned monopoly over potential treatments and cures that are linked to those privately owned genes.[6] It is one thing for the cultural products that help shape the consciousness and imagination of the public to be privately owned by an increasingly consolidated constellation of media firms. But it's another thing altogether for a rapidly shrinking number of powerful biotech and pharmaceutical firms to privately own *the materials that constitute human life itself.*

Intellectual Property Law

Copyright, trademark and patent law protect different types of cultural expression or information. They have emerged out of distinct histories, but people tend to use them interchangeably. For instance, in different parts of the *Daily Hampshire Gazette* article I wrote about in my preface, the reporter referred to freedom of expression® as both a trademarked and a patented good. For her, the newspaper readers, and some readers of this book, these two terms might mean the same thing, but they are certainly not. So to alleviate any confusion, I will provide a very brief overview of patent, copyright and trademark law in the United States, as well as the body of law that protects celebrity images—the right of publicity.

Copyright Law
Copyright applies to all types of original expression, including art, sculpture, literature, music, songs, choreography, crafts, poetry, flow charts, software, photography, movies, CD-ROMs, video games, videos and

graphic designs.[7] Copyright only applies to literal expression, and not the underlying concepts and ideas of that expression (that is, you cannot copyright an idea).[8] The differentiation between an idea and the protected *expression* of that idea highlights the way Enlightenment and Romantic notions of originality and authorship are deeply embedded in contemporary copyright law, a subject I will return to near the end of this chapter.

There is a strong connection between the rise of capitalism, the invention of the printing press, and the commodification of literary and artistic domains, and copyright law was the first piece of legislation to arise from the collision of the above-mentioned concepts.[9] In 1710, Britain passed the Statute of Anne, which was akin to modern copyright law, and in 1790 the U.S. Congress passed a copyright law similar to the 1710 British statute, before most major European countries had copyright laws. This is not surprising considering the fact that an early draft of the Declaration of Independence sought to protect life, liberty and "property" rather than "the pursuit of happiness," as in the well-known phrase contained in the final draft.

Copyright owners are extremely powerful and have at times flexed significant lobbying muscle. For instance, until 1998 the period of copyright protection lasted for the life of the author plus 50 years unless the creator was a business, in which case the period of protection lasted for 75 years. But many of Disney's copyrights to its most lucrative characters were due to lapse near the turn of the century, with (horror of horrors!) Mickey Mouse passing into the public domain in 2004, and Pluto, Goofy and Donald Duck following in 2009.[10] Disney, along with the Motion Picture Association of America (MPAA), heavily lobbied Congress to pass legislation to extend copyright coverage for an extra 20 years, which Congress did.[11]

Trademark Law

As a form of intellectual property law, trademark law developed from a body of common law that was concerned with protecting commercial marks from being misused and misrepresented by competing companies.[12] Trademark law is also a federal statute and it grew out of nineteenth-century court decisions surrounding "unfair competition" business practices. Trademark law is concerned with how businesses may "identify their products or services in the marketplace to prevent consumer confusion, and protect the means they've chosen to identify their products or services against use by competitors."[13]

Among the things that can be trademarked are distinctive words, phrases, logos and graphic symbols used to identify a product or service. Examples include MacDonald's golden arches, Prince's gender-bending squiggle symbol, or Kraft Real Cheese. Trademark law is not simply limited to protecting symbols, logos, words or names; it also covers shapes, sounds, smells, numbers and letters. (In 1997, hip-hop star Warren G sued country star Garth Brooks for the unauthorized use of the lower case letter "g," which he had trademarked.)[14]

Patent Law

Patent law protects from unauthorized commercial use certain types of inventions registered through the PTO, which grants three types of patents. The first, utility patents, are granted to useful inventions that fit into at least one of the following categories: "a process, a machine, a manufacture, a composition of matter or an improvement of an existing idea that falls into one of these categories."[15] The second, design patents, "must be innovative, nonfunctional and part of a functional manufactured article"; a bottle or flashlight design that doesn't improve functionality would qualify.[16] A plant patent, the third type, "may be issued for any asexually or sexually reproducible plants (such as flowers) that are both novel and nonobvious."[17] This last type of patent covers living matter and is relatively recent, the product of a 1980 Supreme Court decision that ruled that an applicant could patent a genetically engineered bacterium.[18] This type of patent expanded, by the mid-1990s, to include human genes, cell lines, proteins, genetically engineered tissue and organisms.[19]

Right of Publicity Law

The oddball in this list, right of publicity law, evolved from legal principles different from copyright, trademark and patent law. Nevertheless, right of publicity, which protects celebrity images from being appropriated in a commercial context without permission, functions in much the same way these other intellectual property laws do. Like trademark law, it does not have a "fair use" component written into law, thus making it easier for celebrities to regulate the contexts in which their images appear. Right of publicity law descends from right of privacy law, and it came into existence to meet a particular social and economic need that developed over the twentieth century. Raymond Williams argued that the logic of capitalism necessarily requires previously untouched areas of cultural activity to be brought into this web of commodity relations. The transformation of *right to privacy*, a nonproprietary law, into *right of publicity*, a proprietary law, is an example of this.[20]

The Industrialization of Culture

Herbert Schiller asserts that, by the late twentieth century, most symbolic production and human activity had become immersed in commodity relations.[21] "In the 1990s," Schiller writes, "the production, processing, and dissemination of information have become remarkably concentrated operations, mostly privately administered."[22] In addition, there has been a growth of corporate power primarily resulting from government deregulation, privatization of once public functions, and the commercialization of activities that previously were not a part of the economic sphere.[23] Schiller argues that a "total corporate information-cultural environment" is spreading throughout the globe, including not just movies and television shows, but banking and other economic and financial networks.[24] To this extent, by the mid-1990s, intellectual property accounted for over 20% of world trade, roughly $240 billion U.S. dollars.[25]

Bettig wrote *Copyrighting Culture* as an attempt to extend the line of thinking that runs through the political economy of communication literature to the area of intellectual property. Although Bettig discusses the ideological functions of media ownership to a certain extent, *Copyrighting Culture* is first and foremost an examination of the appropriation and commodification of information and culture. Intellectual property is significant to his analysis of media ownership, especially because companies that control the copyrights of cultural "software" (back catalogs of music, films, television shows, etc.—for instance, Disney) are considered by many investment firms to be extremely lucrative, perhaps the most profitable companies in the communications market. Furthermore, ownership of intellectual property significantly enhances a company's ability to maneuver in the corporate landscape of culture industries. For instance, Hollywood was able to muscle its way into the cable television industry because of its massive holdings of cultural software.[26]

Schiller focuses on the intensifying push toward the privatization of as many forms of social activity as possible, which were brought under corporate control during the latter part of the twentieth century.[27] Sites where culture is produced (public schools) or made available (public libraries, museums, theaters, etc.) have been brought under the direct influence of private corporations that, in turn, influence the form culture takes.

[B]y the close of the twentieth century, in highly developed market economies at least, most symbolic production and human creativity have been captured by and subjected to market relations. Private ownership of the cultural means of production and the sale of the outputs for profit have been the customary characteristics. The exceptions—publicly supported libraries, museums, music—are few, and they are rapidly disappearing. The last fifty years have seen an acceleration in the decline of nonmarket-controlled creative work and symbolic output. At the same time, there has been a huge growth in commercial production.[28]

New technologies have facilitated both the growth of culture industries and the explosion of information-producing sectors. Both of these areas have been marked by the consolidation of ownership through mergers and acquisitions. An example of this is the 1989 merger of Time and Warner Brothers to create Time-Warner, the subsequent merger of Time-Warner with Turner Broadcasting in 1996, and America Online's acquisition of the Time-Warner empire.[29] As the result of this consolidation of media corporations, the dominance of a few firms works to ensure that a more limited range of expression is communicated. These factors, Schiller maintains, contribute to the homogenization of culture, shaped to meet the interests of the corporate parents that own the sites where culture is produced and the venues where cultural texts are distributed.[30]

Public information has been extensively privatized in the postwar period. This is characterized by the privatization of governmental information that once was made available largely for free to the public, the close relationship between universities and big business (especially in the sciences), and the commercialization of information in the library field. For instance, before World War II, there were no large companies organizing, managing and distributing information, and information gathering centered around universities, government agencies and public libraries. Government materials were not considered lucrative and therefore were not copyrighted. But during the 1950s and 1960s computers facilitated the emergence of information industries, and recent decades have seen the widespread privatization of national and governmental information contained in databases managed by private companies.[31]

With the government increasingly contracting out information to private firms, the primary channels that citizens used to gain access to this information have been restricted in many ways. For instance, while Supreme Court, Federal Court and lower court records are still available for free, companies such as Westlaw control the intellectual property rights to such information as it exists in a more accessible form, and it charges heftily for access to it. Records of scientific data and medical studies that had previously resided in the public domain are very often held by private companies that have a financial stake in restricting the flow of that information. Even if that information is readily available, there is no guarantee it will be organized in a way that benefits the welfare of the public.[32]

Corporations have been extremely resourceful in securing new areas of culture to inhabit and own, and the National Information Infrastructure (NII, or as then Vice President Al Gore called it, the "Information Superhighway") is a good example.[33] Private corporations led the charge to build the NII, and have—with the Reagan, Bush and Clinton administrations' encouragement—invested billions of dollars in telecommunications in the 1980s and 1990s.[34] Those who put up the capital for this new "highway" will get to decide where it's built, who will be admitted and what information can flow through it.

Adding to the unabated privatization of public-owned information resources was the selling off of sections of the radio spectrum to facilitate the increased activity of communication industries. When those sections of the radio spectrum were in government hands, at least there was the *possibility* that they might be used in the public interest. But now that these sections are in the hands of private companies (AT&T and Sprint secured significant portions for themselves), there are no such guarantees. Ultimately, a privately owned information system will contain all the key features of the private industries that came before it: inequality in the distribution of resources.[35]

By primarily focusing on ownership patterns and the effects of the corporate ownership of culture, political economists of communication have often ignored many interesting questions that are raised when cultural texts (songs, television programs, etc.) become commodified and subject to intellectual property laws. Of course, the questions they ask are still very important and central to my own research and communication research in general, but many times studies that employ a purely political economic analysis do not examine *cultural practice* to any great extent. When one looks beyond the political economy of cultural production (with its focus on the determined effects of larger social structures) and examines the *location where culture is produced* (e.g., the day-to-day lived experiences of musicians, writers, etc.), a whole new set of questions emerge.

Specifically, when these areas of cultural production become immersed in the activity generated by intellectual property law, we can ask what happens to: (1) the method used to produce cultural texts (e.g., how a song is composed and recorded); (2) the social ties between groups of individuals involved in the production of similar cultural texts (e.g., the relationships among scientists in a field that becomes subject to patent law); (3) the way in which cultural texts are constructed (e.g., what a piece of visual collage art actually looks like); and (4) the relationship between the consumers of culture and the cultural texts (e.g., what an audience does with a favorite television show).

Cultural Production and the Law

The legal studies literature dealing with intellectual property law is massive and varied. For instance, some scholars have engaged in discussions about the relationship between trademark protection and cultural expression, highlighting how the lack of a strong "fair use" provision in this type of law often limits free speech.[36] Others have discussed "fair use" in copyright law and other limitations surrounding the application of the provision."[37] Even more have extended the previously mentioned concerns through right of publicity law, questioning (or concretely illustrating) how the expanding right of publicity, the privatization of most aspects of celebrity identities, circumscribes the way the public and fans may use celebrity images within various forms of cultural expression.[38] Some scholars have looked at appropriation within the art world, discussing particular cases where the "parody fair use" defense was invoked unsuccessfully.[39] This is but a brief list of the many lines of inquiry that have addressed intellectual property law and, because the literature is so huge, I will focus on two significant works in this field.

In *Contested Culture*, Jane Gaines asks the following questions. First, does intellectual property law proscribe certain aesthetic forms? Second, does the presence of intellectual property law ensure the existence of some forms and not others? Third, do we need to figure into theories of meaning the notion that intellectual property law determines the availability of popular signs? The title of Gaines's book, in part, comes from Stuart Hall's conceptualization of popular culture as being a contested site of movement between containment and resistance. Similarly, copyright law functions in two opposite directions, as a monopoly grant that allows both the limiting of cultural expression and (by not granting a copyright) the free distribution of forms of cultural expression.[40] Gaines invokes the phrase "double movement" to describe the directional tendency to promote both circulation and restriction. But, she argues, because of the nature of intellectual property law and its inherent ties to a capitalist mode of production, property claims often win out over freedom of speech claims.[41]

Using a trademark on different products (T-shirts, gum, etc.) reasserts one's ownership and economic control over signs of great cultural resonance, what Gaines calls "a kind of high-finance squatter's rights."[42] She argues that many intellectual property lawsuits involve, at some level, a policing of what meanings a cultural text has for people, for instance, Mattel's watchful eye over how Barbie's image is used. Intellectual property owners attempt to bind a sign to its originary source, the commodity, but when it leaves the owner's corporate orbit and is distributed to a wide audience, the property faces reinterpretation and rearticulation.[43] An example of these ideological contestations comes from the self-publishing world of zines (short for "fan magazines"). *Hey There, Barbie Girl!*, a photocopied black-and-white sixteen-page zine, used the Barbie doll as the object of discourse around which creative critiques of gender and sexuality took the form of poetry, satirical advertisements and a forum for readers in the "letters to the editor" section.

The Barbie doll provides a common experience for many young American girls and women who at one time played with it and the doll is perceived in many ways, ranging from being a feminist pioneer to an oppressive patriarchal symbol of an idealized woman.[44] The doll served as a perfect signifier around which the readers and editors of *Hey There, Barbie Girl!* could construct their own representations of Barbie that did not necessarily reflect the corporate producer's intents. Unfortunately, Mattel did not appreciate these critiques and after the publication of the second issue titled "Our Barbies, Ourselves," the company sent the zine a letter threatening legal action, citing copyright and trademark violations. Similarly, Coombe states, "Teenage girls who have used the Barbie name to call attention to homemade proto-feminist fanzines, available over the Internet, have been told by Mattel to cease using the name or face legal action."[45]

Rosemary Coombe's *The Cultural Life of Intellectual Properties* focuses on how intellectual property regimes both engender and endanger practices of subcultural resistance. Looking at a large number and eclectic range of resistive practices that engage with privately owned intellectual properties, Coombe argues that intellectual property law both creates spaces of action for, and prevents acts of, resistance. By providing the legal mechanisms for protecting these signs so that they may be distributed on a mass scale, intellectual property law helps generate a myriad of cultural signifiers around which marginal groups can mobilize. Simply put, intellectual property law creates the type of legal protection that allows corporations to feel comfortable enough to invest in the distribution of signs that dissident groups, in turn, may infuse with oppositional meanings. Therefore, intellectual property law ironically creates the space for oppositional groups to appropriate widely known symbols, though it often shuts down these unauthorized appropriations later on.[46]

Intellectual property owners are increasingly socially and legally endowed with, as Coombe puts it, "monopolies over public meaning"[47] and the ability to police the cultural contexts in which these public meanings are exhibited. Like Gaines, Coombe understands privately owned signifiers as occupying sites of conflict, and one of her primary concerns is the fact that intellectual property law may prevent the optimal cultural conditions for engaging in a democratic dialogic practice.[48] For instance, trademark law has no formally written "fair use" statute, and this gives much less potential room for freedom of expression. Federal law protects trademarks from being portrayed in an "unwholesome or unsavory context," which allows courts to suppress uses of famous cultural icons that are unauthorized, even when there is no reasonable possibility of confusion.[49]

Coombe gives a number of examples that illustrate this point, including an environmental rights group that used a caricature of the Reddy Kilowatt trademark in literature that was critical of the electric utility industry. An injunction against this use was upheld by the court because it ruled that, essentially, you cannot use a trademarked property to express yourself—it constituted a type of trespassing.[50] A similar example Coombe gives is the following:

> The Manitoba Court of Appeal, for example, allowed the Safeway grocery chain to enjoin picketing workers from using the stylized S from the company's logo in its strike literature. Deciding that the insignia was known to the public, the court determined it was an asset connected with the company's goodwill, and thus that the company had proprietary rights in it: "there is no right under the guise of free speech to take or use what does not belong to [you]."[51]

As Stuart Ewen points out, in North American culture, and in an increasing number of other cultures, communication and meaning-making are largely mediated though images.[52] We use powerfully coded images and signs to articulate certain observations about our world. Coombe argues that corporate trademarks and brand names are at the center of signifying practices in postmodern culture, and that cultural activity increasingly involves the recoding of commodified cultural forms. She argues:

> Brand names have become so ubiquitous that they provide an idiom of expression and resources for metaphor. With phrases like the Coca-Cola-ization of the Third World, the Cadillac® (or the Edsel) of stereo systems, meeting with the

Birkenstock® contingent (or the Geritol® generation), we convey messages easily and economically.[53]

The use of these privately owned images and signs is subjected to the constraints placed on them by intellectual property laws, which essentially function as the traffic laws that are used to police the exchange of cultural expression on the privatized information superhighways of modern communicative practice. But just like real car-infested roads, some people ignore traffic laws, speed, and drive without registration, while others slow down when they see the police or stay off the roads completely when their license has been revoked. Intellectual property laws do not determine the behavior of individuals, but the way laws become bound up with certain areas of cultural production works to shape conditions under which we are able to navigate our own lives.

Articulation and Cultural Production

Articulation, as the word has evolved within cultural studies, carries a double meaning. To speak, or to be articulate, is the more common understanding of the term in the United States, but it is the second meaning—a joining of different parts—that is of primary interest here. Hall states, "An articulation is thus the form of the connection that *can* make a unity of two different elements, under certain conditions. It is a linkage which is not necessary, determined, absolute and essential for all time. You have to ask, under what circumstances can a connection be made?"[54]

Within the writings of Hall, Laclau, Grossberg and Slack, articulation is most commonly discussed in the context of discourse, ideology and political formations.[55] Hall states, "A theory of articulation is both a way of understanding how ideological elements come, under certain conditions, to cohere together within a discourse, and a way of asking how they do or do not become articulated, at conjunctures, to certain political subjects."[56] Articulation theory can trace its origins to Gramsci, particularly to his theory of hegemony, which is a process whereby a particular class or group exercises power over shaping the ways in which a subordinate group makes sense of the world (therefore eliminating the need for a constant exercise of violent coercion).

For instance, the hegemonic idea of the "American Dream" is extremely powerful in America, and underlies support for eliminating social programs, even from members of disadvantaged groups. People from lower economic classes have internalized individualistic notions of "pulling yourself up from the bootstraps" and the like, even when it can be statistically demonstrated that working hard does not guarantee social and economic success. Instead, of course, the most important factor is the economic class one is born into. Slack states, "The vehicle of this subordination, its 'cement,' so to speak, is ideology . . . Gramsci offers a way of understanding hegemony as the struggle to construct (articulate and re-articulate) common sense out of an ensemble of interests, beliefs and practices."[57]

Laclau's major contribution to a theory of articulation was to move away from the class reductionism that had often figured into what came to be known as Marxism. The inability of this sort of reductionism to account for the fact that certain classes embraced ideologies that were not in their interest pushed Laclau to replace the concept of economic determinism with articulation. Laclau does not set ideology free to float in a sea of random connections; rather, he uses articulation to highlight the process of *hegemony*.[58] He argues that no particular discourse or ideology has an essentialized class position; it is through articulation that certain discursive meanings become linked to different classes or social groups in certain ways.[59]

Although in the past 20 years articulation has almost exclusively been theorized around discourse, ideology and political formations, it can also be usefully employed to understand the nondetermined, contingent effects that result when differing spheres of social activity merge and are articulated with one another. It is this conception of articulation that concerns Marx in "Results of the Immediate Process of Production," in which he discusses the effects of what happens when capitalism comes in contact with other modes of economic activity.[60] He further argues, "Capital subsumes the labour process as it finds it, that is to say, it takes over an existing labour process, developed by different and more archaic modes of production." Marx states, "*Capitalist production* has a tendency to take over all *branches of industry* not yet acquired . . . Once it has appropriated agriculture and mining, the manufacture of the principal textiles etc., it moves on to other sectors where the artisans are still *formally* or even genuinely independent."[61]

Marx then goes on to identify the particular elements that become connected within capitalist production, and it is this careful, systematic identification of the articulated elements that comprises the bulk of Marx's writings (though Marx never uses that term specifically). In a number of essays, Marx sketches out a way of viewing the evolution of capitalism in terms that were later echoed by articulation theorists.[62] For instance, in historicizing the development of capitalism, Marx states in *The German Ideology* that capitalism "may also occur *sporadically*, as something which does not dominate society, at isolated points within earlier social forma-tions."[63] Marx's *The German Ideology* and *Capital* could be considered to be among the first studies of articulation, with the former's more broad survey of the way one mode of production becomes articulated with another mode, and the latter's systematic analysis of the way in which capitalism "works."

In this book I theorize articulation through the ways in which social formations become articulated to each other. Articulation theory has lesser-known origins that evolved out the "modes of production debates," which emerged out of a concern with the way Marxists conceived the evolution of capitalism in underdeveloped, Third World countries. Frank rejected the notion of a "dualist thesis" that conceived of Latin America as coex-isting in both capitalist and feudalist sectors; instead, he posited that once it initially encountered mercantile capitalism, Latin America became al-most instantly integrated into the capitalist world system.[64] Instead, he argued for a theoretical model that considers the way various cultural and economic elements are articulated, an argument taken up by Alavi, Fos-ter-Carter, Rey and Dupre, and Jhally.[65]

Unfortunately, this notion of articulation has not been developed over the past 20 years in any substantial manner. Here, I wish to recover that earlier formulation of articulation theory so it can be used to understand the transformations of *cultural* production when it is immersed in intel-lectual property law. I employ articulation theory to make sense of the varied contexts in which the law and cultural production become con-nected to each other. This allows us to understand the similarities and differences in the way intellectual property law affects various areas of cultural production without reducing them to *merely* being similar and different. Instead, they are explained through the historically contingent and socially situated interconnections I map throughout. In short, this book demonstrates *how* connections are made, and *why* they are impor-tant. In my development and application of articulation theory, I make three distinct moves.

First, I use articulation as a way of understanding how and why intel-lectual property law is usually referred to in the singular when it is actually comprised of different laws with very distinct histories. These laws are not grouped together just because they have traditionally been included in the same sections of law books. There is a deeper principle operating that goes beyond the obvious observation that they all protect mostly intan-gible objects, or cultural texts. That deeper principle at work is a notion of authorship and ownership that is grounded in Western Enlightenment philosophy and Romanticist thought.

Authorship is a construct that is deeply connected with notions of originality and uniqueness that are Western in origin and relatively recent. It is these notions of originality and individuality that constitute the definition of the author, a definition that informed the construction of copyright law. In addition, copyright law was heavily steeped in Lockean notions of labor and property, in which an object becomes a person's property by mixing one's labor with it. Therefore, authorship and ownership are extensively bound up with each other to the point that authorship cannot logically exist in the absence of the concept of ownership. Articulation theory is used to understand not just the interconnectedness of the twin operating logics of intellectual property law (authorship and ownership), but also the way in which all types of intellectual property laws are joined to each other through these central, grounding assumptions. (Later in this chapter, I'll engage in a more detailed discussion of authorship and ownership.)

The second theoretical move I make is to use articulation to frame an analysis of the expanding sphere of intellectual property law as it encompasses areas of cultural production that haven't been affected to a great degree by intellectual property law. In doing so, we can carefully map and understand *how* these areas come to be articulated with each other.

In chapters 2 through 6, I look at the particular ways various areas of cultural production are articulated with intellectual property law in order to demonstrate how we can make sense of the similarities and differences in a historically grounded and socially situated way, so that notions of structure and determination are not completely lost. I identify some of the primary characteristics of the areas of cultural production examined, illustrating how they become articulated with the logic(s) of intellectual property law. (For instance, in chapter 4 I examine how visual collage artists and traditional photographers, whose pictures appear in mass circulation periodicals and are used by collage artists, both employ radically different notions of authorship and originality.) By framing the analysis of different areas of culture within articulation theory, we can understand the way spheres of culture become entangled, connected—articulated—in the new relations fostered by intellectual property law.

The third and final theoretical move I make is to demonstrate how the very different areas of cultural production examined in this book are connected to *each other*, how they are articulated with the others *through* intellectual property law. For instance, an Iowa-based corn farmer and, say, multiplatinum hip-hop artist Dr. Dre have so little in common that they might lapse into uncomfortable silence if the two were stuck together in a broken elevator. Nevertheless, both of them have been affected by the encroachment of intellectual property law on their respective areas of cultural production. The advantage of taking this theoretical perspective is that we can analyze the effects of a social formation as broad as religion, capitalism or, in a less sweeping example, intellectual property law *without* losing sight of determination *or* the specifically situated manner in which they are immersed within people's lived experiences.

I do this in my treatment of all the areas of cultural production examined throughout this book: folk and blues, "world music" and sound collage, hip-hop and African-American oral folk preaching, seed and human gene patenting, visual collage, celebrity images, consumer data collection, and farming. Articulation theory provides a framework for understanding how a vast array of people and cultures can be negatively affected by a single intellectual property regime (much like what occurs within biological, interconnected ecosystems when foreign agents have been inserted in them). I will put it another way. If you will pardon the pun, this may help hip-hop producers who are worried about how copyright law restricts the way they construct their *beats* to understand why they should also care about how patent law restricts the way farmers can grow and replant their *beets*.

I should emphasize that I am not using articulation as a method similar to that of textual critic, in the literary studies sense. That is, in my "readings" of the contemporary cultural and legal scene, I am not asserting that there are connections between things like hip-hop and farming when there are, in fact, no such articulations in the real world. The various and seemingly disparate areas of cultural production discussed in this book *are* linked to each other through how they are similarly impacted by intellectual property law. Most certainly, these topics are not typically linked to each other within popular political discourse. Neither are issues of intellectual property law, environmentalism, fair trade, globalization and labor practices, but as we saw during the 1999 WTO protests in Seattle, however, these very different issues brought together a number of disparate groups to generate one of the most significant recent public protests in the U.S.

Intertextuality and the Social Construction of Authorship

In addition to articulation, intertextuality is an important concept that helps frame my analysis. Intertextuality has been extensively theorized in cultural studies, with Fiske's writings being a notable example. "The theory of intertextuality," Fiske states, "proposes that any one text is necessarily read in relationship to others and that a range of textual knowledges is brought to bear upon it."[66] He maintains that those relationships need not take the form of direct references to other existing works, nor, Fiske claims, does the reader have to necessarily be familiar with the specifics of the referenced work. Intertextuality has figured into other important cultural studies works, such as that of Bennett and Woollacott, Jenkins, Williams, Goodwin and others, almost exclusively with regard to its use in understanding the way audiences read and work with media texts.[67]

While this is an interesting and fruitful line of inquiry, I am more interested in the intellectual trajectory that cultural studies originally borrowed from—*literary theory*. To begin with a concrete definition from Julia Kristeva, who is credited with coining the term, intertextuality is grounded in the proposition that "every text builds itself as a mosaic of quotations, every text is an absorption and transformation of another text."[68] While the intertext of a particular story may be made up of any number of narrative elements, from plot, genre, and other conventions, one can go further and define "text" as a system of signs, whether those signs be a literary work, motion pictures, television shows, or the very things that structure "real life."[69]

Kristeva's (and other literary theorists') conception of intertextuality—which equally considers how intertextuality figures into the *production* of texts and the *reception* of texts—fits better with my focus on the cultural production of texts by individuals and groups. The understanding of intertextuality as being central to *both* reading and writing (in the broadest sense of those terms) figures into the following comments by Kristeva, who states, "It is impossible to read *Finnegans Wake* without entering into the intrapsychic logic and dynamics of intertextuality. . . . If one reads Faulkner without going back to the Bible, to the Old testament, to the Gospels, to American society of the period and to his own hallucinatory experience, I believe one cannot reconstitute the complexity of the text itself."[70]

Implicit in Kristeva's statement above is not just a taking into account of the act of reading, but the motivations of the text's writer, or at least an awareness that intertextual referencing can be deliberately deployed in writing. Similarly, Still and Worton argue Rousseau was not unaware of contemporary church practices or St. Augustine's work of the same name when he entitled his autobiography *The Confessions*.[71] They claim, "This repetition of past or of contemporary texts can range from the most conscious and sophisticated elaboration of other poets' work, to a scholarly use of sources, or the quotation (with or without the use of quotation marks) of snatches of conversation typical of a certain social milieu at a certain historical moment."[72]

Of course, the act of reading brings with it another form of intertextuality in which the remembered history of previously read texts (and one's own life) is brought to bear on the text. I diverge from the way intertextuality has been developed in cultural studies in order to be able to better treat intertextuality within cultural *production* (as it exists, for example, in folk singing, collage art and the sampling methods hip-hop artists employ). As will become evident in chapters 2 through 4, intertextuality is central to a number of areas of cultural production, past and present. It is a concept that allows us to understand social processes in a way that can destabilize relatively contemporary Western notions of authorship and originality.

The Origins of Authorship

Aspects of Enlightenment philosophy informed copyright in its early stages. The strain of "possessive individualism" that was echoed in, for instance, the philosophies of Locke and Hobbes was responsible for the expansionist, colonial activity of early capitalism in England. This type of "possessive individualism" compliments the assumptions that underlie copyright law.[73] In addition, in his philosophical conjectures about personhood and authorship, Hobbes marks a distinction between originality and derivation in a way similar to the thinking of others of his time who helped shape notions of authorship and the formation of copyright. In *Leviathan*, Hobbes uses originality as a measure of a writer's authenticity. "A person is he, whose words or actions are considered, either as his own, or as representing the words or actions of an other man," Hobbes writes. "When they are considered as his own, then is he called a *Naturall* Person: And when they are considered as representing the words and actions of another, then is he a *Feigned* or *Artificall person*."[74]

At the beginning of the eighteenth century, the concept of "the author" had yet to be fully defined in England, but soon a more individualist notion of authorship came into being and came to be articulated with a liberal discourse concerning property and a Romanticist discourse concerning the "original genius."[75] Similar to what happened in England, though a few decades later, a group of eighteenth-century writers in Germany found it increasingly difficult to live by the pen. At the time, the patronage system was breaking down, but no form of copyright protection or established literary market allowed them financial security. Reacting to this, these writers and other Enlightenment-era philosophers attempted to redefine the nature of writing, and their reflections helped ground the modern notions of authorship that still exist today.

During the first half of the eighteenth century the "author" was the unstable marriage of two dissimilar concepts that were inherited from Renaissance ideas about authorship. First, the author was a "craftsman" who adhered to a body of rules and who manipulated traditional materials in ways that satisfied the audience of the court (which made the author's livelihood possible). Second, the author occasionally was seen to rise above those requirements and to achieve something "higher," something that was attributed to a muse, or even to God. The idea that the author was both a "craftsman" and "inspired" lasted well into the eighteenth century, and it was generally assumed that in those cases of inspiration that the author was not personally responsible for his or her acts.[76] Woodmansee writes:

> Eighteenth-century theorists departed from this compound model of writing in two significant ways. They minimized the element of craftsmanship (in some instances they simply discarded it) in favor of the element of inspiration, and they internalized the source of that inspiration. That is, inspiration came to be regarded as emanating not from outside or above, but from within the writer himself. "Inspiration" came to be explicated in terms of *original genius,* with the consequence that the inspired work was made peculiarly and distinctively the product—and the property—of the writer.[77]

Writing in the second half of the eighteenth century, Edward Young argued for an emphasis on originality over a mere mastery of rules and traditions. In Young's essay *Conjectures on Original Composition*, he wrote: "The man who reverences himself, will soon find the world's reverence to follow his own. His works will stand distinguished; his the sole property of them; which property alone can confer the noble title of an author."[78] While the essay drew little attention in England at the time, it had a profound impact in Germany. German philosophers—including Herder, Goethe, Kant and Fichte—elaborated on Young's ideas and emphasized these particular notions of authorship, ownership and originality.

Fichte argued that an author had a proprietary claim over the *form* his or her writing takes. That is, the ideas the author attempts to convey are the common property of both the author and the reader, but the *form* in which these ideas are presented remains the exclusive property of the author. Fichte argued that writers must be willing to hand over their form by making their thoughts public because "no one can appropriate his thoughts without thereby altering their form. This latter thus remains forever his exclusive property."[79]

In his writings, Goethe departed markedly from Renaissance and neo-classical notions of the writer being merely a vehicle for ideas, and he redirected the genesis of those expressed ideas as coming from a writer who transforms thoughts in ways that makes them unique. Goethe described writing as "the reproduction of the world around me by means of the internal world which takes hold of, combines, creates anew, kneads everything and puts it down again in its own form, manner."[80] Similarly, Herder observed:

> Any poem, even a long poem—a life's (and soul's) work—is a tremendous betrayer of its creator, often where the latter was least conscious of betraying himself. Not only does one see in it the man's poetic talents, as the crowd would put it; one also sees which sense and inclinations governed him, how he received images, how he ordered and disposed them and the chaos of his impressions . . .[81]

Many of the legal battles within eighteenth-century Britain that led to a formalized copyright law were informed by emerging Enlightenment notions of what constitutes originality, authorship and ownership, particularly Locke's development of an individualistic form of property. In a well-known passage in his *Two Treatises of Government*, Locke writes,

> Though the Earth, and all inferior Creatures be common to all Men, yet every Man has a *Property* in his own *Person*. This no Body has any Right to but himself. The *Labour* of his Body, and the *Work* of his Hands, we may say, are properly his. Whatsoever then he removes out of the State that Nature hath provided, and left it in, he hath mixed his *Labour* with, and joyned to it something that his own and thereby makes it his *Property*.[82]

Locke's theory of natural law influenced the framers of the U.S. Constitution and it continues to influence contemporary court decisions in the United States, from lower courts to the Supreme Court. Gordon points out that, nevertheless, Locke's writings don't provide as much protection as some advocates have tried to assert. Gordon writes, "Locke's labor theory of property and allied approaches have been used so frequently as a justification for creators' ownership rights that Locke's *Two Treatises* have been erroneously credited with having developed an explicit defense of intellectual property."[83] Such misinterpretations have high stakes, especially in a contemporary world where the distribution of certain ideas and texts are policed by intellectual property owners who employ the law to suppress certain texts. Gordon writes:

> Judges have failed to use the First Amendment to provide extensive protection for free expression in intellectual property cases, in part because they mistakenly find a warrant for strong "authors' rights" in a philosophy of natural law. Natural

rights theory, however, is necessarily concerned with the rights of the public as well as with the rights of those whose labors create intellectual products. When the limitations in natural law's premises are taken seriously, natural rights not only cease to be a weapon against free expression; they also become a source of affirmative protection for free speech interests.[84]

Despite the misinterpretations of Locke's ideas about intellectual property, his writings became influential for writers, publishing houses and others during the eighteenth century, arguing for increased protection under copyright law. For instance, Locke's ideas about the creation of property are echoed not only in the writings of Goethe and Herder quoted above, but in the following passage written by John Bunyan in *Holy War*, published in 1803. He writes:

> Manner and matter too were all mine own,
> Nor was it unto any mortal known,
> Till I had done it. Nor did any then,
> By books, by wits, by tongues, or hand, or pen,
> Add five words to it, or write half a line:
> Therefore the whole, and every whit is mine.[85]

In addition to the arguments and claims of writers, legal decisions around this time also began to connect—articulate—Lockean ideas of personal property with authors' rights. Just as Locke understood property as being created when a person mixes one's labor with materials found in nature, the author's "property" became "his" own when he stamps his personality on the work—doing this in an "original" manner. For instance, a lawyer involved in litigating early copyright cases argued, "When a man by the exertion of his rational powers has produced an original work, he has clearly a power to dispose of that identical work as he pleases, and any attempt to take it from him, or vary the disposition he has made of it, is an invasion of his right of property."[86]

The characterization of originality as a central and critical value in cultural production developed during the same period as the notion of the author's property right. And during the second half of the eighteenth-century the doctrine of originality had become dominant, with Samuel Johnson stating at the time in his "Life of Milton" that "the highest praise of genius is original invention."[87] Mark Rose notes the continuity between earlier literary property debates and modern copyright doctrine when he states:

> By 1774 . . . all the essential elements of modern Anglo-American copyright
> law were in place. Most important, of course, was the notion of the author as the

creator and ultimate source of property. This representation of authorship was at the heart of the long struggle over perpetual copyright; it survived the determination that literary property was limited in term; and it remains central to copyright today.[88]

The paternity metaphor, the idea that a creative work is one's "baby," is a very common one and, in fact, the word "plagiarism" is derived from the Latin term for "kidnapping." In 1710, Daniel Defoe referred to literary theft as a kind of child snatching:

> A Book is the Author's Property, 'tis the Child of his Inventions, the Brat of his Brain; if he sells his property, it then becomes the Right of the Purchaser; if not, 'tis as much his own as his Wife and Children are his own—But behold in this Christian Nation, these Children of our Heads are seiz'd, captivated, spirited away, and carry'd into Captivity, and there is none to redeem them.[89]

During the time preceding the passage of the Statute of Anne, many of the philosophical, legal and popular writings had begun to formulate and codify a discourse about the proprietary ownership of an author's words and ideas. Although the most familiar metaphor was one of paternity (and it still continues to this day), the rhetorical idea of selling a child in the marketplace was a bit tasteless for some, so another comparison gained ground. Literary property was reconceived as a landed estate, and during the first half of the eighteenth century this new metaphor was adopted by courts, legislatures, publishers and writers, and this contributed to a new way of thinking about literature.[90] Rose writes about "the simultaneous emergence in legal discourse of the proprietary author and the literary work. The two concepts are bound to each other. To assert one is to imply the other, and together, like the twin suns of a binary star locked in orbit, they define the center of the modern literary system."[91]

During the second half of the eighteenth century, two landmark literary property legal decisions were ruled upon. *Millar v. Taylor* (1769) and *Donaldson v. Becket* (1774) both centered on a dispute over the use of James Thomson's long introspective landscape poem titled *The Seasons*, a poem that was extremely popular in England and therefore a valuable commodity. In many ways, this poem perfectly fit the definition of Lockean literary property, in that it took changing landscapes of mountains, rivers, meadows and plains found in nature and imprinted the author's original ideas and sentiments on those "raw materials" found in nature.[92]

Justice Aston, ruling on the *Millar v. Taylor* case, wrote, "I confess, I do not know, nor can I comprehend any property more emphatically a man's own, nay, more incapable of being mistaken, than his literary works."[93] The judge was referring to the imprinting of the author's personality on his or her work, and the justification for authors having the right to own their words was the fact that their works were the embodiment of their personalities. Rose writes, "The basis of literary property, in other words, was not just labor but 'personality,' and this revealed itself in 'originality.'"[94] Rose adds, "One logical point of connection between originality and property was *value*; another was *personality*—and of course the notions of value and personality were themselves deeply connected."[95]

The idea that artistic works are the product of an original authorial genius flies in the face of the way cultural texts have always been produced, even during the time this discourse was developed. To ground this with an example, many "classical" composers occasionally borrowed from the melodic themes found in European folk musics, from their own previous works, and from each other, for that matter.[96] Bach adapted Vivaldi's Concerto for Four Violins in B Minor into his Concerto for Four Harpsichords, and Mozart based the finale of his Jupiter Symphony on Hadyn's Thirteenth Symphony in D major.[97] Mahler appropriated a major theme from Brahms' First Symphony, converted it into minor mode, and used it to start his Third Symphony, and Brahms' "First Symphony," which Mahler borrowed from, was built from Beethoven's Ninth Symphony.[98]

When someone pointed out to Mahler the similarity between the two pieces, he dismissed the importance of that observation by snapping, "Any fool can hear that." Beethoven quoted the music of near-forgotten French composers Gossec, Mehul and Lefebvre, and Stravinsky once said, "A good composer does not imitate, he steals." In saying this, Stravinsky explicitly stated what has been made obvious—the fact that the intertextual practice of borrowing, merging and adapting musical phrases and melodies was common within the Western classical music cannon.[99]

Despite these composers' appropriations, no composer's borrowings have been more discussed in music circles than Handel's.[100] Since the nineteenth century and on through today, many music historians have suggested that his melodic borrowings—from others and from himself—should be perceived as a flaw. Handel has been characterized as "a common thief and a shameless borrower" and "morally derelict," and that his appropriations should be understood as the result of a "poverty of melodic invention" or "owing to insufficient compositional impetus."[101] Winemiller argues that these characterizations are shaped by an ideology that positions an author as the originator of a commodity that can be possessed.[102]

Winemiller further argues that the castigation of Handel is symptomatic of the uneasiness surrounding creative works that more explicitly employ an intertextual mode of cultural production. "This anxiety stems largely form the prevailing modern belief that borrowing necessarily signals unoriginality—if not outright plagiarism—since it involves in some way the reuse of existing work."[103] Because Handel's work contained already existing material, the only logical deduction that can be made when operating within this ideological framework is that Handel's borrowings signify a lack of sufficient creativity, a lack of originality.[104]

This notion of originality and authorship was not fully in place by the first half of the eighteenth century when Handel composed his works and, importantly, competing ideologies existed at the time. Winemiller states, "An older conception of creativity that was widely advocated and practiced at the time suggests just the opposite, that borrowing was not only acceptable, but in fact was a preferred method of composition."[105] What was called a theory of "transformative imitation" took hold amongst many writers during the late seventeenth and eighteenth centuries. French writers Boileau and Rapin created "free imitations" that were culled from, in part, numerous uncited sources, and English writers Dryden, Swift, Addison and Pope engaged in, and theorized about, transformative imitation. This theory of transformative imitation also took hold in the visual arts and in musical composition, and for most of the eighteenth century these two notions of creativity coexisted in a somewhat difficult manner.

Alexander Pope and Ben Jonson—who both based their literary writing styles on imitative practices—suffered a fate similar to Handel, in that both their character and their writings were attacked. John Bowle, writing in 1766, stated: "Such a one was Johnson [sic], that he seems to have made it his study to cull out others sentiments and to place them in his works as from his own mint. This surely is an odd species of improvement from reading, and savours very little of Invention or Genius: It borders nearly upon, if it is not really plagiarism."[106] It is obvious from Pope's *Essay on Criticism* that he still held on to a Renaissance view of the writer as being a craftsperson whose job is to express truths carved from traditions rather than to invent novelties. Pope wrote in 1711:

> True wit is nature to advantage dressed;
> What oft' was thought, but ne'er so well expressed;
> Something, whose truth convinced at sight we find,
> That gives us back the image of our mind.[107]

But by the time the English poet William Wordsworth wrote the following passage in 1815, the notion of the author as an individual, original genius was deeply entrenched. Wordsworth argued that "every Author, as far as he is great and at the same time *original,* has had the task of *creating* the taste by which he is to be enjoyed." He continues, "Of genius the only proof is, the act of doing well what is worthy to be done, and what was never done before . . . Genius is the introduction of a new element into the intellectual universe."[108]

Rose argues:

> Property, originality, personality: the construction of the discourse of literary property depended on a chain of deferrals. The distinctive property was said to reside in the particularity of the text—"the same conceptions, clothed in the same words"—and this was underwritten by the notion of originality, which was in turn guaranteed by the concept of personality. . . . As we have seen, copyright is not a transcendent moral idea, but a specifically modern formation produced by printing technology, marketplace economics, and the classical liberal culture of possessive individualism. It is also an institution built on intellectual quicksand: the essentially religious concept of originality, the notion that certain extraordinary beings called authors conjure works out of thin air.[109]

Streeter similarly argues, "As a long-term, Western historical discourse, copyright is the enactment of the dream that the disparate goals and values of individual creative freedom, commerce, and informational dissemination can be reconciled in law."[110] The "romantic author" was in many ways a figure constructed as an offshoot of the individual capitalist entrepreneur whose property rights were secured by Lockean theories of personal property.[111] But—despite the contemporary critiques of authorship by the above-mentioned authors, as well as Foucault, Barthes, Derrida and others—intellectual property law itself has remained unchanged and continues not to recognize a more fluid idea of cultural production.[112]

Jaszi and Woodmansee write, "The problem, at least in part, is that even as the notion of authorship is subjected to the scrutiny of critical theory, the teaching of literature and composition to which future lawyers are exposed continues to reinforce the Romantic paradigm."[113] They point out that, not just in the creative arts, but in business, government, the law and the sciences, writing is done in a collaborative fashion while at the same time it is framed as a solitary, individualistic activity. This creates an unrealistic model whereby everyone fails to measure up to this Romanticist ideal, especially students of non-Western origins who are more prone to not mark the boundaries between "original" and "derivative" material because they haven't internalized early on the basic lessons of intellectual property.[114]

One significant reason why copyright law remains unchanged—despite the contradictions between the Romanticist assumptions about authorship and very real practices of cultural production—is because the law, as it is currently constituted, works to the advantage of wealthy copyright owners. Authorship is typically granted on behalf of publishers rather than writers, or on behalf of the other culture industry firms (television, movie studios, etc.) that own the productions of the creative workers they employ.[115]

In the medium of television, where numerous cultural workers (writers, actors, camera operators, directors, producers, etc.) are involved in the creation of a particular show, the Romantic ideal of an original, individual author completely breaks down. But capital investing corporations are able to stand in as an "author" through the fiction of the "corporate individual" in which corporations have become recognized as legally protected entities (often with more protections than a citizen).[116] Because copyrights are usually assigned to those who own the means of cultural production, intellectual property law benefits wealthy individuals and corporations.[117]

Areas of Cultural Production

In doing research for this book, I conducted 43 interviews with cultural producers involved in areas of cultural production affected by the logic(s) of intellectual property law.[118] In addition, I examined articles from local, regional, national and international newspapers and magazines that reported on areas of cultural production affected by these new social relations. I did some archival research having to do with ownership of, and legal battles over, cultural texts—though this task was made very difficult because many records regarding intellectual property (for instance, internal corporate documents) are considered proprietary. These kinds of documents are impossible to access without resorting to illegal industrial espionage—an intriguing idea, but a breaking-and-entering charge certainly won't help my chances of tenure and promotion.

Legal databases, particularly Westlaw, enabled me to collect the available case law on the subject of intellectual property. But the circumstances surrounding many intellectual property legal actions are impossible to uncover because, first, a large number of these cases are settled out of court and, second, many letters that threaten legal action go unpublicized and unreported. Nevertheless, I used newspaper articles about threatened lawsuits to track down any potential primary legal sources that were useful for my analysis.

To be included as a case study in this book, an area of cultural production had to have gone from not being touched to a great degree by the sphere of intellectual property law to being immersed in that sphere. Therefore, areas of cultural production that include, for instance, software or television industries are not included in this book because from their beginnings each has been impacted by intellectual property law. If I were to have only selected one, two or even three cases, my analysis potentially could be accused of presenting a one-sided, selective account of intellectual property law's immersion in contemporary cultural life. But I believe my project's strength lies, quite literally, in numbers. That is, the validity of my analysis increases with the number of cases I examine that are culled from very different and seemingly disconnected spheres of cultural production. I view this as a kind of triangulation method in which the similar social processes that occur within one area occur in another as well.

Chapter 2 features a social history of the song "Happy Birthday to You," a history that traces the contestations over the use of this privately owned song between a public that largely perceives it to be in the public domain and a company, now AOL/Time-Warner, that needs to police its use to protect its investment. "Happy Birthday to You" has its roots in the folk song tradition—a mode of cultural production that takes existing lyrics and melodies and refashions them into familiar or entirely new compositions. Intellectual property law has redefined this mode of cultural production as copyright infringement, "freezing" folk song production, which (in its mass-distributed form) now exists more as a genre than as a cultural tradition with a rich, vibrant and lengthy history. The birthday song is used as a jumping-off point to launch a broader discussion of how folk music making practices are shut down by the logic(s) of intellectual property law.

In this chapter, I also look at the case of the American Society of Composers and Publishers (ASCAP) which, in 1996, sent out numerous threatening letters to for-profit and not-for-profit summer camps (such as Girls Scouts of America camps) for the unauthorized "public" campfire performances of ASCAP-controlled songs like "This Land Is Your Land" and "Ring Around the Rosie." I document the subsequent public relations fiasco ASCAP found itself in as an example of overt public resistance against the attempt to extend the sphere of intellectual property law into this relatively untouched area of cultural production. Lastly, I suggest that folk music's mode of cultural production *did not* cease but merely shifted to a different type of music-making—that of electronically composed collages built on digital sound samples.

In chapter 3 I examine what happens when an intellectual property law based on Western notions of originality and authorship collide with a culture that conceives of these things in a radically different manner. I focus on the controversy surrounding the discovery that Dr. Martin Luther King Jr. was "guilty" of plagiarism when writing his dissertation. By contextualizing these events within African-American culture—specifically African-American oral folk preaching—I demonstrate that the borrowing of words and ideas was not considered to be the theft of another's property. Instead, it is perfectly in line with the African-American cultural practice of oral folk preaching (in which Martin Luther King Jr., his father and grandfather were immersed), a tradition that had direct roots in an older oral culture that valorized the intertextual practice of "voice merging."

The second aspect of African-American culture I examine in this chapter is the practice of sampling in hip-hop music. I give a history of hip-hop music from its 1970s origins as an urban youth-centered subculture based in the South Bronx to its expansion into a billion-dollar industry in the late 1990s. I demonstrate how the method of music-making used to create hip-hop music, one based on the borrowing of existing music, was altered after its commercial rise and the numerous sampling lawsuits that followed its ascendancy.

Chapter 4 examines the avant-garde visual and sound collage practices that evolved from more rarefied, high art traditions. Today, a common method of constructing sound collages uses digital sampling, but sound collage dates back arguably to 1920 when young composer Stefan Wolpe used eight gramophones rotating at various speeds in a performance piece he arranged. Collage was introduced to the world of visual art by Picasso in 1912 when he glued an object onto one of his Cubist paintings and framed the painting with a piece of rope, making it the first work of fine art to appropriate materials from everyday life. It is the Western European and Anglo-American tradition of collage that is the focus of chapter 4, which traces a history of both visual and sound collage and highlights the technological innovations that facilitated and transformed the creation of these collages. I also discuss the contradictions that arose from the articulation of copyright law and these modes of cultural production.

In chapter 5, I look at the ways pharmaceutical and biotech firms have employed a U.S.-backed international patent system to appropriate indigenous Third World knowledge about the medical uses of local plant life, patenting the active ingredients and genes contained in those plants and turning them into profitable products protected by patent law. As international intellectual property law treaties are more strictly enforced in Third World countries, there is the very real potential of turning these local populations from producers to *consumers* of the knowledge that their culture played a key role in cultivating. This creates a dependence of farmers in both First World and Third World countries on firms that own patents, a trend that has grown even more unsettling with the invention of the so-called terminator seed. The genetically engineered terminator seed kills itself after one season, making it impossible for farmers to engage in an activity that is as old as farming itself—collecting and saving seeds for the next year's crop.

Chapter 6 discusses three very different situations in which aspects of people can be privately owned. First, I examine the ownership of human biological material by pharmaceutical and biotech firms. Second, I look at the way data on consumer behavior are collected, archived and arranged in databases to be sold to marketers. Third, the ownership of celebrity images through "right of publicity law" is examined. In each of these cases, the power relations surrounding the ownership of people's images are vastly different. Unlike celebrities, both those whose genetic material has been patented and consumers whose behavioral data have been collected do not own the means of production (databases, scientific equipment, etc.) used to construct their own abstracted image. Therefore, they have no proprietary rights. As in the rest of the book, I use articulation theory to make sense of the ways intellectual property law places people in very different positions of power.

Chapter 7, the final chapter, briefly returns to articulation theory, and I also expand on my discussion of intertextuality. Also, I look to the future of intellectual property law and cultural production by examining the Internet—one of the most significant and expanding areas of cultural life that is deeply bound up with intellectual property law.

Notes

1   Mrs. Smith has a lot of crust. (1994, December 16). *St. Petersburg Times,* p. 18.

2   Pollack, A. (2000a, June 28). Finding gold in scientific pay dirt. *New York Times,* p. C1.

3   Sold. (1989, January 2). *Time,* 88.

4   Coombe, R. J. (1998). *The cultural life of intellectual properties: Authorship, appropriation, and the law.* Durham, NC: Duke University Press, p. 78.

5   Ibid., p. 77.

6   Meek, J. (2000, June 26). The story of life: Who owns the genome? *Guardian,* p. 8.

7   Elias, S. (1996). *Patent, copyright & trademark: A desk reference to intellectual property law.* Berkeley: Nolo Press, p. 66.

8   Ibid.

9   Bettig, R. V. (1996). *Copyrighting culture: The political economy of intellectual property.* Boulder: Westview Press.

10 Chartrand, S. (1998, October 19). Patents: Congress has extended its protection for Goofy, Gershwin and some moguls of the Internet. *New York Times,* p. C2.

11 Robb, D. (1998, January 28). Early Disney cartoons face loss of copyright. *Denver Rocky Mountain News,* p. 1D.

12 Buskirk, M. (1992). Commodification as censor: Copyrights and fair use. *October, 60,* 82–109.

13 Elias, S. (1996). *Patent, copyright & trademark: A desk reference to intellectual property law.* Berkeley: Nolo Press, p. 324.

14 Elias, S. (1996). *Patent, copyright & trademark: A desk reference to intellectual property law.* Berkeley: Nolo Press; McLeod, K. (1997, November 5). *Warren G and Garth Brooks battle over trademark letter 'g'* [Online]. SonicNet. Available: http://www.addict.com/MNOTW/ hifi/

15 Elias, S. (1996). *Patent, copyright & trademark: A desk reference to intellectual property law.* Berkeley: Nolo Press, p. 187.

16 Ibid., p. 187.

17 Ibid., p. 187.

18 King, J. & Stabinsky, D. (1999, February 5). Patents on cells, genes, and organisms undermine the exchange of scientific knowledge. *Chronicle of Higher Education, 22,* 7–8.

19   Rifkin, J. (1998, April 13). The biotech century: Human life as intellectual prop-
      erty. *Nation,* 11–19.

20   Gaines, J. (1991). *Contested culture: The image, the voice, and the law.* Chapel
      Hill: University of North Carolina Press.

21   Schiller, H. (1973). *The mind managers.* Boston: Beacon Press; Schiller, H.
      (1984). *Information and the crisis economy.* Norwood, NJ: Ablex Corporation;
      Schiller, H. I. (1989). *Culture Inc.: The corporate takeover of public expres-
      sion.* New York: Oxford University Press.

22   Schiller, H. I. (1996). *Information inequity the deepening social crisis in America.*
      New York: Routledge, pp. 124–125.

23   Ibid.

24   Ibid.

25   Harris, L. E. (1998). *Digital property: Currency of the 21st century.* New York:
      McGraw-Hill.

26   Bettig, R. V. (1996). *Copyrighting culture: The political economy of intellec-
      tual property.* Boulder: Westview Press.

27   Schiller, H. I. (1989). *Culture Inc.: The corporate takeover of public expres-
      sion.* New York: Oxford University Press.

28   Ibid, p. 32.

29   Bagdikian, B. (1992). *The media monopoly.* Boston: Beacon Press; Saporito, B.
      & Baumohl, B., et al. (1996, October 21). Time for Turner. *Time,* 72.

30   Schiller, H. I. (1989). *Culture Inc.: The corporate takeover of public expres-
      sion.* New York: Oxford University Press.

31   Ibid.

32   Schiller, H. I. (1996). *Information inequity: The deepening social crisis in
      America.* New York: Routledge.

33   Bettig, R. V. (1996). *Copyrighting culture: The political economy of intellec-
      tual property.* Boulder: Westview Press.

34   Schiller, H. I. (1994). *Information inequity: The deepening social crisis in
      America.* New York: Routledge, 1996.

35   Ibid.

36   Aoki, K. (1997). Using law and identity to script cultural production: How the
      world dreams itself to be American: Reflections on the relationship between the
      expanding scope of trademark protection and free speech norms. *Loyola of Los
      Angeles Entertainment Law Journal, 17,* 523–; Coombe, R. J. (1996). Survey-
      ing law and borders: Authorial cartographies: Mapping proprietary borders in a
      less-than-brave world. *Stanford Law Review, 48,* 1357–; Dorsen, H. K. (1985).
      Satiric appropriation and the law of libel, trademark, and copyright: Remedies

without wrongs. *Boston University Law Review, 65,* 923–; Koenig, D. M. (1994). Joe Camel and the first amendment: The dark side of copyrighted and trademark-protected icons. *Thomas M. Cooley Law Review, 11,* 803–; Kravitz, R. N. (1989). Trademarks, speech and the gay Olympics case. *Boston University Law Review, 69,* pp. 131–; Pearson, A. (1998). Commercial trademark parody, the Federal Trademark Dilution Act, and the First Amendment. *Valparaiso University Law Review, 32,* 973–; Shakow, J. D. (1998). Just steal it: Political sloganeering and the rights of trademark holders. *Journal of Law & Politics, 14,* 199–; Shaughnessy, R. J. (1986). Trademark parody: A fair use and First Amendment analysis. *Virginia Law Review, 72,* 1079–.

37   Crittenden, D. R. (1995). Copyright law—fair use privilege—in an action for copyright infringement, the commercial nature of a song parody does not invoke a presumption against a finding of fair use. *Seton Hall Law Review, 25,* 1256–; Dratler, J. Jr. (1988). Distilling the witches' brew of fair use in copyright law. *University of Miami Law Review, 43,* 233–; Francis, M. M. (1995). The "fair use" doctrine and Campbell v. Acuff-Rose: Copyright waters remain muddy. *Villanova Sports and Entertainment Law Forum, 2,* 311–; Gordon, W. J. (1982). Fair use as market failure: A structural and economic analysis of the Betamax case and its predecessors. *Columbia Law Review, 82,* 1600–; Jacobson, N. (1994). Faith, Hope & Parody: Campbell V. Acuff-Rose, "Oh Pretty Woman," and parodists' rights. *Houston Law Review, 31,* 955–; Lacey, L. J. (1989). Of Bread and Roses and Copyrights. *Duke Law Journal, 1989,* 1523–; Patterson, L. R. (1987). Free speech, copyright and fair use. *Vanderbilt Law Review, 40,* 1–; Trunko, T. D. (1989). Remedies for copyright infringement: Respecting the first amendment. *Columbia Law Review, 89,* 1940–.

38   Cordero, S. M. (1998). Cocaine-Cola, the velvet Elvis, and Anti-Barbie: Defending the trademark and publicity rights to cultural icons. *Fordham Intellectual Property, Media & Entertainment Law Journal, 8,* 599–; Fernandez, C. (1998). The right of publicity on the Internet. *Marquette Sports Law Journal 8,* 289–; Giacoppo, E. (1997). Avoiding the tragedy of Frankenstein: The application of the right of publicity to the use of digitally reproduced actors in films. *Hastings Law Journal, 48,* 601–; Kwall, R. R. (1994). The right of publicity vs. the First Amendment: A property and liability rule analysis. *Indiana Law Journal, 70,* 47–; Langvardt, A. (1997). The troubling implication of a right of publicity "wheel" spun out of control. *Kansas Law Review, 45,* 329–; Madow, M. (1993). Private ownership of public image: Popular culture and publicity rights. *California Law Review, 81,* 125–; Moore, L. (1994). Regulating publicity: Does Elvis want privacy? *Journal of Art and Entertainment Law, 5,* 1–; Pesce, C. (1990). The likeness monster: Should the right of publicity protect against imitation? *New York University Law Review, 65,* 782–; Robinson, R. S. (1998). Preemption, the right of publicity, and a new federal statute. *Cardozo Arts & Entertainment Law Journal, 16,* 183–; Sen, S. (1995). Fluency of the flesh: Perils of an expanding right of publicity. *Albany Law Review, 59,* 739–.

39   Badin, R. (1995, Winter). An appropriate(d) place in transformative value: Appropriation art's exclusion from Campbell v. Acuff-Rose Music, Inc. *Brooklyn Law Review, 60,* 1653–; Greenberg, L. A. (1992). The art of appropriation: Puppies,

piracy, and post-modernism. *Cardozo Arts & Entertainment Law Journal, 11,* 1–; Smith, M. H. (1993). The limits of copyright: Property, parody, and the public domain. *Duke Law Journal, 42,* 1233–.

40   Gaines, J. (1991). *Contested culture: The image, the voice, and the law.* Chapel Hill: University of North Carolina Press.

41   Ibid.

42   Ibid., p. 223.

43   Ibid.

44   Lord, M. G. (1994). *Forever Barbie: The unauthorized biography of a real doll.* New York: Avon Books.

45   Coombe, R. J. (1998). *The cultural life of intellectual properties: Authorship, appropriation, and the law.* Durham, NC: Duke University Press.

46   Ibid.

47   Ibid., p. 26

48   Ibid.

49   Cordero, S. M. (1998). Cocaine-Cola, the velvet Elvis, and Anti-Barbie: Defending the trademark and publicity rights to cultural icons. *Fordham Intellectual Property, Media & Entertainment Law Journal, 8,* 599–.

50   Coombe, R. J. (1998). *The cultural life of intellectual properties: Authorship, appropriation, and the law.* Durham, NC: Duke University Press.

51   Ibid., p. 69.

52   Ewen, S. (1988). *All consuming images: The politics of style in contemporary culture.* New York: Basic Books; Ewen, S. (1996). *PR!: A social history of spin.* New York: Basic Books.

53   Coombe, R. J. (1998). *The cultural life of intellectual properties: Authorship, appropriation, and the law.* Durham, NC: Duke University Press, p. 57.

54   Hall, S. (1996). On postmodernism and articulation: An interview with Stuart Hall. In D. Morley and K. Chen (Eds.), *Stuart Hall: Critical dialogues in cultural studies* (pp. 131–151). New York: Routledge.

55   Hall, S. (1980). Race, articulation and societies structured in dominance. In UNESCO, *Sociological theories: Race and colonialism* (pp. 305–345). Paris: UNESCO; Hall, S. (1985). "Signification, representation, ideology: Althusser and the post-structuralist debates." *Critical Studies in Mass Communication 2, 2,* 91–114; Hall, S. (1996). On postmodernism and articulation: An interview with Stuart Hall. In D. Morley and K. Chen (Eds.), *Stuart Hall: Critical dialogues in cultural studies* (pp. 131–151). New York: Routledge; Grossberg, L. (1992). *We gotta get out of this place: Popular conservatism and postmodern culture.* New York: Routledge; Laclau, E. (1977). *Politics and ideology in Marxist theory.*

London: New Left Books; Slack, J. D. (1996). The theory and method of articulation in cultural studies. In D. Morley and K. Chen (Eds.), *Stuart Hall: Critical dialogues in cultural studies* (pp. 112–127). New York: Routledge.

56   Hall, S. (1996). On postmodernism and articulation: An interview with Stuart Hall. In D. Morley and K. Chen (Eds.), *Stuart Hall: Critical dialogues in cultural studies* (pp. 131–151). New York: Routledge, p. 140.

57   Slack, J. D. (1996). The theory and method of articulation in cultural studies. In D. Morley and K. Chen (Eds.), *Stuart Hall: Critical dialogues in cultural studies* (pp. 112–127). New York: Routledge, p. 117.

58   Laclau, E. (1977). *Politics and ideology in Marxist theory*. London: New Left Books.

59   Ibid., p. 161.

60   Marx, K. (1976). Results of the immediate process of production. In *Capital: A critique of political economy: Vol. 1* (pp. 993–1084). New York: Penguin Books.

61   Ibid., p. 1036.

62   Marx, K. (1978). Capital, Vol. 1. In R. Tucker (Ed.), *The Marx-Engels Reader* (2nd ed.). New York: W. W. Norton.

63   Marx, K. (1978). The German ideology. In R. Tucker (Ed.), *The Marx-Engels Reader* (2nd ed.). New York: W. W. Norton, p. 1022.

64   Frank, A. G. (1970). *Latin America: Underdevelopment or revolution*. New York: Monthly Review Press.

65   Alavi, H. (1973). The state in post-colonial society. In K. Gough & H. P. Sharma (Eds.), *Imperialism and revolution in South East Asia* (pp. 145–173). New York: Monthly Review Press; Foster-Carter, A. (1978, January/February). The modes of production debate. *New Left Review, 107,* 7–33; Jhally, S. (1979). Marxism and underdevelopment: The modes of production debate. *Alternate Routes, 3,* 63–93; Laclau, E. (1971, May/June). Feudalism and capitalism in Latin America. *New Left Review, 67,* 19–38; Rey, P. & Dupre, G. (1973). Reflections on the pertinence of a theory for the history of exchange. *Economy and Society, 2, 1.*

66   Fiske, J. (1987). *Television culture*. New York: Routledge, p. 108.

67   Bennett, T. & Woollacott, J. (1987). *Bond and beyond: Fiction, ideology and social process*. London: Macmillan; Goodwin, A. (1993). *Dancing in the distraction factory: Music television and popular culture*. New York: Routledge; Jenkins, H. (1992). *Textual poachers: Television fans and participatory culture*. London: Routledge; Williams, R. (1974). *Television: Technology and cultural form*. London: Fontana.

68   Newman, J. (1995). *The ballistic bard: Postcolonial fictions*. New York: Arnold.

69   Ibid.

70   Waller, M. (1989). An interview with Julia Kristiva, (R. Macksey, Trans.). In P. O'Donnell & R. C. Davis (Eds.), *Intertextuality and contemporary American fiction* (pp. 280–293).

71   Worton, M & Still, J. (1990). Introduction. In M. Worton & J. Still (Eds.), *Intertextuality: Theories and practices* (pp. 1–44). New York: Manchester University Press.

72   Ibid., p. 1.

73   Jaszi, P. & Woodmansee, M. (1994). Introduction. In R. Jaszi, P. & Woodmansee, M. (Eds.), *The construction of authorship: Textual appropriation in law and literature* (pp. 1–14). Durham, NC: Duke University Press.

74   Stewart, S. (1991). *Crimes of writing: Problems in the containment of representation.* New York: Oxford University Press.

75   Rose, M. (1994). The author as proprietor: Donaldson v. Becket and the genealogy of modern authorship. In B. Sherman & A. Strowel (Eds.), *Of authors and origins* (pp. 158–201). Oxford: Clarendon Press.

76   Woodmansee, M. (1984). The genius and the copyright: Economic and legal conditions of the emergence of the "author." *Eighteenth-Century Studies, 17, 4,* 425–448.

77   Ibid., p. 427.

78   Ibid., p. 430.

79   Ibid., p. 445.

80   Ibid., p. 447.

81   Ibid.

82   Rose, M. (1993). *Authors and owners: The invention of copyright.* Cambridge, MA: Harvard University Press, p. 5.

83   Gordon, W. J. (1993). A property right in self-expression: Equality and individualism in the natural law of intellectual property. *Yale Law Journal, 102,* 1533–, p. 1540.

85   Stewart, S. (1991). *Crimes of writing: Problems in the containment of representation.* New York: Oxford University Press, p. 16.

86   Rose, M. (1993). *Authors and owners: The invention of copyright.* Cambridge, MA: Harvard University Press, p. 115.

87   Ibid.

88   Ibid., p. 132.

89   Rose, M. (1993). *Authors and owners: The invention of copyright.* Cambridge, MA: Harvard University Press, p. 39.

90   Rose, M. (1993). *Authors and owners: The invention of copyright.* Cambridge, MA: Harvard University Press.

91   Ibid., p. 91.

92   Ibid.

93   Rose, M. (1993). *Authors and owners: The invention of copyright.* Cambridge, MA: Harvard University Press, p. 114.

94   Ibid.

95   Ibid., p. 121.

96   Toelken, B. (1986). Ballads and folksongs. In E. Oring (Ed.), *Folk groups and folklore genres: An introduction* (pp. 147–174). Logan, UT, Utah State University Press.

97   Lebrecht, N. (1996, May 11). Echoes strike a chord. *Daily Telegraph,* p. 7.

98   Ibid.

99   Oswald, J. (1995a). Creatigality. In R. Sakolsky and F. Wei-Han Ho (Eds.), *Sounding off! Music as subversion/resistance/revolution* (pp. 87–90). Brooklyn: Autonomedia.

100   Winemiller, J. T. (1997, Fall). Recontextualizing Handel's borrowing. *Journal of Musicology, 15, 4,* 444–470.

101   Ibid.; Lebrecht, N. (1996, May 11). Echoes strike a chord. *Daily Telegraph,* p. 7.

102   Winemiller, J. T. (1997, Fall). Recontextualizing Handel's borrowing. *Journal of Musicology, 15, 4,* 444–470.

103   Ibid., p. 446.

104   Ibid.

105   Ibid., p. 447.

106   Rose, M. (1993). *Authors and owners: The invention of copyright.* Cambridge, MA: Harvard University Press.

107   Woodmansee, M. (1984). The genius and the copyright: Economic and legal conditions of the emergence of the "author." *Eighteenth-Century Studies, 17, 4,* 425–448.

108   Ibid.

109   Rose, M. (1993). *Authors and owners: The invention of copyright.* Cambridge, MA: Harvard University Press, p. 128.

110   Streeter, T. (1996). *Selling the air: A critique of the policy of commercial broadcasting in the United States.* Chicago: University of Chicago Press.

111   Ibid.

112 Jaszi, P. & Woodmansee, M. (1994). Introduction. In R. Jaszi, P. and Woodmansee, M. (Eds.), *The construction of authorship: Textual appropriation in law and literature* (pp. 1–14). Durham, NC: Duke University Press.

113 Jaszi, P. & Woodmansee, M. (1994). Introduction. In R. Jaszi, P. and Woodmansee, M. (Eds.), *The construction of authorship: Textual appropriation in law and literature* (pp. 1–14). Durham, NC: Duke University Press, p. 9.

114 Ibid.

115 Jaszi, P. (1994). On the author effect: Contemporary copyright and collective creativity. In R. Jaszi, P. and Woodmansee, M. (Eds.), *The construction of authorship: Textual appropriation in law and literature* (pp. 29–56). Durham, NC: Duke University Press.

116 Streeter, T. (1996). *Selling the air: A critique of the policy of commercial broadcasting in the United States.* Chicago: University of Chicago Press.

117 Bettig, R. V. (1996). *Copyrighting culture: The political economy of intellectual property.* Boulder, CO: Westview Press.

118 I conducted a number of interviews with a wide range of hip-hop artists, from multimillion-selling artists to "underground" cult artists including Kool DJ Herc; Redman; Treach from Naughty by Nature; MC Eiht; Meen Green; DJ Muggs of Cypress Hill; DJ Spooky; Frankie Cutlass; Cee-lo and Big Gipp of Goodie Mob; Treach of Naughty by Nature; Killah Priest, Cappadonna and Method Man of Wu-Tang Clan; Rass Kass; Hell Razah of Sunz of Man; Voodoo; Wyclef and Pras of the Fugees; MC Lyte; Kool Keith; Lou Nutt and Flaggs of Land of Da Lost; Guru and DJ Premier of Gang Starr, and Mixmaster Mike and Q-bert of the Beastie Boys and Invisibl Skratch Piklz. In addition, I conducted four one-to-two hour interviews with the most well-known sound collage group, Negativland— interviews that took place between 1993 and 1999. I also interviewed other sound collage artists such as John Oswald.

Chapter 2

Copyright and the Folk Music Tradition

Most cultures produce their own folk music, and though the specific form the music takes is different from region to region, the defining feature of folk music production remains the same across cultures. Folk music is based on the practice of drawing on existing melodic and textual elements and recombining those elements in ways that create a song that can range from a slightly modified version of an older song to a wholly new piece that contains echoes of familiar melodic or lyrical themes. At the center of this mode of cultural production is intertextuality, in which texts are (re)made from other texts to create a "new" cultural text.

This chapter is primarily concerned with examining the articulation of the folk music tradition and the social relations imposed when intellectual property law is enforced. This articulation, I argue, redefines as *copyright infringement* the act of creating and publicly performing folk music that borrows from preexisting melodies. The expansion of intellectual property law into this domain of cultural activity changes the practices folk musicians engage in to the point that today's folk music is considered more of a musical style or genre (associated with Joan Baez, Tracy Chapman and others) or a section of a record store instead of a cultural activity with a long historical tradition.

Folk Music As Cultural Practice

Lumer defines the process by which folk music is created as when "ordinary people remembered older music and changed it somewhat to fit their needs, sometimes adding new words or new embellishments of the tunes."[1] Forcucci expands on this description by stating that in most cases the creator of the song was often forgotten, but the song was

remembered and passed down by individuals and groups through generations.[2] "It becomes a folk song not simply because a lot of people like it or
because thousands have listened to it, but because some have persisted in
singing it among themselves, in their own way," adds Toelken.[3] A folk
song is seldom memorized word-for-word but instead is recalled and con-
tinually recomposed in varying ways that suit the context of the place,
performer and audience.[4]

In an illustration of the ethic that is at the core of the folk music tradition, Bess Lomax Hawes—the former director of the Folk Arts Program
at the National Endowment for the Arts—recalled a conversation with the
famous folk singer Woody Guthrie, the composer of "This Land is Your
Land" and a host of other classic folk songs. She stated: "I told Woody
that I thought that the chorus of [his song] 'Union Maid' had gone so
completely into oral tradition that no one knew where it came from . . .
It was part of the cultural landscape, no longer even associated with him.
He answered, 'If that were true, it would be the greatest honor of my
life.'"[5]

Although folk music still exists in print cultures, it originated in oral
cultures—cultures that rely heavily on structure and formula to aid the
transmission of, for instance, oral poems and folk songs from singer to
singer, generation to generation.[6] Further, Ong writes, "In an oral culture, knowledge, once acquired, had to be constantly repeated or it would
be lost: fixed, formulaic thought patterns were essential for wisdom and
effective administration."[7]

Milman Parry argues that Homer's *Iliad* and *Odyssey* were not the
product of written literary culture; rather, these works were oral compositions that were passed down from earlier poets and which had no single,
identifiable "original" author. These oral poets were able to tell stories of
great length not through the rote memorization of every word. Instead,
they were memorized through learning the structure of the poems, the
order of the particular segments that make up the epic story, as well as a
vocabulary of verbal formulas (i.e., phrases and expressions) that are appropriate to the telling of these stories.[8]

To test his hypothesis that the *Iliad* and *Odyssey* could be oral compositions, Parry and his student Albert Lord recorded the oral tradition of
South Slavic epic singing (whose singers recited epics tens of thousands
of metric lines in length), a tradition that was still alive in the mid-twentieth century when they documented it. They found that "when a singer
came to sing, he recomposed his song as he sang it, utilizing his knowledge of the organization of incidents and descriptions and his large stock

of poetic formulas. The analysis of recorded Yugoslav songs revealed striking similarities with the Homeric texts, thus suggesting the oral origins of Greek epic poetry."[9] This highlights the fact that intertextuality is not simply a reference to a text—it is a fundamental organizing principle of meaning-making.

From South Slavic epic singing on through country blues, the formulaic borrowing and reconfiguring of musical and textual elements constitutes the central component of folk music composition.[10] It is important to note that "formula" should not be misread as "cliché," because most oral cultures have considerably different notions of uniqueness than do print-based cultures. Ong states, "Print culture gave birth to the romantic notions of 'originality' and 'creativity,' which set apart an individual work from other works even more, seeing its origins and meaning as independent of outside influence, at least ideally." Print culture, Ong argues, attempts to close off intertextuality by emphasizing the importance of a pure text untainted by the influence of other texts, of others' ideas.[11]

The anxiety that lies in many modern writers, an anxiety that they are actually creating nothing new under the sun, is something that those within oral cultures did not share. This uneasiness is central to Bloom's *The Anxiety of Influence*,[12] and Francoise Meltzer similarly stated that we are "increasingly haunted by an odd anxiety every time the idea of originality is at issue."[13] Folk singers within most oral cultures also did not share this uneasiness surrounding the "originality" of their compositions; in fact, there was no framework within which they could even conceive of such a concept. In a modern print culture steeped in Enlightenment and Romantic notions of originality, cultural producers such as folk singers must wrestle with these issues because their mode of cultural production is at odds with the dominant culture. Seeger states, "The attempt to make sense out of copyright law reaches its limit in folk song. For here is the illustration par excellence of the law of plagiarism. The folk song is, by definition and, as far as we can tell, by reality, entirely a product of plagiarism."[14]

When Laclau began developing articulation theory, he did so because the idea that one mode of economic production automatically subsumes another one did not sit well with him and did not reflect the way the world—with all its complexities—worked. Similarly, it is not true that intellectual property law and the assumptions that underlie it completely subsume folk music production or other modes of cultural production. Differing conceptions of originality, creativity, authorship and ownership exist in varying degrees of intensity within these contradictory articulations, and the strength of those assumptions (as well as economic issues) is an important factor in determining where the force of law will fall.

It is important to historically situate these competing concepts in order to carry out a thorough analysis of the intersections of intellectual property law and cultural production. Johannesen does so when he describes the concept of plagiarism as "a norm deeply imbedded in the Euro-American tradition of print orientation, individual originality, and capitalistic commodification of ideas. The conventional view sees a person's words and ideas as private property or commodities to be owned and sold."[15] Chapter 3—with its discussion of Martin Luther King Jr.'s alleged plagiarism in his doctoral dissertation—examines these issues in more detail.

Folk Music and Copyright Law

There are two substantial observations that can be made in regard to the penetration of intellectual property law into the realm of the folk song tradition. First, copyright law makes illegal the process of folk song creation and this, to say the least, puts a damper on a creative process that existed for centuries. Second, by not recognizing intertextual cultural practices as legitimate, copyright law places an emphasis on individualistic proprietary ownership and essentially "freezes" the development of particular melodic themes and lyrics, placing them in the hands of a single "original" copyright owner.

I want to focus on this second point. Many collectors who recorded folk songs for the Library of Congress during the Great Depression published songs under their own names without the permission of the musicians who performed the songs.[16] British folk song collector Cecil Sharp attached his name to the copyrights of a number of traditional folk songs he collected, including "The Battle Hymn of the Republic" and the classic folk song "Old King Cole," a folk song that Oscar Brand sarcastically writes was "old when London Bridge was still a plank and 'Beowulf' was the Book of the Month."[17] Similarly, in England, a songbook publisher copyrighted traditional songs such as "Edward," "The Rocks of Baun" and "The Shooting of His Dear."[18]

Rod Stewart's song "Purple Heather" from his album *A Spanner in the Works* borrows heavily from the traditional Irish folk song "Wild Mountain Thyme," though the copyright for "Purple Heather" is fully assigned to Rod the former Mod.[19] And while we are on the subject of the color purple, the vomit-inducing copyrighted Barney-the-purple-dinosaur theme song "I Love You" is based on the melody taken from the children's folk song "This Old Man."[20] After the 1956 *Wihtol v. Wells* decision, it became possible for one who created a "new" song that borrows elements from traditional folk songs to copyright it and potentially sue another who has used a similar melody. In *Wihtol v. Wells*, a composer copyrighted a song based on a melodic element from a Russian folk song. A second composer used that same melody and developed entirely different lyrics for it, but was nonetheless found liable for infringing upon the first composer's work.[21]

The development of the U.S. Marines' anthem, officially known as "The Marine Hymn," was born from the intertextual practice of borrowing and modifying preexisting cultural texts. The words, which came from an anonymous member of the Marines, were originally set to the tune of an old Spanish folk song but were then sung to a melody culled from an 1868 French operetta, "Geneviève à Brabant," written by Jacques Offenbach. This version of the song—borrowed lyrics, melody and all— was eventually copyrighted by the Marine Corps in 1920.[22] When engaging in these kinds of copyrighting practices, this doesn't mean one necessarily owns the public domain elements, but copyright law predisposes judges and lawyers to interpret the law in a way that slows or "freezes" a mode of cultural production.

During the course of writing this chapter, I happened to be listening to a lot of old country music, and in my casual listening I noticed that *six* country songs shared *exactly* the same vocal melody, including Hank Thompson's "Wild Side of Life"[23]; The Carter Family's "I'm Thinking Tonight of My Blue Eyes"[24]; Roy Acuff's "Great Speckle Bird"[25]; Kitty Wells' "It Wasn't God Who Made Honky Tonk Angels"[26]; Reno and Smiley's "I'm Using My Bible as a Roadmap"[27]; and Townes Van Zant's "Heavenly Houseboat Blues."[28]

It's unlikely that the individual writers of these differently titled songs (that differ lyrically as well) simply ran out of melodic ideas and decided to pillage someone else's song. Rather, it's more probable that these six country songwriters, the majority of whom grew up during the first half of the twentieth century, were immersed in the practice of borrowing from folk melodies—something they probably did not think twice about. In his extensively researched book *Country: The Twisted Roots of Rock 'n' Roll*, Nick Toches documents that the melody these songs share is both "ancient and British."[29] There were no recorded lawsuits stemming from these appropriations, and it is assumed that these songs were not heard as being either unoriginal or a type of plagiarism.

Despite the rich history of musical borrowing, Romantic notions of originality resonate in many music communities. In a review I wrote of an album by The Coopers, I argued, "When The Coopers car-jack Billy Idol's

'Dancing With Myself' to make their own custom-made hot rod (titled 'American Car'), it doesn't matter that they're being 'unoriginal' because rock 'n' roll was built on unoriginality. . . . They hit and run the Ramones (on 'Oblivious'), The Who (on 'Déjà vu') and the Jesus & Mary Chain (on 'New Hesitation'), but it's all in good fun." I concluded, "Part of the pleasure of listening is trying to figure out where all the different riffs come from."[30] This didn't sit well with Abbey Tyson, who identified herself as affiliated with a recording studio in a letter to the paper's editor. She wrote:

> I have to take issue with reviewer Kembrew McLeod's belief that stealing ideas from other composers is all in good fun. There's something about praising "rip-off artists" that rubs me the wrong way. Of course all artists in every field are influenced by those they admire, but isn't the point of art to take what you've learned and make something new? . . . It's just laziness and lack of creativity that makes people leach off of other artists. When The Coopers steal . . . they are just joining the swamp of mediocre musicians who can't come up with anything original.[31]

She concludes, somewhat redundantly, "Artists who steal do so because they either can't come up with anything original or because they are afraid it won't be accepted or popular if it's different."[32] Her statement about the creation of art being the practice of taking "what you've learned" and making "something new" echoes some of the eighteenth-century writings about authorship that I quoted in chapter 1. This Romantic idea is widespread, one that has persisted for years in spite of the fact that borrowing has been a central component of musical production that preceded Enlightenment and Romantic thought, and it continues to this day.

This is more apparent than ever with the rise of technologies (computers, samplers, etc.) that allow people to easily reproduce, manipulate and recontextualize various sounds and melodies. Nevertheless, the Romantic discourse of creating "new," "original" music from "influences" has persisted, and has cropped up in debates surrounding digital sampling within contemporary music, particularly hip-hop. Notably, many of the arguments against sampling are proprietary in nature and have both an economic basis ("they are stealing my property") and an authorial basis ("they are ripping off my ideas").

Copyright and African-American Music

The blues, a distinctly African-American form of folk music, was based on the intertextual borrowing by other blues musicians of existing melodic and lyrical elements. But the appropriation of blues music has also come from established outsiders. In the early recorded history of blues, musicians such as W. C. Handy derived much of their copyrighted "original" songs (such as "Saint Louis Blues," "Yellow Dog Blues," and "Joe Turner Blues") from direct exposure to African-American folk songs in frequent visits to the South.[33] According to Barlow, Handy often "reconstructed the melodies and the lyrics of commonly known folk blues from memory, and published them under his own name; this was not an uncommon practice in the record industry during the heyday of the blues."[34]

British heavy metal group Led Zeppelin borrowed extensively from blues artists and on their debut album they used significant elements of Willie Dixon's "You Shook Me," "I Can't Quit You Baby" and "You Need Love" without credit, assigning themselves the copyright. Dixon successfully sued the group because his songs had been copyrighted, but even after Led Zeppelin's career came to a halt, Zeppelin guitarist Jimmy Page continued to borrow from Dixon. In a post-Zeppelin collaboration with David Coverdale, Page's "Shake My Tree" bears a striking resemblance to Dixon's classic "I Just Want To Make Love To You."[35] Other songs in the Zeppelin catalog are comprised of lyrical themes, melodies and riffs culled from blues artists in a manner that is not as blatantly derivative.[36]

Dixon and virtually all other blues artists engaged in the same type of borrowing that Zeppelin did. For instance, many of Dixon's copyrights incorporate material from the folk-blues public domain, such as the song "My Babe," which was part of the Southern folk tradition long before he claimed them.[37] It is doubtful that blues artists such as Leadbelly "wrote" every single song for which they were assigned a copyright. Leadbelly's song "In the Pines," which Nirvana reworked as "Where Did You Sleep Last Night," has obvious antecedents in the nineteenth century (Nirvana, incidentally, shares a copyright license with Leadbelly for their cover version on their *Unplugged* album).[38] Also, John Lee Hooker's "Crawlin' King Snake" was based on a 1941 recording by Tony Hollins, which was in turn rooted in a song that Blind Lemon Jefferson recorded in 1926, "That Black Snake Moan."[39]

Despite the fact that Led Zeppelin and other rock groups engaged in the same type of borrowing these early blues artists did, the power dynamics in the two cases are quite different. There is an obvious contrast between blacks borrowing from common cultural texts developed by other American blacks and a white English group (backed by a powerful record label and its lawyers) slightly reworking a rural black man's song without giving credit or financial compensation. Blues artists, if they are to potentially make a living from their music, are pulled into the logic(s) of intellectual property law-fostered relations. When Willie Dixon sued Led Zeppelin for making thousands of dollars from his song, he implicitly had to buy into notions of originality and creativity that are relatively foreign to the blues folk tradition that enabled and structured the creation of his songs in the first place.

Many early blues artists could not read or write, thus existing primarily within an oral culture. The emphasis on the system of copyright (which, by its very name, requires literacy and a familiarity with print culture) therefore put these artists at a distinct disadvantage. There is nothing inherently wrong with Led Zeppelin borrowing song elements (as I have demonstrated, this is a common cultural practice), but copyright law handicaps those who value oral-based cultural practices in favor of groups or individuals who have grown up within this cultural and economic system. Willie Dixon couldn't read or write; by the time his daughter, Shirley Dixon, was 8 years old, she said, "I had filled in many copyright forms and typed his lyrics out and mailed contracts."[40] To survive within the mainstream recording industry, therefore, blues and folk artists must disengage themselves from an intertextual mode of cultural production and buy into Western conceptions of authorship and ownership.

Western Copyright Law and "World Music"

An area of the music business that parallels the exploitation of African-American folk blues artists (and the way industries exploit people, more generally) is the "world music" sector. "World music" involves the distribution of a large number of non-Western public domain recordings by the large multinational record companies that dominate the world's music distribution. Because of the way Western intellectual property law is structured, individuals and record companies can copyright elements of the traditional music of other cultures. The logical extension of the consequences of the privatization of culture can be felt in less developed countries, which typically bear the brunt of innovations within the capitalist system.

This recalls the efforts of multinational corporations that patent the products derived from natural resource extracts, thus robbing the local community the opportunity to benefit from collective innovation (which is the subject of chapter 5). In the case of "world music," the legal appropriation method takes the form of copyright and, similarly, the profits typically don't return to the community that labored to create the original cultural product. In his article "Pygmy Pop," which studies the digital sampling of Pygmy field recordings in Western popular music, Feld states:

> The primary circulation of several thousand, small-scale, low-budget, and largely non-profit ethnomusicological records is now directly linked to a secondary circulation of several million dollars worth of contemporary record sales, copyrights, royalty, and ownership claims, many of them held by the largest music entertainment conglomerates in the world. Hardly any of this money circulation returns to or benefits the originators of the cultural and intellectual property in question.[41]

A concrete example of this is the 1992 album *Deep Forest*, which was the product of two Frenchmen, Michael Sanchez and Eric Mouquet, who created an album that "fused digital samples of music from Ghana, the Solomon Islands and African pygmies with 'techno-house' dance rhythms."[42] The *Deep Forest* album makes claims that it received the support of UNESCO as well as two musicologists. But sampling permission was given only after one of the musicologists was told that the Frenchmen intended to use his recordings from the Ivory Coast for an "Earth Day" album. The musicologist was not told that, instead, the recordings from the Solomon Islands would be used for a widely disseminated commercial album. In addition to the profits garnered from the two-million-plus copies that were sold, Sony Music has undoubtedly accrued additional profits from licensing the album's tracks to such corporations as Porsche, Coca-Cola and Sony TV for use in advertising campaigns.[43]

Although copyright law is complex and varies from country to country, Seeger argues that for the most part "copyright laws recognize only invention or composition by an individual (or a small group). In general, they do not recognize oral traditions or folk music as copyrightable, and do not establish enduring rights to an invention or idea."[44] The intellectual property laws and treaties that the United States and other Western nations have pressured Southern Hemisphere countries to adopt are biased against the mode of cultural production used to create non-Western musics. That bias echoes the notions of originality and creativity that evolved from Enlightenment and Romantic thought discussed earlier.

Many non-Western musics do not meet the criteria for copyright protection (there must be an "original," identifiable author), a requirement that puts an undue burden on traditional cultures. This functions to relegate the music of traditional cultures "to the public domain where it may be freely used without legal restraints. Conversely, recorders may copyright their recordings of traditional music and obtain *de facto* control over its use and dissemination."[45] People from traditional cultures—much like the early blues musicians—are at a decided disadvantage because there can be no tangible representation of the music that originates primarily from oral traditions, except as it is recorded. Mills discusses the legal difference between performing traditional songs and recording them, stating:

> The recordings of non-Western songs themselves fully meet the Constitutional and statutory requirements of an author, originality and tangibility. The actual field recordings "owe their origin" to the producer who pressed the "record" button, therefore, the producer is the author in the Constitutional sense. . . . Through the simple process of recording and transcribing, a recorder exerts enough intellectual effort to secure a copyright over field recordings. The traditional community, however, is denied ownership rights over their music if they cannot produce the requisite "writing" and "author."[46]

In examining the articulation of intellectual property law with spheres of cultural production associated with "world music," these differing conceptions of authorship (and ownership, both of which are closely connected) are important. Even if the person who recorded the music was ethically opposed to registering a copyright for the music in his or her own name, and therefore assigned the music to the public domain, a person or group like Deep Forest may come along and freely sample that music at will. Whatever profits made from that album of sampled music are not legally required to be shared with the community whose labor was appropriated to enable the creation of that copyrighted album. Artists like Deep Forest don't have to give back to the community from which they sample (the same is true with the patenting of the biological products based on the indigenous knowledge of plants).

A court case that may affect the practice of appropriating from the music of other cultures without compensation was initiated in 1996 by two members of the Ami tribe, Taiwan's largest indigenous minority group.[47] In 1988, a live performance of Guo Hsiu-chu and her husband Guo Ying-nan was recorded by a French cultural organization, Maison des Cultures du Monde, and placed on a compact disc that promoted the music of Taiwan's nine indigenous tribes. In 1992, a sample of their voices was licensed from Maison des Cultures by a European "ethno-techno" artist who records under the name Enigma. The sample was integrated into the song "Return to Innocence," which went to number one in numerous European countries and remained on *Billboard*'s "International" chart for 32 weeks.

The song was later licensed by the International Olympic Committee to be the theme song of the 1996 Atlanta Olympics, where it was broadcast around the world, finally making its way back to the remote Ami tribal village and to the sexagenarian couple.[48] The success of their suit may be made more difficult for a couple of reasons. First, the U.S. record company's lawyers argue that U.S. courts do not have jurisdiction over the matter and, second, their performances are not copyrightable in the first place (these arguments may create significant obstacles for similar cases that might be initiated in the future).[49]

Something that makes this case unique is that—unlike most indigenous people who do not have even a remote chance of discovering the use of their voices or music in a commercially distributed recording—Enigma's song was chosen to be the official theme song of the most watched sporting event in the world. What does *not* make the case unique is the way their music was appropriated through digital sampling techniques and integrated into a copyrighted work by Western artists who have profited from their labor. In mid-2000, the case was still pending.[50]

Artists like Deep Forest and Enigma are part of a musical movement (sometimes labeled "ethno-techno") that uses digital samples to fuse "ethnic" sounds and sources to a beat that can range from the very slow to the danceable. While the borrowing of non-Western music by Western artists has a long history—Debussy's incorporation of Javanese music is one of many examples[51]—digital sampling has enabled anyone with access to the "world beat" rack of a record store or the field recordings section of a library to freely appropriate the voices, sounds and rhythms of traditional music. Lesser known contemporary artists such as Loop Guru, Future Sounds of London, Banco De Gaia, Transglobal Underground, Jah Wobble, Bill Laswell and many others have incorporated samples of traditional musics into their recordings, a trend that entered the mainstream music charts with the popularity of Enigma and Deep Forest.[52]

Although financial compensation is important, the monetary protection of traditional musics may not be the most significant issue for many cultures whose music is appropriated. Because traditional communities frequently ascribe significant powers to music (the ability to heal, kill, create bountiful game) these cultures place an importance on the *restriction* and *regulation* of music's use, rather than on financial profits. Western law, on the other hand, places a premium on the protection of one's *property rights*. Mills therefore argues, "Traditional music and Western law clash at the most fundamental level."[53]

With these issues in mind, it is much more difficult to argue for the free appropriation of musical elements with no restrictions at all, particularly when sensitivity to other cultural practices or compensation for poorer communities enters into the equation. The complexity of this discussion increases when we turn to other cultures that are grounded in intertextual practices, where open and unacknowledged borrowing lies at the center of the productive practices of those cultures, cultures that have also been historically exploited (the African-American culture is an example of this).

"Happy Birthday, Screw You"

"Happy Birthday to You," shared in everyday rituals in Western societies, is certainly among the three most sung songs in the English language, but it is a privately owned cultural text.[54] It is widely perceived to be in the public domain and is sung in many different languages throughout the world, but its copyright is strictly enforced by Warner-Chappell, a subsidiary of AOL/Time-Warner, which currently holds worldwide rights to the song (with the exception of Japan).[55]

During most of the twentieth century, singing "Happy Birthday to You" in any kind of public venue without paying royalties and gaining permission is a violation of copyright law, and there are agents employed by song publishing firms that "scour the U.S.A., popping up unexpectedly in restaurants, nightclubs, bars and even summer camps, looking for lawbreakers."[56] Restaurants whose servers sing "Happy Birthday to You" must buy a permit from ASCAP and, consequently, many chain restaurants do not allow the song to be sung on the premises. Other establishments like ShowBiz Pizza Place and Bennigan's have their own versions of the birthday song to avoid costly licensing fees or potential lawsuits.[57]

Repeated requests for information about the song from the current copyright holder, Warner-Chappell Music, Inc., went unanswered. Finally, Don Biederman—an Executive Vice President of the company—informed me in a faxed letter that although the company maintains "files concerning HBTY in various departments of our company," he could not provide me with any information on "Happy Birthday to You" because "we regard this information as proprietary and confidential."[58] Furthermore, I was refused permission to quote the song's brief lyrics within a chapter that was even remotely critical of the song's history. This is important because it provides another illustration of the restrictions placed on the use of cultural texts when they enter into privatized legal and economic relations.

In this case, the song's history is obscured by the legal and administrative rules that surround the use of these privately owned cultural texts. The federal Copyright Law of 1976 defines an event as "public performance" if it occurs "at a place open to the public, or at any place where a substantial number of persons outside of a normal circle of a family and its social acquaintances is gathered."[59] If the song is sung at school, summer camp, a restaurant, or the like, the performers or the establishments are liable under the law.

The birthday song, as it is currently known, was formally copyrighted in 1935 by two schoolteacher sisters, Mildred and Patty Hill and, according to Patty's nephew, it was done so as a joke.[60] Whether or not it was originally conceived of as a joke, it was taken very seriously and the Hills' publisher frequently brought suit against people or businesses that violated copyright law by performing it publicly—in most cases as a result of those people mistakenly believing it was a children's song in the public domain.[61]

One person who was most likely very well acquainted with royalty payments and copyright law is the popular music composer Irving Berlin. In his 1934 Broadway play *As Thousands Cheer*, the actors sung the lines "Happy Birthday to You" in a scene celebrating John D. Rockefeller's birthday. Although the *lyrics* of "Happy Birthday to You" had not yet been copyrighted, the Hills' publishing firm, Clayton Sammy Company, nevertheless claimed that the use of the song in the play was an infringement on the *melody* of "Good Morning to You."[62] The unauthorized usage of the song that celebrated the birthday of John D. Rockefeller was in all probability very innocent, but as was the case with later lawsuits against other infringers, that fact did not cease the lawsuit against Berlin.

The producers of another Broadway show (*Angel on the Wings*) that also used the tune at the beginning of its run had the show's composer write a new melody to avoid paying royalties for "Happy Birthday to You." Similarly, the authors of *The Male Animal* and *Panama Hattie* were also involved in litigation over the unauthorized use of the song.[63] A later Broadway play, *The Gin Game*, did not properly credit the song in its program at the beginning of its run in the 1970s. After a "polite yet firm" letter was sent by the song's then-current copyright owners, Sammy-Birchard Music, a fee of $25 per performance was paid.[64]

In 1986, classical music humor musician P.D.Q. Bach avoided using any strains of "Happy Birthday to You" in a public performance of a birthday ode to his father, for fear of violating the song's copyright. Instead, he based his piece on a traditional German birthday song to avoid a lawsuit.[65] Some composers of "serious music" have also unknowingly infringed on the song's copyright, such as Stravinsky, who met with trouble when he cited a few bars of "Happy Birthday to You" in one his symphonic fanfares.[66] In another case, Roy Harris used part of the song in his work "Symphonic Dedication," which honored the birthday of a famous American composer, Howard Hanson.[67] *Variety* reporter David Ewen stated, "Keeping the occasion in mind, Harris brought his composition to a climax with a modern treatment of 'Happy Birthday.' After Harris' piece had been introduced by the Boston Symphony he was compelled by the copyright owners to delete the 'Happy Birthday' passage from his score."[68]

Postal Telegraph, a company that began the practice of using "Happy Birthday to You" for singing telegrams in 1938, found itself treading in copyright infringement waters, as did Western Union.[69] The birthday song had been sung upwards of an estimated million and a half times during the early 1940s by telegram delivery persons. Western Union career man M. J. Rivise stated, "From 1938 to 1942, most of our singing telegrams were birthday greetings, and 'Happy Birthday to You' was the cake-taker."[70] Postal Telegraph had apparently gained permission from ASCAP to use "Happy Birthday to You" without paying royalties, but in 1941 ASCAP demanded a payment proportionate to the amount the song was sung. Western Union and Postal Telegraph refused and commissioned birthday songs based on the public domain melodies of "Yankee Doodle" and "Mary Had a Little Lamb."[71]

These versions failed to catch the public's fancy, and by 1950 the singing of "Happy Birthday to You" resumed, apparently with the licensing problem sorted out. One of the most striking features of the song's evolution was the speed at which "Happy Birthday to You" was established as a folk song in the public mind—no more than 40 years after it was written, a very conservative estimate. This time frame is especially interesting because Hawes and other folk music authorities have documented that traditional folk song ballads can take centuries to become ensconced. The "Happy Birthday to You" singing telegrams and the number of times the song was apparently sung by telegraph company employees most certainly contributed to the song's institutionalization.[72]

There have been many instances in which the song's copyright owners have objected to unauthorized usage, including the lingerie manufacturer Frederick's of Hollywood advertising underwear that played "Happy Birthday to You" (perhaps the copyright owners should have, instead, protested for reasons of taste).[73] By the 1980s, it had become common knowledge in commercial sectors that the song was copyrighted and currently, more often than not, approval is sought and royalties are paid.

In the case of the watch manufacturer Casio, in the 1980s the company paid one cent for every watch that was sold that played the tune of

"Happy Birthday to You" on the owner's birthday.[74] The entertainment industry is also well aware of the song's copyright, routinely paying royalties when the song is used in movies.[75] Over time, the various owners of the song's copyright have gone to great lengths to protect their intellectual property. One lawyer at Sammy-Birchard Music even wanted to redress Congress for singing "Happy Birthday to You" to President Reagan after a televised State of the Union address.[76]

In 1988, Birch Tree Group, Ltd. sold "Happy Birthday to You" (and its other assets) to Warner Communications (which later became AOL/Time-Warner) for $25 million. In explaining why they sold it, the owners of Birchtree told the *Chicago Tribune* that it is hard for a smaller company to monitor the usage of "Happy Birthday to You" and that "a major music firm could better protect the copyright during its final 22 years."[77] The copyright was set to run out in the year 2010, but, in 1998, Congress extended copyright protection for another 20 years.[78] The massive media companies that have taken shape after two decades of mega mergers allow these companies not only greater access to revenues, but because of their size, strengthened policing as well. At the turn of the twentieth century, AOL/Time-Warner continued to collect royalties for the performance of the song in any public setting; it aggressively guards its investment and will continue to do so until 2030.[79]

Copyright law attempts to shut down intertextuality by trying to define where one text begins and another ends, and this is true of the way copyright treats the folk-song production method. In the case of "Happy Birthday to You," although it is not a folk song that dates back to the nineteenth or eighteenth centuries, the *evolution* of the song appears to be very deeply entrenched in the folk music-making tradition. "Happy Birthday to You" was based on a melody that floated around for years before it developed into its copyrighted arrangement, changing in form as different performers and composers made their personal contributions to the song.

The melody was composed by Mildred J. Hill and her sister Patty, and was published in 1893 within their book *Song Stories for the Kindergarten* as "Good Morning to All."[80] Children liked the song so much that they began singing it at birthday parties, changing the words to "Happy Birthday to You," a spontaneous form of lyrical parody or alteration that is common to the folk-song creation process.[81] This song's origin, however, dates back beyond the Hill sisters' version; for instance, a very similar song was published by Horace Waters in 1858 as "Happy Greetings to All."[82] "Happy Birthday to You" also bears a substantial similarity to two other previously published songs, "A Happy New Year" and "A Happy Greeting to All."[83]

Hawes argues that the story of "Happy Birthday to You" follows a classic pattern:

> The Misses Hill . . . wrote a little song for little children; their work was so successful that it was, in essence, taken from them to become the anonymous property of the people, the public voice—the "folk," if you like. But in a society which is based very profoundly on the concept of private ownership, it becomes extremely difficult for the public to hang onto any kind of common property, whether it be a parkland or a song. And so "Happy Birthday to You" was taken back again, not so much by its authors as by the whole network of middlemen dedicated to the control and distribution of cultural works.[84]

The manner in which copyright is used within contemporary music and culture industries leaves little room for building music from previously existing elements. This is especially ironic in the case of "Happy Birthday to You" because the song itself has no single "original" author who crafted the melody on his or her own. Even though the song evolved over a number of years, with numerous people contributing to the existence of the song as it is currently known, copyright law draws a border around the song, prohibiting its use in varying adaptations such as the works of Stravinsky or Roy Harris, among others.

ASCAP vs. Summer Camps

In a 1993 editorial published in the *Orlando Sentinel Tribune*, Ed Hayes[85] sarcastically suggested that one day we might see "a troop of Boy Scouts hauled into court, nabbed in the act of singing 'Happy Birthday to You' while grouped around a campfire."[86] Not more than three years later, ASCAP went after the Girl Scouts of America and other proprietors of summer camps for not paying royalties on ASCAP-controlled songs sung in that setting, with one overzealous ASCAP official stating, "We'll sue them if necessary."[87]

In many ways this story was over nearly as soon as it began. Early in 1996 ASCAP sent out letters to thousands of camps—including many Girl Scout camps—notifying them that royalty fees must be paid for the public performance (including campfire singing) of the over 4 million songs to which the company controls the copyright.[88] ASCAP argued that because a commercial exchange takes place at summer camps in the form of fees, these camps should compensate songwriters.[89] Connie Bradley—an ASCAP vice president—stated,

A big part of a camping experience is music. . . . We're not talking about four to five girls sitting around a campfire singing songs. We're talking about several hundred girls sitting around a campfire singing songs. These children are charged a fee for coming to camp, and that fee includes such things as food, housing and arts and crafts.[90]

Many Girl Scout camp officials became very concerned with ASCAP's position, particularly because of the ambiguity of the term "public performance." Julia Newsome, director of programs for the Girl Scout Council, stated during the height of the controversy, "If someone walks into a camp from ASCAP and you've got a group of girls singing a song that's copyrighted by ASCAP, that's a violation."[91] Defending the hardball measures, ASCAP official John Lo Frumento stated, "They buy paper, twine and glue for their crafts—they can pay for the music, too. We will sue them if necessary."[92]

Under the guidelines set by this ASCAP letter, songs such as "Ring Around the Rosie," "This Land Is Your Land," "God Bless America," "Edelweiss," and of course "Happy Birthday to You" could not be sung at the summer camps without paying royalties.[93] Girl Scout camp officials stated that the penalty for failing to comply with copyright laws would range from $5,000 and six days in jail to $100,000 and a year in jail for every unauthorized performance.[94]

After ASCAP first approached the American Camping Association in an attempt to try to collect royalties for music performed at the association members' camps, John Miller, the association's executive vice president, exclaimed, "You've got to be kidding." Other camping officials were more sympathetic to ASCAP's position, but were nonetheless worried about how to pay for licensing fees. "We're real supportive of songwriters, and yet, we want to do it in a way that doesn't make it financially difficult for girls, in an informal way, to get together and sing songs that make them feel good," said Kathy Cloninger, president and CEO for the Girl Scout Council of Cumberland Valley.[95]

After they were approached by ASCAP, the American Camping Association sent out a newsletter warning its members of the possible risks of singing ASCAP-controlled songs.[96] Some took the warning very seriously, including a Girl Scout Council director who advised future counselors at a training session to limit their repertoire exclusively to Girl Scout songs.[97] Other camps with tighter budgets curtailed the singing of songs at camps, and the *Houston Chronicle* reported that "several cash-strapped camps stopped singing the songs" altogether.[98] This climate of fear resulted in the following surreal scenario reported by the *Star Tribune*:

> Something is wrong in Diablo Day camp this year. At the 3 p.m. sing-along in a wooded canyon near Oakland, Calif., 214 Girl Scouts are learning the summer dance craze, the Macarena. Keeping time by slapping their hands across their arms and hips, they jiggle, hop and stomp. They spin, wiggle and shake. They bounce for two minutes. In silence. "Yesterday, I told them we could be sued if we played the music," explains Teesie King, camp codirector and a volunteer mom. "So they decided they'd learn it without the music." Watching the campers' mute contortions, King shakes her head. "It seems so different," she allows, "when you do the Macarena in silence."[99]

The interesting thing about this use of "Macarena," or lack thereof, is that even though the version of "Macarena" made famous (infamous?) by Los Del Rio sports its own distinctive rhythms, instrumentation and production techniques, the primary melody of the song is based on a South American folk song.[100] This recalls previous examples I gave regarding the incorporation of public domain folk melodies and/or lyrics into a copyrighted, protected song. It is also a reminder—again—that intertextuality is central to most modes of cultural production, but copyright law seeks to cease this type of borrowing activity.

After a flood of indignant editorials and public outcry that portrayed ASCAP as a big bully beating up on the Girl Scouts, ASCAP endured what its public relations consultant called "P.R. hell."[101] Soon after national wire services picked up the story, ASCAP released a statement claiming that it "has never sought, nor was it ever its intention, to license Girl Scouts singing around a campfire."[102] ASCAP entered into negotiations with Girl Scout leaders in an attempt to hammer out royalty fee guidelines allowing for the waiving of royalties for nonprofit camps, a reversal of ASCAP's previous position.[103] Despite ASCAP's insistence that they never intended to license campfire singing, the statements made by high-ranking officials before the public relations debacle came to a head contradict those later assurances.

This is an excellent example of a culture-producing industry trying to expand the scope of the enforcement of copyright law into previously untouched areas of cultural activities—namely, the summer camp experience. The quote by the ASCAP official, "They buy paper, twine and glue for their crafts—they can pay for the music, too" is very telling in that it points to the fact that ASCAP sees music as just another commodity, a commodity that is privately owned and that can be controlled through commercial exchange. This highlights another effect of the privatization of culture: people are discouraged from being active producers in a shared, participatory culture because much of that culture is controlled by corporate and individual owners.

Conclusion

By defining the unauthorized use of melodic and lyrical fragments as copyright infringement, or plagiarism, the intertextual borrowing of preexisting cultural texts that has grounded folk music making for centuries is rendered illegal. Forcucci attributes the decline in the intertextual folk music making process to the decline of orality in modern society and, conversely, the increase in literacy—which emphasizes musical notation and the printing of lyrics that can be learned.[104] This argument has been challenged by folklorists, including Greenhill, who states, "I have seen no evidence that when performers learn songs orally—from a recording or in person—they are any less inclined to change it than when they learn songs from written sources."[105]

His point is well taken, and it is unlikely that because a society has transformed from an oral to a print culture, individuals tend not to make their own changes to a particular song. Toelken complicates this discussion by including a number of other variables.[106] He states, "Today, with the help of copyright laws, personality cults and fan clubs, media identification and glorification of stars and composers, royalty provisions and the like, the bulk of new songs retain their connection to their composers and achieve very little if any dynamic change."[107] I want to emphasize a couple of the points Toelken identifies—copyright laws and royalty provisions—and argue that fear of litigation is a very important factor that dissuades folk musicians working in the commercial sphere from using preexisting elements from copyrighted songs.

I don't claim that there is a direct causal relationship between the codification of folk music into a style and the expanding sphere of intellectual property law. Nevertheless, one reason that much contemporary folk music has been transformed into a style with few links to the traditional folk music making process is because (in its mass distributed form) the practice has been rendered illegal by intellectual property law. Nevertheless, this intertextual mode of cultural and musical production hasn't been stamped out. In more small-scale economies, such as bluegrass music festivals, this practice of borrowing from earlier songs is still alive and well. But if those same bluegrass artists were to release a recording of their live performances, to avoid the risk of being sued they would have to assign song-writing credit, gain permission from the songwriter and/or publisher (especially if any changes were made), and pay royalties.

The folk method of producing music most certainly survived in the first half of the twentieth century, even in recorded form, as is evidenced by the example I gave of the six different folk and country songs that contained exactly the same vocal melody. Most of these songs were recorded during the first half of the twentieth century; they all had a relatively widespread release, but no litigation emerged from these borrowings (there are many similar examples beyond the scope of this book). This suggests that a different way of conceiving of authorship still had a foothold in these music communities, a concept that is much less popular within folk music circles today.[108]

This mode of cultural production also is manifested in music communities that are radically different from traditional folk music, such as hip-hop and electronic dance music, both of which use digital sampling as a primary method of musical production. For instance, during an interview with me, DJ Spooky stated: "I think electronic music is the inheritor of folk culture. It's just a digitized folk culture."[109] Artists within electronic-dance music circles have kept the tradition of musical borrowing alive, albeit in a quite different form. These artists who work with computers and samplers tend not to have very rigid views of what constitutes originality and authorship. Furthermore, they often exist outside the mainstream music industry, releasing records on small, independent labels—which allows them to more freely continue their activities.

Some important questions to ask in an analysis of the way folk music (or another form of cultural production) is articulated with intellectual property include: first, *what* is being authored; second, *how* is it authored; third, *who* is defined as the author; and finally, in regard to the question of ownership, who has control of the *means of production*? There is an idea of authorship in folk-song production that is completely at odds with construction of the "original," individualistic author that is the norm in contemporary print cultures. In both earlier oral cultures and contemporary print cultures, the thing that is being authored in both instances is the song itself, but that is where the similarity ends, especially when we ask *how* it was authored and *who* constitutes the author.

In earlier cultures, where intertextual practices were more firmly recognized as legitimate, there were fewer demarcations between where one song (or text) ends and the other begins. The folk song was more the result of the existence of a cultural commons than the "originality" of the performer. Therefore, the performer or performers are a less important part of the equation of authorship than is the entire community that has contributed to maintaining the cultural commons. Granted, these are generalizations. For instance, in some cultures, the performance of certain songs may be tightly controlled by a shaman, but that shaman is not seen as the original, individualistic "author" of those songs; they are still considered the property of the entire community.

But when folk music enters the music marketplace, the means of production moves from a communal setting (i.e., the front porch or festivals) and shifts into the hands of individual songwriters and record companies that finance, release and distribute music. The fact that many contemporary folk musicians have a much more proprietary view of the songs they write—that they more closely identify with this relatively recent notion of authorship—is one reason there has not been more resistance against the way copyright laws have been applied in this area of cultural production. Another reason for this lack of resistance is the fact that folk music is now a part of the music industry. These folk musicians are bound up in a system of record labels and publishing companies that certainly do not approve of the unfettered borrowing of existing song fragments.

Blues, an African-American strain of folk music, provides an interesting example of the contradictions that occur when this sphere of cultural production becomes articulated with the logic(s) of intellectual property law. During the first half of the twentieth century, blues musicians largely conceived of authorship in a much more fluid way; certain melodies, lyric fragments and song structures were considered to be common cultural property. But those who engage in these types of cultural production are placed in a position of disadvantage by Western copyright laws.

For blues musicians like Willie Dixon to be able to protect themselves from such appropriation—for them to possibly be able to make a living from playing their songs—they must implicitly buy into notions of authorship and cultural ownership that ground copyright law. Many of those who make what is labeled "world music" aren't recognized as authors; this is because of the ethnocentrism embedded in Western intellectual property laws. Therefore, it is Sony Music that gets the profits from the 2 million plus records sold and the licensing of Deep Forest's songs for commercials and motion pictures, not the people of New Guinea whose music was a key ingredient in their multi platinum album.

In these final pages, I want to provide a transition to the next chapter that deals with African-American cultural production by unpacking the following quote by Marc G. Gershwin, a cotrustee of the Gershwin Family Trust, which oversees the estates of popular music composers Ira and George Gershwin. In arguing for the extension of copyright protection from life plus 50 years to life plus 70 years, Marc Gershwin lamented, "Someone could turn *Porgy and Bess* into rap music."[110] My first reaction, as a music fan and critic, was what hip-hop artist who wants to connect with a hip, young audience would want to sample *Porgy and Bess* in the first place? But then I realized that after hardcore rapper Jay-Z[111] landed a number-one record in the *Billboard* charts when he sampled the chorus of "Hard Knock Life" from the musical *Annie*, anything is possible. (Friend and *Rolling Stone* editor Rob Sheffield jokingly claimed Jay-Z's bizarre juxtaposition of a song most likely caused more car accidents than any other radio song released in 1998.)

The humorous image of Foxxy Brown rapping "I Loves You Porgy" aside, a more important issue lies just beneath the surface of Gershwin's statement, which is ironic on many levels. This 1935 "folk opera," as George Gershwin dubbed it, was a collaboration between three whites—lyric writer Ira Gershwin and composer George Gershwin, who based *Porgy and Bess* on the novel *Porgy*, by author DuBose Heyward. Heyward got the idea for the novel from a newspaper clipping about a legless black beggar from a Southern town and he had no extensive, direct experience with Southern blacks.[112]

Heyward condescendingly stated, "My preoccupation with the primitive Southern Negro as a subject for art derives from the often unworthy quality of curiosity . . . What, I wondered, was the characteristic in the life of these people who formed this substratum of the society that endowed them with the power to stun me unexplicably to tears and laughter."[113] From its beginnings as a novel written about blacks from the voyeuristic perspective of a privileged white author, at its very core the "folk opera" *Porgy and Bess* is the result of the appropriation of black culture by whites.

Another aspect of *Porgy and Bess's* cultural appropriation is the music itself. While Gershwin claims that he did not directly borrow songs from the black folk music tradition, he nonetheless had a great interest in the music of African Americans.[114] Johnson[115] writes, "His increasingly energetic interest in other folk musics (e.g., in his trips to Cuba and Mexico and collection of Latin music records) points up the fundamental, fluid role this type of cultural borrowing played in his thinking."[116]

There are easily discovered similarities between the spirituals collected in James Weldon and J. Rosamond Johnson's two-volume songbook, *American Negro Spirituals* and the incidental music found in *Porgy and Bess* (especially "Somebody's Knockin' at Yo Do'" and "O, Gambler, Git Up Off O' Yo' Knees").[117] While there is no evidence that Gershwin ever owned a copy of those songbooks, Johnson[118] argues, "Gershwin's direct contact with the cultural currents and figures that prompted this collection existed beyond the appearance of the books themselves."[119]

The street cries heard throughout the opera were variants on the real thing, and the undercurrent of spirituals emanating from a black chorus is characteristic of *Porgy and Bess*.[120] Before Gershwin transformed *Porgy* into an opera, Heyward had already turned it into a play that included "Negro spirituals" written by Heyward but which borrowed heavily from existing spirituals. Some of the lyrical themes contained in the spirituals featured in the play were carried over into the opera, particularly "Ain't it Hahd to be a Nigger" (featured in two of the play's acts), which showed up in more tame version as "I Got Plenty O' Nuttin" in Gershwin's score. The play's "Rock in De Mountain" seems a foreshadowing of the *Porgy and Bess* song "A Red-Headed Woman," and "Sit Down! I Can't Sit Down" clearly recalls Gershwin's "Oh, I Can't Sit Down."[121]

To inspire himself when preparing for scoring the *Porgy and Bess* music, George Gershwin made numerous trips to the South—particularly Charleston, South Carolina, where he told of hearing some "grand negro sermons."[122] Gershwin and *Porgy*'s author, Heyward, visited the nearby James Island, whose Black Gullah population had preserved many of their traditional songs. Heyward said that it was like a laboratory "in which to test our theories, as well as an inexhaustible source of folk material."[123] On one of those trips, Gershwin and Heyward observed a service at a "holy roller church," which Gershwin describes as having had a direct impact on the composition of his score.[124] Schwartz writes, "Gershwin responded to the stimulus of his surroundings with an exuberant, creative outflow. Musical ideas poured forth quickly and steadily at the piano as if from some limitless subterranean well. Most of the ideas he incorporated into his opera immediately; others he laid aside for future use."[125]

An important aspect of *Porgy and Bess* that relates to Heyward and Gershwin's borrowing is the control of the representations of African Americans, and the opera has been severely criticized on those grounds. For instance, the father of Ann Brown, the woman who played the original Bess in 1935, blasted *Porgy and Bess*, stating, "Negroes had been pictured in the usual clichés as ignorant dope peddlers and users and criminals . . . we've had enough of that."[126] Heyward, George, Ira and their white associates coached the all-black cast in the "proper" way to speak in the dialect that had been written by the collaborators and, aside from the cast, the production was entirely created and controlled by whites.[127]

Stanley Crouch—the grouchy conservative cultural critic—ignores these issues of representation. In responding to the charges of Gershwin's appropriation of black music, however, he correctly points out that borrowing has gone both ways. Crouch argues that jazz musicians have used many of the chords and melodies written by Gershwin as jumping-off points for improvisations, something that no one disputes.[128] The intertextual borrowing of musical themes and melodies is a key component in jazz music, and showtunes by Gershwin, Rogers & Hammerstein, Cole Porter and others have been heavily used by jazz artists.

Although contributions of African Americans have been central to twentieth-century popular music, they grew more significant following the explosion of rock 'n' roll, and even more so with the emerging popularity of hip-hop music. At the same time, easy demarcations between "white" and "black" music began to grow less precise and musical borrowings became more fluid. For instance, in the late Notorious BIG's song, "Hypnotize," he interpolates an old bubblegum classic when he raps, "the crew run run run/the crew run run." It's hard to think of anything more "white" than Shawn Cassidy's candy-coated cover version of "Doo Run Run," but when an inner-city born and raised individual like Notorious BIG namechecks that song it is a reminder that cultural borrowing goes both ways.

In this day and age, it is impossible to neatly separate the African American from the European-American influences in popular music, though the African-American contribution is by far the most prominent. Because the impact of African-American culture is so pronounced in American popular music, white artists of today would have to go out of their way to avoid any "darker" influences, just as black artists aren't blind to certain aspects of white pop. The Police borrowed from the Afro-Caribbean sounds of reggae, and Puff Daddy, in turn, sampled the guitar hook and chorus of their song "Every Breath You Take" in his tribute to his slain friend, Notorious BIG. Later, Sting hired Puff Daddy to remix an old Police song to give it more of a contemporary "street" flavor.

Returning to the remark quoted earlier, the irony of Marc Gershwin raising the specter of "rap music" to justify increased copyright protection for his ancestors' music—who borrowed significantly from African-American culture in their copyrighted work—is *extremely* ironic. I would argue that an instance of hip-hop artists (say, the nine members of the Wu-Tang Clan) reworking *Porgy and Bess* would be a justifiable case of the proverbial chickens coming home to roost. Marc Gershwin's fear that *Porgy and Bess* might be turned into "rap music," and his unstated but implicit uneasiness with the idea of the opera being sampled, highlights how intellectual property law is used ideologically to restrict the circulation of a property that is used in a way in which the owner disapproves.

Notes

1   Lumer, R. (1991). Pete Seeger and the attempt to revive the folk music process. *Popular Music and Society 15, 1,* 45–58, 45.

2   Forcucci, S. L. (1984). *A folk song history of America: America through its songs.* Englewood Cliffs, NJ: Prentice Hall.

3   Toelken, B. (1986). Ballads and folksongs. In E. Oring (Ed.), *Folk groups and folklore genres: An Introduction* (pp. 147–174). Logan, UT, Utah State University Press.

4   Ibid.

5   Zeitlin, S. (1998, April 25). Strangling culture with a copyright law. *New York Times,* p. A15.

6   Ong, W. (1982). *Orality and literacy.* New York: Routledge.

7   Ibid., p. 24.

8   Parry, M. (1971). *The making of Homeric verse: The collected papers of Milman Parry.* Oxford: Clarendon Press; Barnie, J. (1989). Oral formulas in the country blues. In E. Oring (Ed.), *Folk groups and folklore genres: A reader* (pp. 254–266). Logan, UT: Utah State University Press.

9   Barnie, J. (1989). Oral formulas in the Country Blues. In E. Oring (Ed.), *Folk groups and folklore genres: A reader* (pp. 254–266). Logan, UT: Utah State University Press.

10 Ibid.

11 Ong, W. (1982). *Orality and literacy.* New York: Routledge, p. 133.

12 Bloom, H. (1973). *The anxiety of influence: A theory of poetry.* New York: Oxford University Press.

13 Winemiller, J. T. (1997, Fall). Recontextualizing Handel's borrowing. *Journal of Musicology, 15, 4,* 444–470, 446.

14 Seeger, C. (1977). *Studies in musicology, 1935–1975.* Berkeley: University of California Press.

15 Johannesen, R. L. (1995). The ethics of plagiarism reconsidered: The oratory of Martin Luther King, Jr. *Southern Communication Journal. 60, 3,* 185–194.

16 Brand, O. (1962). *The ballad mongers: Rise of the modern folk song.* New York: Funk & Wagnalls.

17 Boyes, G. (1993). *The imagined village: Culture, ideology and the English folk revival.* New York: Manchester University Press, p. 224.

18   Ibid.

19   Stewart, R. (1995). *A Spanner in the Works*. [CD]. New York: Warner Brothers; Smith, W. G. (1995, June 18). Rod the Mod should consult bible for the song of songs. *Scotland on Sunday*, p. S10.

20   Berg, L. (1994, June 24). I sue you, you sue me. *Information Law Alert: A Voorhees Report, 2*, 11.

21   Coon, W. O. (1971). Some problems with musical public domain materials under United States copyright law as illustrated mainly by the recent folk-song revival. *Copyright Law Symposium 19*, 189–218.

22   Ask the Globe. (1990, July 1). *Boston Globe Magazine, 37*.

23   Carter, A. A. & Warren, W. (1951). Wild side of life [Recorded by Hank Thompson]. On *The Capital Collectors series* [CD]. Hollywood: Capital. (1989)

24   Carter, A. P. (1939). I'm thinking tonight of my blue eyes. [Recorded by the Carter Family]. On *On border radio* [CD]. Nashville: Arhoolie. (1995)

25   Carter, Roy. (1936). Great speckle bird. [Recorded by Roy Acuff]. On *The essential Roy Acuff* [CD]. New York: Columbia. (1992)

26   Miller, J. D. (1952). It wasn't god who made honky tonk angels. [Recorded by Kitty Wells]. *On Country music hall of fame* [CD]. Universal City, CA: MCA. (1991)

27   Reno, D. (1952). I'm using my bible as a roadmap. [Recorded by Reno and Smiley]. On *Early years 1951–1959*. New York: King. (1996)

28   Van Zant, T. (1972). Heavenly houseboat blues. On *High, low and in between*. New York: EMI.

29   Toches, N. (1985). *Country: The twisted roots of rock 'n' roll*. Rev. ed. New York: Charles Scribner's Sons.

30   McLeod, K. (1999, September 30). Rip-off artists. *Valley Advocate*, p. 33.

31   Tyson, A. (1999, October 7). Letter to the editor. *Valley Advocate*, p. 4.

32   Ibid.

33   Barlow, W. (1990). 'Fattening frogs for snakes': Blues and the music industry. *Popular Music and Society 14, 2*, 7–36.

34   Ibid., p. 18.

35   Varga, G. (1993, March 18). Coverdale is no Plant for another Zeppelin. *San Diego Union-Tribune*, Night and Day, p. 11.

36   Catlin, R. (1992, July 29). Blues greats guilty of 'borrowing,' too. *Chicago Sun-Times*, p. B41.

37   Ibid.

38   Moss, M. D. (1997, May–July). Who owns the songs the whole world sings? *Sing Out! Folk Song Magazine, 42, 1,* 3.

39   Catlin, R. (1992, July 29). Blues greats guilty of "borrowing," too. *Chicago Sun-Times,* p. B41.

40   Hochman, S. (1994, October 8). Willie Dixon's daughter makes sure legacy lives on. *Los Angeles Times,* p. F10.

41   Feld, S. (1996). Pygmy pop: A genealogy of schizophonic mimesis. *Yearbook of Traditional Music, 28,* 44.

42   Mills, S. (1996). Indigenous music and the law: An analysis of national and international legislation. *Yearbook for Traditional Music, 28,* 57–86, 59.

43   Ibid.

44   Seeger, C. (1996). Ethnomusicologists, archives, professional organizations, and the shifting ethics of intellectual property. *Yearbook for Traditional Music, 28,* 87–105.

45   Mills, S. (1996). Indigenous music and the law: An analysis of national and international legislation. *Yearbook for Traditional Music, 28,* 57–86, 60.

46   Ibid. p. 67.

47   Huang, R. (1996, August 29). Imperfect harmony: Age-old chants strike a discordant note. *Far Eastern Economic Review, 159, 35,* 50.

48   Sandburg, B. (1998, December 11). Copyright wilderness. *Broward Daily Business Review,* p. B1.

49   Ibid.

50   McCarty, S. (2000, February 4). The Enigma that is Cretu. *South China Morning Post,* p. 5.

51   Toop, D. (1995). *Ocean of sound: Aether talk, ambient sound and imaginary worlds.* New York: Serpent's Tail.

52   Pride, D. (1995, October 28). U.K.'s nation of "ethno-techno." *Billboard,* 43.

53   Mills, S. (1996). Indigenous music and the law: An analysis of national and international legislation. *Yearbook for Traditional Music, 28,* 57–86, 57.

54   Lissauer, R. (1996). *Lissauer's encyclopedia of popular music in America: 1888 to the present.* New York: Paragon House; Smith, L. (1985, April 5). Food servers drafted as birthday warblers. *Los Angeles Times,* p. E1.

55   Birthday song rights for sale. (1988, October 20). *Chicago Tribune,* p. C15; Fabrikant, G. (1988b, October 20). Put a song in your portfolio: 'happy birthday' is for sale." *New York Times,* p. A1; Sold. (1989, January 2). *Time,* 88.

56   Hayes, E. (1993, April 10). 'Happy birthday to you' tune can't copyright good memories. *Orlando Sentinel Tribune,* p. E1; Shepard, S. (1992, January 6). Name that tune. *Memphis Business Journal,* 3.

57   Ibid.

58   Don Biederman, personal correspondence, March 17, 1997.

59   O'Reilly, D. (1986, April 28). Crackdown on song rights. *Record,* p. B7.

60   Fuld, J. J. (1985). *The book of world famous music.* Toronto: General Publishing Company; Wolfson, A. (1988, October 22). Louisville sisters' celebrated ditty is set to be sold. *Courier-Journal,* p. 1A.

61   Ask the Globe. (1996, December 9). *Boston Globe,* p. B10.

62   Hawes, B. L. (1970). *The birthday: An American ritual.* Unpublished master's thesis, University of California-Berkeley, Berkeley; Lax, R. (1989). *The great song thesaurus.* Oxford: Oxford University Press; Shy women teachers who wrote child's ditty figure in plagiarism suit over broadway hit. (1934, August 15). *New York Times,* p. A19.

63   Hawes, B. L. (1970). *The birthday: An American ritual.* Unpublished master's thesis, University of California, Berkeley.

64   Fabrikant, G. (1988b, October 20). Put a song in your portfolio: 'Happy birthday' is for sale." *New York Times,* p. A1; Salamon, J. (1981, June 12). On the other hand, you can blow out the candles for free. *Wall Street Journal,* p. 1.

65   Blau, E. (1986, December 26). The antics of Schickele and Borge. *New York Times,* p. C3.

66   Lebrecht, N. (1996, May 11). "Echoes strike a chord." *Daily Telegraph,* p. 7.

67   Ewen, D. (1969, January 8). Yanks sing this song most often. *Variety,* p. 4.

68   Ibid., p. 4.

69   Ball, I. (1988, December 21). Beware if you sing happy birthday. *Daily Telegraph,* p. 6; Ewen, D. (1969, January 8). Yanks sing this song most often. *Variety,* p. 4.

70   Hawes, B. L. (1970). *The birthday: An American ritual.* Unpublished master's thesis, University of California Berkeley, p. 22.

71   Ibid.

72   Ibid.

73   Jensen, K. (1996, May 9). Singing 'happy birthday' can carry a hefty price. *Rocky Mountain News,* p. 5B.

74   Cake, candles not included. (1988, October 31). *Time,* 59.

75   Salamon, J. (1981, June 12). On the other hand, you can blow out the candles for free. Wall Street Journal, p. 1.

76   Smith, L. (1985, April 5). Food servers drafted as birthday warblers. *Los Angeles Times,* p. E1.

77 Maybe you could get it for a song. (1988, October 29). *Chicago Tribune,* p. C10.

78 Lyons, T. (1996, August 23). These fees are a royal pain. *Sarasota Herald-Tribune,* p. 1B; McNeely, J. (1993, April 25). If you want to sing 'happy birthday to you,' you'd better have a good attorney. *Columbus Dispatch,* p. 3F; Scott, J. (1994, September 30). Singer Gladys Knight helps launch search for new 'birthday' song. *Plain Dealer,* p. 41.

79 Ball, I. (1988, December 21). Beware if you sing happy birthday. *Daily Telegraph,* p. 6.

80 Fuld, J. J. (1985). *The Book of World Famous Music.* Toronto: General Publishing Company.

81 Grattan, V. L. (1993). *American women songwriters: A biographical dictionary.* Westport: Greenwood Press.

82 Claghorn, G. (1996). *Women composers and songwriters: A concise biographical dictionary.* Lanham: Scarecrow Press.

83 Fuld, J. J. (1985). *The book of world famous music.* Toronto: General Publishing Company.

84 Hawes, B. L. (1970). *The birthday: An American ritual.* Unpublished master's thesis, University of California Berkeley.

85 Hayes, E. (1993, April 10). 'Happy birthday to you' tune can't copyright good memories. *Orlando Sentinel Tribune,* p. E1.

86 Ibid.

87 ASCAP faces the music. (1996, September 1). *Austin American-Statesman,* p. J2.

88 Gilligan, A. (1996, September 1). You won't get burnt singing around campfire. *Telegraph Herald,* p. E1. Bannon, L. (1996, August 24). Birds sing, but campers can't—unless they pay up. *Star Tribune,* p. 10E.

89 Orr, J. (1996, August 23). Large groups of scout campers must pay to play ASCAP's songs. *Nashville Banner,* p. A12.

90 Ibid.

91 Jensen, K. (1996, May 9). Singing 'happy birthday' can carry a hefty price. *Rocky Mountain News,* p. 5B.

92 SCAP faces the music. (1996, September 1). *Austin American-Statesman,* p. J2.

93 Bannon, L. (1996, August 24). Birds sing, but campers can't—unless they pay up. *Star Tribune,* p. 10E; Orr, J. (1996, August 23). Large groups of Scout campers must pay to play ASCAP's songs. *Nashville Banner,* p. A12; Singing a different tune. (1996, August 29). *St. Louis Post-Dispatch,* p. 6B.

94   Orr, J. (1996, August 23). Large groups of scout campers must pay to play ASCAP's songs. *Nashville Banner,* p. A12; Bumiller, E. (1996, December 17). Battle hymns around campfires: ASCAP asks royalties from Girl Scouts. *New York Times,* p. B1.

95   Orr, J. (1996, August 23). Large groups of scout campers must pay to play ASCAP's songs. *Nashville Banner,* p. A12.

96   A-caroling we go. (1996, December 18). *Indianapolis News,* p. A22; Orr, J. (1996, August 23). Large groups of scout campers must pay to play ASCAP's songs. *Nashville Banner,* p. A12.

97   A-caroling we go. (1996, December 18). *Indianapolis News,* p. A22.

98   Hassell, G. (1997, January 15). Memorable pr missteps of 96. *Houston Chronicle,* p. 1.

99   Bannon, L. (1996, August 24). Birds sing, but campers can't—unless they pay up. *Star Tribune,* p. 10E.

100   Loder, K. (Producer). (1996, August 30). *MTV Week in Rock.* New York: MTV.

101   Bumiller, E. (1996, December 17). Battle hymns around campfires: ASCAP asks royalties from Girl Scouts. *New York Times,* p. B1.

102   Harmon, R. (1996, August 30). Calling off the troops in the song war. *Montgomery Advertiser,* p. 1C.

103   ASCAP chief says scouts controversy part of 'shameful agenda.' (1996, October). *Chattanooga Times,* p. C3; Lichtman, I. (1996, September 7). Words and music: ASCAP tries to rectify Girl Scout flap. *Billboard,* p. 1.

104   Forcucci, S. L. (1984). *A folk song history of America: America through its songs.* Englewood Cliffs, NJ: Prentice-Hall.

105   Greenhill, P. (1993). 'The folk process' in the revival: 'Barrett's privateers' and 'Barratt's privateers. In N. V. Rosenberg (Ed.), *Transforming tradition: Folk music revivals examined* (pp. 136–159). Chicago: University of Illinois Press, p. 139.

106   Toelken, B. (1986). Ballads and folksongs. In E. Oring (Ed.), *Folk groups and folklore genres: An introduction* (pp. 147–174). Logan, UT: Utah State University Press.

107   Ibid., p. 149.

108   Berryman, P. (1998, Fall). Baffled and annoyed: Thoughts on "the art of the rewrite." *Sing Out!, 43, 2,* 75–77.

109   DJ Spooky, personal correspondence, October 7, 1999.

110   Zeitlin, S. (1998, April 25). Strangling culture with a copyright law. *New York Times,* p. A15.

111   Jay-Z. (1998). *Vol. 2: Hard Knock Life.* [CD] New York: Def Jam.

112   Iverem, E. (1998, February 4). "Porgy": New dialogue on an old opera. *Washington Post,* p. D1.

113   Ibid.

114   Johnson, A. J. (1996). *Gershwin's "American folk opera": The genesis, style, and reputation of Porgy and Bess (1935).* Unpublished doctoral dissertation, Harvard University, Cambridge, MA.

115   Ibid.

116   Ibid., p. 160.

117   Ibid.

118   Ibid.

119   Ibid., p. 167.

120   Japlonsky, E. (1988). *Gershwin.* New York: Da Capo Press; Johnson, A. J. (1996). *Gershwin's "American folk opera": The genesis, style, and reputation of Porgy and Bess (1935).* Unpublished doctoral dissertation, Harvard University, Cambridge, MA, p. 258.

121   Johnson, A. J. (1996). *Gershwin's "American folk opera": The genesis, style, and reputation of Porgy and Bess (1935).* Unpublished doctoral dissertation, Harvard University, Cambridge, MA.

122   Ibid., p. 329; Rosenberg, D. (1991). *Fascinating rhythm: The collaboration of George and Ira Gerswin.* New York: Dutton.

123   Alpert, H. (1990). *The life and times of Porgy and Bess: The story of an American classic.* New York: Knopf, p. 88.

124   Johnson, A. J. (1996). *Gershwin's "American folk opera": The genesis, style, and reputation of Porgy and Bess (1935).* Unpublished doctoral dissertation, Harvard University, Cambridge, MA.

125   Schwartz, C. (1973). *Gershwin: His life and music.* New York: Bobbs-Merrill, p. 260.

126   Iverem, E. (1998, February 4). "Porgy": New dialogue on an old opera. *Washington Post,* p. D1.

127   Schwartz, C. (1973). *Gershwin: His life and music.* New York: Bobbs-Merrill.

128   Crouch, S. (1998, August 30). Gershwin is still cause for rhapsody: An inspired borrower of black tradition. *New York Times,* p. B1.

Chapter 3

Copyright, Authorship and African-American Culture

African-American culture comes out of a primarily oral culture. Black American slaves, not allowed to read, continued the oral traditions of the various African cultures from which they came.[1] While I do not collapse the nuances and differences that exist within African-American culture into a neat, essentialized whole, I nevertheless maintain that prominent elements of African-American culture engage in an intertextual mode of cultural production.

I have selected two extended examples—one shorter (oral folk preaching) and the other quite long (hip-hop music)—that illustrate contradictions that occur when the intertextual practices of African-American cultural production become articulated with intellectual property law. The intertextual practices that characterize many aspects of African-American culture conflict with a particular way of understanding authorship and ownership that originated in Western Enlightenment and Romanticist thought, and these differences have resulted in significant consequences.

Originality, Plagiarism and African-American Oral Folk Preaching

Plagiarism is inescapably intertwined with copyright (both concepts came into being around the same time) and, moreover, these concepts are bound up in the capitalist relations that began to emerge in Europe during seventeenth century.[2] During this time, there was a push to view texts as commercial products and the author as the manufacturer of those texts, a process which Scollon argues represents the "economic/ideological system which arose at the time of the Enlightenment."[3] Scollon concludes, "The traditional view of plagiarism constitutes, in fact, an ideological position which privileges a concept of the person established within the European Enlightenment."[4]

This particular concept of the person, in part, provides the basis for a model of communication that dominated communication studies from its early stages (e.g., there is a message that originates from a singular individual, the sender, and this message gets transmitted to a receiver). Numerous studies have demonstrated that this is a culturally situated model that is connected to a particular historical time and social group. Therefore, the simple conceptualization of a speaker or writer rooted in Enlightenment thought is not a tenable concept, because "real life" is more complex.[5] Scollon concludes:

> A closer analysis of the concept of plagiarism shows that, in fact, it disguises these complexities by masking them in the idea that . . . [people] . . . speak and write as unified biological persons who always represent themselves in a straightforward and sincere way. . . . In other words, the concept of plagiarism is a shorthand compilation of a rather hefty set of assumptions about who should or should not have the right to use discourse to create individual, autonomous voices in a society. In yet other words, the concept of plagiarism is fully embedded within a social, political, and cultural matrix that cannot be meaningfully separated from its interpretation.[6]

For example, those who do not have the right to "use discourse to create individual, autonomous voices" are those who engage in discursive tactics that do not conform to these conceptualizations of originality and authorship.

The invention of the printing press not only is directly connected with capitalism, copyright and plagiarism, it was instrumental in facilitating the shift from oral to written manuscript, then to print culture in Europe. Print culture resulted in attempts to close down intertextuality by emphasizing Romantic notions of "originality" and "creativity," and at this time there came into being the notion that words can be privately owned. Put simply, Ong states, "Typography had made the word into a commodity."[7]

This newly conceptualized "private ownership of words," as Ong labels it, provided a philosophical basis for the emergence of copyright laws that followed the invention of the printing press, which unambiguously tied up the newly formed concept of plagiarism with commodity capitalism.[8] Bettig echoes these arguments when he states that there is a direct connection between the rise of typography, capitalism and the commodification of literary and artistic domains.[9] The thread that ties these concepts together is copyright law, and plagiarism provides the deeply resonating moral underpinnings for this economically grounded legal construction.

Plagiarism and African-American Oral Folk Preaching

Martin Luther King Jr. not only borrowed words and ideas in his gradu-ate-school work, but also in many of the documented speeches he gave throughout his life. We can either view this as an intellectual shortcoming or use this understanding as a springboard to construct more complex notions of how other cultures understand the role and use of knowledge. Both Scollon[10] and Johannesen[11] emphasize that their critiques of the tenets that underlie plagiarism should not be read as an endorsement of a uniformly relativistic view of plagiarism, and I agree with their cautions. Nevertheless, they argue that King's borrowings of words and ideas can be understood in light of their critiques, and they believe that we should not view plagiarism in the one dimensional way that dominates the acad-emy.[12] "I use the oratory of Martin Luther King, Jr.," Johannessen writes, "as illustrative of discourse that, while reflective of multiple cultural and intellectual influences, was shaped significantly by a cultural tradition that approved of the unattributed borrowing of ideas and held words and ideas to be communal resources."[13]

In 1985 Coretta Scott King—Martin Luther King Jr.'s widow—appointed Stanford University historian Clayborne Carson to head the King Papers Project, which was dedicated to preserving, annotating and publishing King's writings from his early years as a student up through the time of his death in 1968.[14] In a front-page story published on November 9, 1990, the *Wall Street Journal* disclosed that the King Papers Project's researchers had found, in Carson's words at a press conference called after the *Journal* published its story, "a pattern of appropriation, of tex-tual appropriation."[15] The *New York Times* and other major U.S. news-papers (the *Washington Post,* the *Boston Globe,* etc.) placed the story on their front pages, and it was extensively covered during 1990 in re-gional newspapers, national magazines, and on radio and television.

The *Boston Globe's* coverage of the controversy was typical, begin-ning with the sentence, "Researchers at Stanford University said yester-day they have discovered numerous instances of plagiarism in Rev. Mar-tin Luther King, Jr.'s writings as a graduate student, and Boston University has started an investigation of whether King's use of others' material without giving credit violated the integrity of the doctoral degree he re-ceived there."[16] The *New York Times* and other newspapers that picked up the story quoted Carson as saying, "By the strictest definition of pla-giarism—that is, any appropriation of words or ideas—there are instances of plagiarism in these papers."[17]

One theme within many of the stories published in newspapers was that this discovery may, as *New York Times* writer Anthony De Palma stated, "tarnish the myth of the man."[18] Many writers also emphasized that King was well aware of the principles of citation, expressing bewilderment over why Dr. King appropriated the words and ideas of others without giving proper credit.

This confusion was intensified by the fact that Dr. King apparently did not attempt to conceal his appropriations. First, he paid tribute to the man from whom he borrowed material that appeared on the fifth page of his dissertation; also, King cited this person's work in the bibliography and he sporadically footnoted that work as well.[19] Second, the *New York Times* reported that King "not only retained his graduate school papers, but also deposited them in an archive at Boston University where they would become available to scholars."[20] Another story quoted a researcher as saying, "Why didn't he know better?" and "Why did he do it? Was he so insecure that he thought this was the only way to get by?"[21]

Why did he do it? I cannot answer that question any more definitively than can other scholars and pundits who have weighed in on the matter, partially because King neither spoke of this issue to any known living person nor did he leave any evidence of his intentions. I want to argue, nevertheless, that perhaps the reason why King never spoke of this to anyone is because he did not think it an issue. That is, the practices that led him to appropriate the words and ideas of others were so much a part of the cultural tradition that King grew up in that he did not see what he did to be a problem.

That he did not try to hide what he did is perhaps the most significant indicator that he did not believe he was wrong when he borrowed the words and ideas of others without proper, consistent attribution in his doctoral dissertation and graduate-school class papers. As stated above, King deposited his graduate papers in the Boston University archives; moreover, he often referred to the scholars whose words he borrowed— not exactly the best strategy for a knowing, calculating plagiarist to employ.[22]

Rather than turning to some of the more sensational explanations the media reported ("Was he so insecure that he thought this was the only way to get by?"), I here make a point that, with minor exceptions, the media overwhelmingly failed to consider—the fact that King's "motives" were perhaps nothing more than the unconscious habits resulting from years of enculturation within the black folk-preaching tradition of which he, his father, and grandfather were a part. Keith D. Miller argues:

> Legally forbidden to read and write, slaves had created a highly oral religious culture that treated songs and sermons as shared wealth, not private property. During and after slavery, African-American folk preachers gained stature by merging

their identities with earlier, authoritative bearers of the Word. In this context, striking originality might have seemed self-centered or otherwise suspect. While growing up, King absorbed this tradition, hearing religious themes and metaphors that originated during slavery.[23]

Because earlier black folk preachers usually could not write down their sermons, they borrowed sermons and traded with other preachers, working from the assumption that language is created by everyone and that it could not be considered private property.[24] Miller gives the example of two sermons King heard as a child, "The Eagle Stirs Her Nest" and "Dry Bones in the Valley," which date back to the end of slavery and continue to be heard in black churches today. [25] "A large community shares those two sermons," Miller[26] continues, "for only with the arrival of print have people come to view language as private property to be copyrighted, packaged, and sold as a commodity."[27] Moreover, the imitation of important and long-standing pulpit texts and preaching styles was a fully accepted method of apprenticeship among the black folk preachers from whom King learned.[28]

Reagon discusses the notion of apprenticeship in the two traditions in which King was immersed: Western-based academia and the black folk pulpit. She states that Western-based academia stresses the importance of developing one's thesis by drawing on a thoroughly identified database cultivated by other scholars who came before, and that this process is given the highest status within the Western academy.[29] This is, Reagon argues, "keyed to the ownership, possession, private-property ethos that drives so much of Western cultural nationalism."[30] In beginning to study a practice within an area of African-American culture such as the black folk ministry, one is primarily an imitator, and the phase that marks the passage from apprentice to master is when one is seen as finding his or her "voice."

Reagon states, "Within African-American culture, there is a very high standard placed on the moment when one not only makes a solid statement of the song or the sermon, but the offering is given in one's own signature."[31] This "signature" is marked by an original "sound," "style," "rhythm" or "voice"—a conceptualization that differs considerably from many fields of Western academic culture that define originality within the parameters of the analysis of the data and what one does with it based on that analysis, or both. Reagon writes, "The academic process looks at the documentation: Did she or he reveal every step made through the documentation and is the trail of the search clearly outlined? Living within a society where style and voice are not perceived as signature—are not understood as data—makes survival challenging."[32]

Garrow asserts that explaining King's "transgressions" in graduate school vis-à-vis the cultural tradition from which he emerged does disservice to his intellect.[33] But this is not true, because King was obviously smart enough to be able to discern the differences between the standards and ethics of academia and the black folk preaching tradition that grounded him. King—like many African Americans (and other minority groups) who straddle between two cultures—found a way to negotiate a hybrid system when, in Miller's[34] words, he "ventured outside the universe of African-American orality to negotiate his way through the unfamiliar terrain of intellectualized print culture."[35]

Speaking of this negotiated hybrid system, Reagon argues that those who "straddle" construct a new network of rules and practices that are an amalgamation of the differing systems they take part in.[36] "Therefore no system," Reagon writes, "neither the one of our birth nor the one we adopt through mastery, is sacred. Both systems become instruments or tools."[37] By "straddling," King learned to synthesize effectively these cultural traditions in ways that allowed him to make sense of the world and, further, to help make sense of the world for others. One of King's greatest attributes was his ability to integrate—articulate—seemingly disparate ideologies and ideas so that, for instance, he could rearticulate many of the key notions that white America held dear in a way that made whites understand the necessity of the black freedom struggle.[38] Miller states:

> Resisting his professors' rules about language and many notions of the Great White Thinkers, King crafted highly imaginative, persuasive discourse through the folk procedures of voice merging and self-making. Reanimating the slaves' world view, he prodded John F. Kennedy and most of white America to listen for the first time to the slaves' time-honored cry for racial equality.[39]

This is important because, Miller argues, "King's borrowing gives us an additional reason to reconsider intertextuality, collaboration, the rhetoric of protest, orality and literacy, the social context of invention, and our sacrosanct notion of language as private property."[40] It is important to note that many of the above-mentioned concepts *directly* apply to hip-hop music—intertextuality, the rhetoric of protest, orality and literacy, the social context of invention, as well as (to slightly modify the wording above) the sacrosanct notion of *music* as private property. Because hip-hop has forced itself to the center of mainstream American culture, this self-consciously rebellious musical culture based in the experiences and modes of cultural production that many African Americans share provides a significant, contemporary example of these issues.

Hip-hop is significant because it has become a massive money-making industry that is based on a form of cultural production that flies in the face of particular Western notions of originality and authorship in much the same way King's black folk pulpit style did. Because hip-hop digitally samples and recontextualizes fragments of copyrighted sound recordings, it was an easy target for intellectual property infringement lawsuits in its early commercially successful days (and, of course, it continues to be). By looking at the way in which hip-hop evolved and was transformed by these new legal and economic relations, we can gain a better understanding of how race, intellectual property law, cultural production and a variety of other elements come to be articulated.

Hip-Hop, Sampling and Copyright Law

Tricia Rose claims that Ong's notion of a postliterate orality is a useful one to apply to hip-hop's mode of cultural production.[41] Both digital sampling and rapping create a technological and cultural form of literacy that incorporates the intertextual referencing of varying elements, both the language-based and the more amorphously aural. Similarly, Schumacher discusses how technology, especially in hip-hop, is now very much a part of musical production.[42] Digital sampling creates new modes of production, all while drawing on older modes—in this case, the cultural traditions discussed by Rose.[43] This is another notion of authorship, Schumacher argues, a notion that is not seen as equal in the eyes of the law because it does not conform to Enlightenment and Romantic notions of originality and authorship.[44]

Schumacher goes further than Rose in his critique of what he considers the fundamental basis of intellectual property law. He argues that intellectual property law is, first, a *property law* and that the author should be seen as a historical construct, and that further, these notions of originality and authorship are deeply embedded in capitalist relations. Copyright is a culturally bound law that could not deal with the collision of a particular form of cultural production rooted in the European practice of composing and notating music and the more improvisatory African-American tradition of jazz. Just as copyright law did not know how to deal with jazz artists' appropriation of certain phrases and whole choruses from popular songs, copyright law still has not come to terms with sampling.[45]

"The Sound of (Hip-Hop) Music": A Brief History

Rap music, as it is popularly known, is but one element of a larger cultural movement called hip-hop. "When I say the word 'hip-hop,'" explains Richie "Crazy Legs" Colon, an early participant in hip-hop culture, "I'm including every element—the graf[fiti], the dance, the music, everything, the rapping."[46] It is important to understand hip-hop music as being directly tied to a historical social movement that developed in the South Bronx during the mid-1970s because many have dehistoricized the development of hip-hop by, for instance, tracing the roots of "rap music" to the vocal delivery style of Bob Dylan or by other similar comparisons.

Hip-hop culture, broadly speaking, incorporates four prominent elements: "breaking" (or breakdancing), "tagging" or "bombing" (marking the walls of buildings and subways with graffiti), "DJ"-ing (collaging the best fragments of records by using two turntables), and "MC"-ing (more commonly referred to as "rapping").[47] The significance of breakdancing and graffiti should not be downplayed, but it is obvious that DJs and MCs have become hip-hop's most noticeable and persistent components; therefore, I will focus primarily on them.

The key figure in the development of hip-hop music was the DJ.[48] During the early to mid-1970s, DJs simply spun popular records that kept the party alive and people dancing, existing more in the mold of radio and club DJs. In the early days of hip-hop there were a number of DJs who had strong followings in each of their districts throughout the Bronx. These DJs rarely had access to large clubs; the primary venues were block parties, schools and parks (where, as legend has it, they would plug their sound systems into lampposts and play until the police broke up the gathering).

The most popular of these early DJs was Jamaican immigrant Kool DJ Herc, who is credited with two new musical methods that, Rose argues, separated hip-hop music from other popular musics and provided the groundwork for further innovation.[49] The first was Herc's habit of isolating the fragments of songs that were the most popular with dancers and segueing them into one long musical collage. These song fragments were composed of the percussion breaks within the songs and came to be known as "breakbeats." Early DJ pioneer Africa Bambaataa recalls Kool Herc's DJ style:

> Now he took the music of Mandrill like "Fencewalk," certain disco records that had funky percussion breaks like The Incredible Bongo Band when they came out with "Apache" and he just kept that beat *going*. It might be that certain part of the record that everybody waits for—they just let their inner self go and get wild.[50]

Kool Herc told me: "I quickly realized that those breakbeats were making the crowd go crazy, so I just started digging deeper and deeper into my record collection, ya know? As long as I kept the beat going with the best parts of those records, everybody would keep dancing. And the culture just evolved from that."[51] Other DJs built on the collaged breakbeat method and began expanding on the possibilities that two turntables could offer. One of the first DJs to pick up on the breakbeat technique was Grandmaster Flash, who went further than Kool Herc in his turntable wizardry.[52]

With two turntables Flash was able, in his own words, to "take small parts of records and, at first, keep it on time, no tricks, keep it on time. I'm talking about very short beats, maybe 40 seconds, keeping it going for about five minutes, depending on how popular that particular record was."[53] Flash continues: "After that, I mastered punch phasing—taking certain parts of a record where there's a vocal or drum slap or a horn. I would throw it out and bring it back, keeping the other turntable playing. If this record had a horn in it before the break came down I would go— BAM, BAM, BAM-BAM—just to try this on the crowd."[54] Another technique credited to Grandmaster Flash is "scratching."[55]

Kool Herc is credited with a second important innovation—the development of the live MC.[56] During parties he began "dropping rhymes" or shouting simple phrases that were popular in the streets like "rock on my mellow," "to the beat y'all," or "you don't stop" on top of the breakbeats he played.[57] Herc borrowed this rhythmic form of talking (called "toasting") from the microphone personalities who deejayed in his native Jamaica, and he is recognized as the person who brought this style to New York.[58] Early on, when Herc began concentrating more on mixing breakbeats, he enlisted the help of his friend Coke La Rock to take over the duties of the MC (Master of Ceremonies). The MC was responsible for exciting the dancers and giving the party a live feel, functioning as an agent of crowd control—and thus diffusing tensions that might arise from rival groups in the crowd.[59]

When Grandmaster Flash realized that people were paying too much attention to what he was doing (instead of dancing) he saw the importance of having live MC accompaniment.[60] Along with Melle Mel, Scorpio, Kidd Creole, and Raheem and Cowboy, Flash formed Grandmaster Flash and the Furious Five.[61] This group, along with many other groups of MCs and DJs—such as Grand Wizard Theodore and the Fantastic Five, DJ Breakout and the Funky Four, Cold Crush Brothers, and the Treacherous Three—fought for microphone supremacy in local parks and clubs.[62]

Until July 1979, when the Sugarhill Gang released "Rapper's Delight," hip-hop was strictly an underground phenomenon that had not been documented beyond the numerous bootleg tapes of live performances that circulated throughout the city.[63] The release of "Rapper's Delight" forever changed hip-hop music's (and hip-hop culture's) relationship with the music industry. It also changed the way hip-hop music sounded for a majority of listeners, because mass record distribution was the only way most consumers could hear this new musical form.

The Sugarhill Gang was not a part of the South Bronx hip-hop scene that had developed in the 1970s; the group was put together by Sugarhill Records owners Sylvia and Joe Robinson.[64] The Sugarhill Gang had no street credibility and was not known to anyone involved in the Bronx hip-hop scene, but this did not stop them from having a huge hit—selling over 2 million records worldwide.[65] Grandmaster Flash recalled hearing "Rapper's Delight" back in 1979, stating: "What is this? I heard this record on the radio almost every 10 minutes on almost every station that I switched to. They said it was these boys out of Jersey."[66] At another time he said: "I'm saying to myself, I don't know of anybody else from here to Long Island that's doing this. Why don't I know of this group called the Sugarhill who?"[67]

Because I'm interested in the development of hip-hop's sound—its production techniques—I argue that the first 20 years of *recorded* hip-hop can be divided into five relatively distinct though still somewhat overlapping phases, beginning with the Sugarhill era and carrying through to the late 1990s. These particular phases are *not* mutually exclusive; *neither are they the only potential way of organizing hip-hop's history.* For my purposes, however, it is a useful framework for analyzing the evolution of hip-hop's musical production. Tuff City Records owner Aaron Fuchs identifies four major periods in recorded hip-hop during a discussion of sampling in a *Billboard* article he authored, something that provides the basis for my organizational scheme.

The first period (about 1979–1983) featured the live funk band sound of the Sugarhill era, which came to be known as "old school" when a new wave of rappers entered the hip-hop arena with their stripped down, "hardcore" sound. This "hardcore" sound that dominated the second period (about 1983–1987) was characterized, according to Fuchs,[68] by a predominance of "electronic drums and synthesizers."[69] The proliferation of the use of digital samplers created a third distinctive period (about 1986–1992), during which time samples (digitally recorded fragments of preexisting sounds) of old funk, rock, soul, jazz and reggae records became a prominent part of much hip-hop music.

Fuchs, writing in 1992, argued that as sampling moved into its third or fourth year of popularity, it was superseded by the incorporation of live instrumentation that was often sampled and inserted in a hip-hop production.[70] This phase constitutes the fourth period of recorded hip-hop music (about 1992–1996) which, to some extent, has been complemented by a resurgence in sampling but with an emphasis on only one or two obvious recognizable hooks. This is typical of the most recent period of recorded hip-hop, about 1996–2001. Again, this is not the only way of organizing hip-hop's aural history as it exists on record, and the specific dates can be argued, but this rough organizational scheme is appropriate for this analysis.

"Rapper's Delight" changed the way hip-hop sounded. Before this single was released, hip-hop performances were almost uniformly comprised of the DJ spinning and manipulating records while the MC rapped on top of the music.[71] "Rapper's Delight" featured a live band that provided the background music over which the MCs could rap, and its sound was radically different from the hip-hop music that was performed in the parks and clubs by DJs and MCs when the Sugarhill Gang's hit song was recorded. One similarity the backing track of this record shared with its hip-hop predecessors is the fact that it appropriated its music from an existing song. The Sugarhill Records live house band lifted the background track of the popular disco song "Good Times," by Chic, using the bass line and chords as its instrumental foundation. This appropriation set a precedent for a controversy that still brews today because it prompted a lawsuit by Nile Rogers, the song's cowriter.[72]

Because these studio musicians essentially performed the role of the DJ on record, it is unsurprising that "Rapper's Delight" wasn't the only early hip-hop song to borrow from previous hits. The Funky Four Plus One's "Rappin' and Rockin' the House" (released shortly after "Rapper's Delight") essentially took its backing track from Cheryl Lynn's "Got To Be Real." Similarly, numerous hip-hop songs appropriated the Tom Tom Club's "Genius of Love," such as Grandmaster Flash and the Furious Five's "It's Nasty" and Dr. Jeckyll & Mr. Hyde's "Genius Rap," which featured those rappers rhyming on top of the Tom Tom Club's instrumental track.

The live funk band sound dominated the first few years of recorded hip-hop until RUN-DMC released their debut single in 1983 and, after this release, musicians were largely replaced by the DJ/producer on hip-hop records.[73] In light of this, the live funk band sound can be seen as an anomaly, a relatively short-lived trend that used traditional instruments in an attempt to translate hip-hop onto record before samplers became affordable. It was soon superseded by the extremely influential sound ushered in by RUN-DMC, which more closely resembled the way hip-hop sounded in the days before it was committed to vinyl, with its emphasis on just the beats and rhymes.

Run-DMC stripped down their music to simple drum machine beats, sparse keyboard embellishments, bass, scratch sounds, and the occasional live rock guitar, helping to redefine the sound of hip-hop music for the next few years. In addition, RUN-DMC was possibly the first group to overtly employ a DJ cutting up records on a hip-hop release (on their song "Peter Piper"), which also had a huge influence.[74] Toop claims that after the release of this record, "thousands of records based on scratchy samples have followed in the wake of 'Peter Piper.'"[75] He continues, "By parading the fact that they use stolen fragments of ancient vinyl, all these tracks have emphasized the importance of this disregard for recording studio conventions."[76]

The use of samplers revolutionized the way hip-hop was recorded, making them a quintessential production tool in hip-hop, allowing hip-hop artists to expand on the techniques used in hip-hop's early stages. One important factor contributing to the rise of sampling in hip-hop—which during the mid-1980s was still a relatively underground genre that had small recording budgets—was the drop in the cost of digital samplers. When samplers were first introduced in the market they cost upwards of $50,000, but by the mid-1980s they were relatively affordable, costing as little as $2,000.[77]

Digital samplers became a primary tool in hip-hop music-making be-cause it allowed DJs/producers to piece together breakbeats and sounds in a similar (but more sophisticated) way than the early DJs did. Sampling is a way of paying homage to older artists; it is also a kind of musical archeology, an archaeology that is significant when it is applied to black music which, as a result of music industry fostered conditions, has a noto-riously short shelf life.[78] From the early days of the music industry up through today, many popular jazz, funk, soul, rhythm and blues and hip-hop albums go out of print quickly, much faster than their rock and pop counterparts. This is partially what Stetsasonic's Daddy-O is talking about when he raps in "Talkin' All That Jazz": "Tell the truth James Brown was old 'til Eric B came out with 'I Got Soul'/ Hip-hop brings back old R&B/ If we would not people could have forgot."[79]

This song was written as a response to the attacks on sampling that came from older members of both the black and white music communi-ties. It was specifically a reply that Daddy-O penned after hearing R&B songwriter Mtume blast what he called "Memorex music."[80] Daddy-O fur-ther explained his position on sampling by saying: "Sampling's not a lazy man's way. We learn a lot from sampling; it's like school for us."[81] Another

Stetsasonic member, Prince Paul, has played a significant role as a hip-hop producer in pushing the boundaries of what can be done with sampling (he produced the first three De La Soul albums, among other hip-hop classics).

After the introduction of sampling in hip-hop music, virtually every hip-hop record used this technique. By the early 1990s, James Brown had been sampled on an estimated 2,000 records.[82] Similarly, Parliament-Funkadelic's music has provided a source for innumerable samples that has been used in hip-hop songs. An illustration of how pervasive the sampling of the P-Funk catalog has been lies in a lawsuit filed by a publishing company that owns some of Parliament-Funkadelic's songs. The suit extensively lists virtually every record label that released hip-hop records as well as dozens of hip-hop stars.[83]

Within what I have identified as the fourth period of recorded hip-hop, however, live instrumentation increasingly dominated the way hip-hop records were produced. Rapper and producer Dr. Dre, whose album *The Chronic* was released in 1992, epitomizes the use of live production techniques in hip-hop. Speaking about *The Chronic* before it was released, hip-hop producer Sir Jinx said: "It's gonna revolutionize, just change everything, because he didn't use samples. He might have used one or two or three, but as of a whole album, no. And that's gonna change up everything, because that's showing that we don't need the samples."[84] This was no hollow boast; *The Chronic* went on to sell millions of records, becoming one of the biggest and most influential hip-hop records of the decade.

Like any major trend in hip-hop music (as well as pop music), many emulators followed suit by incorporating live instrumentation into their records. The decline in the use of samples taken directly from records and the increased use of "traditional" musicians in recorded hip-hop during the early to mid-1990s was, in part, a result of the enforcement of copyright law in this area. The contradiction between hip-hop music's intertextual mode of musical production and the economic and legal restrictions of copyright law created significant obstacles that dissuaded producers from sampling as freely as they had in the past. Before I further address those issues, I will outline a history of the development of hip-hop as it relates to the marketplace.

The Business of Hip-Hop
In the time since the late 1970s, hip-hop rose from an underground phenomenon confined to the black and Hispanic neighborhoods of the South Bronx to a billion-dollar industry. Today it pervades nearly every facet of

popular culture: TV shows, commercials and movies feature hip-hop performers (Will Smith, LL Cool J, and Queen Latifah have all starred in successful TV sitcoms, movies, or both). The pop charts are dominated by hip-hop and hip-hop-influenced music, and hip-hop fashion styles have come to dominate the dress of young blacks and whites throughout America.

I'm not willing to claim that hip-hop music never was a commodity (though when it was being performed for free in local parks it came close), but I nevertheless agree with Rose when she argued, "What is more important about the shift in hip-hop's orientation is not its movement from precommodity to commodity but the shift in control over the scope and direction of the profit-making process, out of the hands of local Black and Hispanic entrepreneurs and into the hands of larger White-owned, multinational businesses."[85] Put another way, the means of production shifted from the community that developed this music to the corporations that control the distribution of most hip-hop records that are purchased each year.

During the 1970s hip-hop was a performance-oriented medium confined to the South Bronx, where "B-Boys" (short for "Break-Boys," who danced to the breakbeats the DJs spun) competitively "battled" each other in breakdance competitions. Little Rodney Cee, then of the hip-hop group The Funky Four Plus One, gave a description of the environment that dominated hip-hop at the time.

> An uptown group would battle a downtown group. What I mean by battle is that they could come and they would say, "Okay. Us four are better than your four," and we would go at it. We would pick one and we would dance against each other. We'd do one move and they'd do a move and the crowd liked it. That's where the competition came in. This is before any records, before any money was made. This was from our hearts.[86]

Another early hip-hop pioneer, DJ Lovebug, echoed these somewhat romanticized sentiments: "Back in the day, we used to push refrigerator-size speakers through the blocks . . . It was just for the love of it. We wasn't gettin' no money at all."[87] In the early days of hip-hop, DJs such as Kool Herc, Grandmaster Flash and Afrika Bambaataa often played for free in outdoor parks, house parties and community centers because of a lack of other venues. Soon, Grandmaster Flash's popularity surpassed that of Kool Herc's and Flash began to play for paying customers at numerous high schools and small clubs. By 1977, Flash's following had grown to the point where he was playing in clubs to crowds numbering more than 3,000.[88]

Before the mega success of the "Rapper's Delight" single, many (including Grandmaster Flash) believed that this new style's popularity would not translate into significant record sales. "I didn't think that somebody else would want to hear a record re-recorded onto another record with talking on it," Grandmaster Flash said, "I didn't think it would reach the masses like that."[89] Flash recalls an incident that took place in 1977 when he was approached by a small record label:

> "Let me bring you into the studio," said one of the owners. "Do exactly what you guys do at a party, but let's go into a recording studio." "It wouldn't work," said Flash. "Who would wanna spend $4.99?" He was charging a dollar or two for the shows in school gymnasiums and community centers at housing projects. "Nobody would want to buy the record." The idea was killed. "I regret that," says Flash. "Coulda been the first."[90]

Instead, the Sugarhill Gang were the first to release a hip-hop record. The release and subsequent popularity of this record—it became the biggest selling 12-inch single in history—was a watershed event in the commercialization of hip-hop because, before this record's release, the only way in which hip-hop was heard was in the clubs and via homemade cassettes of live performances, which were traded extensively within the New York boroughs.[91] Jazzy Jay (another early hip-hop participant) boasted, "I mean, we had tapes that went platinum before we was even involved with the music industry,"[92] and Grandmaster Flash claimed to have sold his taped performances at "a buck a minute."[93]

After the commercial success of "Rapper's Delight," many of the MCs and DJs who were popular on the club circuit began signing primarily to independent record labels. While hip-hop continued to gain new fans and grow in popularity through the early 1980s, it never achieved a sustained success on the level of "Rappers Delight" until the mid- to late 1980s.[94] This largely grassroots-fueled momentum helped provoke an intense, short-lived media infatuation with hip-hop culture (that singled out and highlighted the elements of rapping and breakdancing) during the early 1980s. Soon after, a deluge of movies that featured breakdancing and rapping such as *Flashdance*, *Wild Style*, *Beat Street*, *Breakin'* (plus a sequel), and *Krush Groove* were produced and released. Although many people in the mainstream music industry treated hip-hop as a passing fad, hip-hop's popularity continued to increase throughout the 1980s, a trend that intensified into the late 1990s.

Soon to be a major player in what would become the hip-hop music industry, Def Jam Records was cofounded in 1984 by Russell Simmons, the brother of RUN-DMC's Run.[95] By 1985, Simmons' label had released a string of 12-inch singles that sold over 250,000 each, an unprecedented number at the time, launching the careers of LL Cool J and The Beastie Boys. Simmons' business partner, Rick Rubin, produced the debut albums of soon-to-be multiplatinum artists LL Cool J, The Beastie Boys and Public Enemy. He also had a hand in producing Run-DMC's *Raising Hell,* the first hip-hop album to go platinum.[96] After starting the company with a $5,000 investment, Simmons and Rubin signed a $1 million distribution deal in 1985 with the giant corporate record label CBS, starting a trend that other independent labels would follow.

The evolution of Def Jam reflects many of the business-related trends within hip-hop, and it supports Nelson George's argument in *The Death of Rhythm & Blues* that major labels inevitably absorb the most vital black-owned labels if they prove profitable. By the late 1980s, Simmons and Rubin had parted ways, and Simmons became the sole owner of the operation until 1996. That year, Simmons sold 50% of Def Jam (a company that started as a grassroots label that he cofounded with a $5,000 investment) to the major label PolyGram for $33 million.[97]

In 1998, the German beverage giant Seagram purchased PolyGram, and in 1999 the company bought Universal Music, reducing the number of U.S. major labels from six to five (the AOL/Time-Warner merger with EMI/Capitol in 2000 would further reduce the number of major labels to four). Around this time, Seagram paid Def Jam a reported $100 million for the remaining shares of the hip-hop label it did not already own, completely dissolving Def Jam into the corporate structure of the Universal Music Group. Motown Records followed a quite similar path, and by 2000 both Motown and Def Jam—two of the twentieth century's most important and culturally significant black owned record labels—became reduced to the mere arms of a corporate behemoth. In regard to business practices, the story of Def Jam is in many ways the story of hip-hop.[98]

While Run-DMC was considered the first hip-hop group to attract a predominantly white rock audience, The Beastie Boys (the first white hip-hop group of note) were the first rappers to top the *Billboard* album charts—a sign that hip-hop had finally infiltrated the white suburbs of America.[99] This was another significant moment in the evolution of hip-hop, a wake-up call to the major labels that hip-hop was becoming a very profitable genre. These major labels, which had the distinct advantage of access to large amounts of capital and better distribution, moved quickly to sign new artists and, in a field dominated by small independent labels, many major labels began to absorb these smaller labels either through distribution deals (such as CBS's relationship with Def Jam Records or

RCA's relationship with Jive Records) or by purchasing the independents outright (as Warner Brothers did with the small but profitable Tommy Boy and Sleeping Bag labels).[100]

In 1988, annual hip-hop record sales reached $100 million, which accounted for 2% of the music industry's sales. The next year *Billboard* (the music industry's trade journal) added hip-hop charts to its magazine and MTV debuted *Yo! MTV Raps*, which quickly became the network's highest rated show.[101] By 1992, hip-hop was estimated as generating $400 million annually, roughly 5% of the music industry's annual income, and in 1995 CNN reported that hip-hop's annual sales had risen to 8% of the music industry's annual income.[102]

Within a decade, hip-hop's popularity and annual sales skyrocketed, a success that triggered a notable side effect, namely, a proliferation of lawsuits involving copyright infringement.[103] The deluge of lawsuits began in 1986, when 1960s and 1970s funk artist Jimmy Castor sued Def Jam and the Beastie Boys for their appropriation of the phrase "Yo, Leroy" from Castor's 1977 record "The Return of Leroy (Part I)."[104] Other important legal actions include the $1.7 million suit brought against De La Soul for their use of a Turtles song fragment in their 1989 album *Three Feet High and Rising*.[105] Also, Vanilla Ice was sued for using the bass hook from a David Bowie and Queen song as the foundation for his hit song "Ice Ice Baby," a dispute that was settled after Vanilla Ice agreed to share publishing royalties with the sampled artists.[106] The list of sampling copyright infringement lawsuits is extensive and includes lawsuits brought against Tag Team, MC Hammer, Jazzy Jeff and the Fresh Prince, Tone Loc and dozens of others.[107]

While many suits have been filed, most have been settled out of court because the expense involved in fully litigating a copyright infringement case is massive.[108] As a result, the music industry has been anxiously awaiting a legal precedent to be set so that many of the muddy issues surrounding sampling may be cleared.[109] In one example that breaks from this trend of settling out of court, the Supreme Court ruled in favor of rappers 2 Live Crew after the group was sued for reworking Roy Orbison's hit "Pretty Woman" in a lewd and arguably humorous fashion, sampling Orbison's original drum beat and bass line.[110]

2 Live Crew's lawyers argued that the song was a parody and it should be protected as such, while Orbison's publishing company's lawyers claimed that the song violated their client's copyrights to the original song. The court voted unanimously that the commercial nature of the song did not disqualify it from potentially being "fair use," and the court returned the

case down to a lower court with expanded guidelines concerning "fair use."[111] While the case attracted a great amount of attention and celebration in some circles, the court's ruling did not significantly affect the way *sampling* is legally defined because most rappers and hip-hop producers do not use samples in a way that a parody defense could convincingly be used.

The only other major case that has reached a verdict stage is Gilbert O'Sullivan's suit against Biz Markie, in which Markie used a 20-second sample from O'Sullivan's most popular song, the 1973 hit "Alone Again (Naturally)."[112] Immediately after the suit was filed, the album that contained the contested song was ordered off the shelf, and it became the focus of extensive media attention.[113] Judge Duffy, who presided over the case, handed down a strongly worded ruling that not only found the defendant guilty of copyright infringement, but also invoked the Seventh Commandment when suggesting Markie be subject to criminal prosecution for "stealing."[114] In the ruling, Duffy wrote:

> "Thou shalt not steal" has been an admonition followed since the dawn of civilization. Unfortunately, in the modern world of business this admonition is not always followed. Indeed, the defendants in this action for copyright infringement would have this court believe that stealing is rampant in the music business and, for that reason, their conduct here should be excused. The conduct of the defendants herein, however, violates not only the Seventh Commandment, but also the copyright laws of this country.[115]

This ruling sent shockwaves through the music industry, which immediately took notice of the possibility of criminal prosecution.[116] For those looking for some sort of precedent to be set, entertainment lawyer Stewart Levy argued, "This isn't the seminal case everyone wanted."[117] It is important to note that the ruling did not provide any guidelines for dealing with cases of sampling that were less substantial and easy to recognize (Markie used a sizable chunk of the original song's chorus), and there remain almost as many gray areas in the law after the case as before.[118]

As a result, this highly charged legal climate has put many in the music industry on edge. With virtually every major record label releasing hip-hop records and almost every record company owning the rights to records being sampled, this industry has a great interest in how samples are used. Most companies have taken defensive measures to guard against both copyright infringement lawsuits against them and the unauthorized sampling of records they own.

For instance, as early as 1990 it was one executive's job at PolyGram (which owns the rights to most James Brown recordings) to periodically listen to new releases on other labels for the Soul Brother #1's trademark scream.[119] Many companies developed entire departments devoted to this practice; in the early 1990s EMI Music Publishing had a staff of six people whose sole job was to listen to new releases that may have contained samples of its property.[120] By the end of the 1990s, these types of departments existed and greatly expanded in virtually all major publishing and record companies.

On the other side of the coin, record companies that distribute hip-hop records became increasingly interested in making sure that all samples that appear on a forthcoming release are "cleared," particularly after the Biz Markie ruling.[121] "That was the turning point for people clearing stuff," states Hope Carr, the owner of a sample-clearing company.[122] "Clearing" a sample involves licensing the use of a song fragment from its copyright owner(s) and working out a financial agreement that often involves a flat fee and/or some percentage of the new song's royalties. Businesses called "sample clearance houses" were established in the early 1990s and thrived as labels and artists increasingly employed them in order to avoid legal problems that may arise from sampling.[123] Put simply, today's hip-hop artists face an increasing array of complex legalities that their counterparts in the earlier periods most likely never even considered.

Institutional Pressures on Hip-Hop Music Production

Detractors have labeled sampling "groove robbing,"[124] and they have argued that it is a form of aural plagiarism or it is just plain "stealing."[125] For instance, one entertainment lawyer diplomatically said, "It may be flattering to have the underlying works used for sampling purposes, but it's still taking," while another lawyer who represented an artist who had been sampled stated that it "is a euphemism in the music industry for what anyone else would call pickpocketing."[126] Mark Volman, a member of the 1960s rock band The Turtles that the hip-hop group De La Soul sampled, said, "Sampling is just a longer term for theft . . . Anybody who can honestly say sampling is some sort of creativity has never done anything creative."[127]

These characterizations of sampling as "theft," "pickpocketing" and being devoid of creativity are situated within a cultural tradition that conceives of originality and authorship in a radically different way. This reaction is not surprising considering mainstream America's lack of understanding regarding the intertextual modes of cultural production that produced African-American folk preaching, blues and hip-hop.

Copyright lawyer Ken Anderson argues, "A jazz musician, for example, can quote from dozens of songs as he free-associates their musical implication, and those artistic references to the past are considered part of the art form, not a copyright infringement." A performance by a legendary jazz musician illustrates Anderson's point. "When Sonny Rollins played a rare solo saxophone concert at the Museum of Modern Art in 1985," Brown[128] states, "he quoted dozens, perhaps hundreds of songs from Tin Pan Alley to be-bop, honking some and crooning others, free-associating their musical and nostalgic implications, making them his own."[129] This intertextual mode of cultural production, which is akin to "voice-merging" in oral folk preaching traditions, is also echoed in the sampling methods used by hip-hop artists.

As sampling evolved within the musical practices of hip-hop, it grew more complex, and producers became more adept at deconstructing and reconfiguring small musical fragments in ways that sounded completely new. One example among many is the Beastie Boys' song "Sounds of Science," which incorporates the drum track, bass line, ambient sounds and guitar riffs from four very well-known Beatles songs in a way that makes the original sources almost impossible to recognize. In many cases the process of sampling is extremely complex, with a variety of different musical elements such as the bass drum, hi-hat, snare drum, and other drum sounds being layered beneath a bass line, keyboard sound, vocal snippet, guitar and other noises.

Many times these samples are drawn from numerous sources. Public Enemy coproducer Bill Stephney explained that many hip-hop producers use many recording tracks running simultaneously to create a single rhythm track: "These kids will have six tracks of drum programs all at the same time. This is where sampling gets kind of crazy. You may get a kid who puts a kick from one record on one track, a kick from another record on another track, a Linn kick on a third track, and a TR-808 kick on a fourth—all to make one kick!"[130]

From the simple breakbeats created by DJs with two turntables in the mid-1970s to the dense and edgy sound collages of Public Enemy in the late 1980s and early 1990s, it is clear that existing but reconfigured recordings have provided the backbone of hip-hop music. But when hip-hop became a multimillion-dollar industry, numerous lawsuits were filed and, as a result of this, hip-hop artists found it increasingly difficult to operate the way their predecessors did. Labels reacted by creating a complex system of business and legal networks that include the above-mentioned sample clearance houses. The sample clearance practices that arose in the wake of industrywide copyright infringement lawsuits are often very expensive, and the financial burden is completely absorbed by the hip-hop artist, producer, or both, who pay for the costs out of his or her future royalties.[131]

When clearing a sample taken from a record, two types of fees must be paid: *publishing* fees and *master recording* (or *mechanical*) fees. The publishing fee, which is paid to the company or individual owning a particular song, often consists of a flexible and somewhat arbitrary formula that calculates a statutory royalty rate set by Congress.[132] This formula takes into account the sampled artist's popularity, the popularity of the artist that is sampling, and the time length of the sample used.[133] To obtain a license to use an original song's master recording (for example, a bass line from Chic's "Good Times" or James Brown's well-known scream), many times one must pay a one-time flat fee, which can often be very expensive—ranging from an estimated $2,000 to $7,000, with an additional two to four cents on every unit sold. A brief sample might require as much as a 50% stake in the new song's publishing, if it is allowed to be used at all.[134]

As I discussed in chapter 1, intellectual property law can be used ideologically. Producer Marley Marl says that because of hip-hop's graphic and confrontational reputation, "some artists won't give me permission to sample their music."[135] Similarly, Anita Baker will not allow any of her songs to be sampled by hip-hop artists, and James Brown forbids the sampling of his music in hip-hop songs about violence and drugs. Brown's special assistant states, "He really doesn't want to be involved in any kind of rap that demoralizes any segment of society."[136]

A director of a sample clearance house estimated that the clearance fees for the average hip-hop album totaled about $30,000 in the early 1990s, and those rates have risen throughout the 1990s.[137] Often, the cost can be much more. For instance, after De La Soul was sued for copyright infringement, they took pains to clear the 50-plus samples that appeared on their follow-up album, *De La Soul is Dead*, which cost over $100,000 in clearance and legal fees. Sometimes it can cost that much for a single sample, as is the case with 2 Live Crew, who had to pay roughly $100,000 to lift a section of dialogue from Stanley Kubrick's *Full Metal Jacket*.[138]

This is an extremely large amount of money, especially when it is added to the cost of recording, promotion, music videos, etc.[139] The peril in paying such high fees is that often a great amount of money can be spent on records that achieve relatively little success (the vast majority of all records released in a given year fail commercially).[140] Hope Carr gives an example of this: "Say MCA quotes $4,000 on the master side and

$2,000 on the publishing side . . . If you're some poor schmuck trying to put out the record yourself, you can't afford that—that's more than you're likely to earn on it."[141]

Tommy Boy record executive Daniel Hoffman says, "It's a legal and administrative hassle and it costs us a lot of money."[142] Chris Lighty, a hip-hop management company executive, states, "It's very hard to find these [copyright owners] and very expensive legally. You can spend between $5,000 and $10,000 just trying to obtain a license and still come up dry."[143] In reference to Lighty's comments about "coming up dry," he discusses a case in which a production team assumed that the licensing of a sample was imminent, so they completed and mastered the album only to find that the license was rejected. The production team had to reenter the studio to remaster the album, deleting the song with the unauthorized sample in the process because, Lighty states, "We decided it was expensive to remaster, but not as expensive as getting sued."[144]

The Beastie Boys' 1989 album *Paul's Boutique* contains a dizzying array of hundreds of samples from 1960s, 1970s and 1980s songs woven together, some that are extremely obscure and brief, and some slightly longer and more recognizable. (This album contains their song "Sounds of Science," which was discussed in the previous section.) Alan Light, an editor at *SPIN* and *Vibe*, comments on this album in relation to the current cost of sampling, "You could never make that record today. It would be *way* too expensive. You could still use recognizable samples in 1989 and not have to pay millions and millions of dollars for them."[145]

A *Billboard* article describes the process of making sample-based music within the context of a highly charged legal environment and a nervous record company that has no desire to lose a substantial chunk of money (as did Warner Brothers in the above-mentioned Biz Markie case):

> "When a project starts, we send a letter to the producer outlining all sorts of things that he needs to know about sampling to make a record with us," [PolyGram VP of business affairs] Hoffman says. "This includes keeping track of each song that was sampled." Additionally, PolyGram has begun asking for tapes of the original song, so that its legal department can evaluate "how extensive the sample is," Hoffman says. As the album nears completion, PolyGram follows up the original letter with a different letter to the artist, reminding the act that it is his or her responsibility to clear any samples. Additionally, if any remixes are done, the remixer gets a letter similar to the missive sent to the original producer.[146]

This highlights the complexities surrounding the practice of sampling within hip-hop after the music had become a high-profile, commercially successful genre. At the time that article was written (in 1992), the legal and bureaucratic procedures surrounding sampling were already in place and they became more fixed as the decade wore on.

By the mid-1990s, a large number of popular hip-hop artists who dominated the rap and pop charts used live musicians on their records— something that was virtually unheard of in the second half of the 1980s.[147] Interestingly, even when these artists were using recognizable instrumental phrases, these were often played by hired studio musicians who were instructed to make it sound like the original recording; this happened on Dr. Dre's *The Chronic*. This seemingly odd and circuitous music-making process is, in actuality, a rational course of action for a producer who wants to sidestep the often expensive *mechanical* royalty fee (though he or she still has to pay for the *publishing* fee).

For example, Naughty By Nature's Treach states that while samples were used on their debut album, over half of the album consisted of live instrumentation.[148] Treach told me that the use of live instrumentation was partially a stylistic decision but that it also had a lot to do with the cost of mechanical royalty licensing fees, especially in light of the cost of securing the right to use a Jackson 5 sample for their hit, "OPP."[149] Leading hip-hop magazine *The Source* reported that Redman's 1996 album *Muddy Waters* was a stylistic departure from his previous funky, sample-heavy outings. "With the soaring price of samples," *The Source* states, "Redman says he made a deliberate decision to do less sampling."[150] During an interview with me, Redman complained: "They was taking me to the cleaners, fuckin' publishers. They wanted me to pay, like twenty G's [$20,000] for one sample, on top of all the other samples, and the video budget and the promotion. That means I won't see a fucking paycheck and my kids don't eat, you know what I'm saying?"[151]

Fugees member Wyclef says that his use of live instrumentation is primarily an aesthetic choice, because, in addition to being a hip-hop producer and MC, he is a talented multi-instrumentalist. Wyclef, who has both sampled other people's records and used live instruments to closely mimic records, told me that copyright has played a part, on a subconscious level, at least, in his use of instruments. He stated, "Yeah, it's a way of getting around that mechanical fee, so that has something to do with it. Licensing is expensive."[152]

While artistic innovation and individual vision were involved in the proliferation of live instrumentation during the 1990s, other circumstances also played a part. One major factor is the high cost of clearing samples, a practice that has become necessary as a result of the highly charged legal climate that exists in the music industry today. Hip-hop producers such as Marley Marl bring in live musicians to recreate a sample to bypass paying for the more expensive mechanical royalty fee.[153] Francesca Spero, a manager of hip-hop producers and musicians, tells a story she feels is representative of situations many hip-hop producers and artists found themselves:

> [This] producer, who was to become famous for his contribution to hip-hop, is still an avid sampler. He samples not because he has to, but because he loves the flavor it gives his music and because it is part of his musical heritage and culture. Due to the legal climate surrounding sampling, more and more he is working with live musicians and sampling his own live drum sounds. But this is not his favorite thing. He started on two turntables in a local park, working the crowd. This is where sampling began, and it explains why sampling is his culture."[154]

By 1993, many hip-hop artists were steering clear of what some called the "sample hell" brought on by this restrictive legal environment.[155] Both David Landis and Sheila Rule, writers who have covered hip-hop trends and sampling cases, argue that this highly charged legal climate together with the large expenses surrounding sampling helped push hip-hop in the direction of live instrumentation.[156] Ken Anderson, an entertainment lawyer who defends hip-hop artists, argued that the evolution of hip-hop should not be "dictated by business concerns," and he expressed worries over the use of live music in hip-hop for "legal reasons."[157] For instance, when Public Enemy wanted to sample a bit of Buffalo Springfield's "For What It's Worth," the group discovered that it would be cheaper for them to have the song's original vocalist Stephen Stills sing the part of the song they were going to sample.[158]

Despite the powerful institutional pressures manifested by intellectual property law described above, hip-hop artists did not react in a uniform way, though they have largely responded in three particular ways. *First*, as I stated in the previous pages, by the early to mid-1990s many hip-hop artists incorporated live instrumentation into their music, either wholesale or by hiring studio musicians to imitate familiar riffs that are then sampled to avoid costly mechanical fees. *Second*, hip-hop artists who have the financial backing of large record labels can afford to sample significant sections of previously recorded songs in their own recordings. Because of the expensive flat fees, producers tend to shy away from collaging numerous samples. Artists and producers (such as Puff Daddy) favor using only one or two recognizable hooks or melodies. This is representative of the fifth, most recent, period of recorded hip-hop.

Third, artists have pushed themselves to more cleverly alter the unauthorized samples in their songs through effects such as reverb, flange, phasing, etc. The member of Cypress Hill who produces the group's instrumental tracks, DJ Muggs, states: "I don't worry much about copyrights. Yeah, I haven't been able to license some samples in the past, but the trick is to really fuck it up so that you don't even have to ask for permission."[159] Sample clearance business owner Hope Carr says that because the licensing fees are so high, "more people are doing songs without samples or trying to make songs where the samples are so obscure you don't hear them."[160]

Q-bert—a member of the turntablist crew Invisibl Skratch Piklz—said that copyright laws make "it more of a challenge for us because you really have to flip the sound. You really have to work it to make that sound so that it's not theirs anymore." He added, "That's what also makes it more beautiful as well. It makes you want to change that sound because if you just *use it* then it's theirs and that's stealing." He then says somewhat cryptically, "So if you can make it *not theirs*, it's yours."[161]

Mixmaster Mike—a fellow Invisibl Skratch Piklz member and full-time member of the Beastie Boys—agreed, saying that he included some unauthorized samples, sounds, and scratches from movies and records on his 1998 solo album, *Anti-Theft Device*. "I didn't clear all of them because it would be too expensive and a pain in the ass, tracking down all the movie studios and publishers and record companies from the records and films I used," Mike said. "Anyway, I feel like I flipped the sound so that it became mine. I just flipped the sound and made it hella fresh."[162]

Others still work within the sample clearance system, but apply the same philosophy by sampling more obscure artists. Underground hip-hop artist Voodo says that the artists he samples—often largely unknown 1960s and 1970s jazz-funk artists—do not charge high flat fees in the way more popular artists do. Voodo states:

> That's probably the reason why my sound is the way it is. For some reason I've been able to clear every sample that I've ever used. Every sample, even though it still cost a lot, it was still clearable. It was like $2,000 or $3,000 for the actual use of the sample and $3,000 for the mechanical, you know, it gets deep! Certain artists aren't that much. . . . I *dare not* sample a Sade song or an Anita Baker song because they don't clear, well Sade will clear it, but you have to pay a grip. We're talking 50 G's [$50,000] or something stupid. . . . You've got to be more selective with the stuff you sample."[163]

Voodo strongly identifies the practice of sampling as an essential element of hip-hop culture. The fact that he and other artists feel so strongly about sampling emphasizes that it is certainly not seen as a mere tool or technique, but a profoundly resonating practice that is deeply imbedded in their culture. Voodo states:

I'm hip-hop to the death and I'll sample to the death. That's what it's about. If I stop sampling just on the premise that it's too expensive for me not wanting to pay a certain amount for the publishing or a percentage—if that's the case then I'm not doing my job as a B-Boy. My point is that hip-hop is a sampling thing. No doubt. I don't want to stop sampling. Hell no.[164]

The case of hip-hop and sampling is illustrative of what Coombe means when she writes that intellectual property law is both *prohibitive* and *productive*. It would be too simplistic to view the effects of intellectual property law as only closing down cultural production and meaning, something that is certainly not the case with hip-hop. True, artists' ability to freely sample has been severely limited, which many (including myself) argue has been to the detriment of this musical and cultural form. But it is just as interesting to look at *how* artists respond to these structural limitations.

Although intellectual property law has been prohibitive, it has also been productive in that artists have been forced to confront these parameters and to come up with creative ways of dealing with the restrictions imposed by the enforcement of copyright law. Again, they have done so by disguising their samples to the point that these samples are, potentially, unrecognizable to the artist who recorded the original song, or by hiring studio musicians to mimic a sound, thereby getting around paying the mechanical royalty fees.

Albums released in the late 1980s, such as Public Enemy's *It Takes a Nation of Millions to Hold Us Back* and the Beastie Boys' *Paul's Boutique*—albums that incorporated hundreds of samples in a dizzying aural collage—are virtually impossible to release today if they are to be distributed through mainstream channels. Despite that limitation, there is one significant distribution network where this can occur: the Internet. DJ Spooky points out that copyright law "is going to be utterly bypassed by technology."[165] He explains, "The only thing is that the mass distribution of this music will have to go online. The RIAA [Recording Industry Association of America], they are able to intercede on physical pressing plants, but not the online areas." In fact, however, the music industry *can* intercede on web sites, and has forced the closing down of many web sites that infringe on copyrighted musical works. I will return to this point in the final chapter.

Conclusion

Throughout most of the music's evolution, hip-hop used existing music as the foundation on which its musical bed was constructed, and in the time before the mid- to late 1980s, it did so in a relatively unfettered way. It is not coincidental that the first copyright infringement lawsuit that involved hip-hop was brought against the first rappers to land a number-one pop record on the *Billboard* charts. This suit set off a flurry of legal activity that still exists in the music industry. The application of copyright law in this area made it increasingly difficult for hip-hop artists to engage freely in the intertextual modes of musical production in the same way they and their predecessors had.

Nevertheless, sampling did not die. Even if many song publishing companies and songwriters themselves do not respect sampling as a method of musical production, they tolerate the practice because, in part, it earns them money in exchange for very little effort. The intertextual mode of cultural production that informs sampling may lend itself, as some have argued, to an anticapitalist ethic (with its communal, nonproprietary assumptions concerning culture), but capitalism has been remarkably adaptable when it encounters potentially resistive ideologies and practices.

Despite the fact that certain musicians do not like to have their music sampled, sampling has not disappeared from the contemporary music industry because it is another way of making money from a work that may be no longer generating income for the company. This is something that would have been inconceivable before hip-hop introduced this new mode of cultural production to the music industry. In light of this, it is not surprising that old song publishing catalogs—particularly of 1960s and 1970s funk and soul artists—are being purchased with the primary intention of licensing songs to hip-hop artists.[166]

Hip-hop's commercial explosion can also be seen as representing a shift in the means of production out of the hands of the local community and into the hands of corporations. Even though high-profile artists such as Puff Daddy have been given their own boutique labels, it is still the major labels that call the shots, and none of these labels favor a system that encourages, or approves of, unauthorized sampling. Therefore, even if artists are ideologically opposed to copyright restrictions, there is little or nothing they can do to change the situation, particularly because virtually all artist contracts have record company-enforced stipulations and rules regarding sampling.

Most top-selling hip-hop artists are signed to (or are distributed by) major labels, which release albums by artists who sample and which own the copyrights to albums that others sample. It is this interconnectedness that has led to the establishment of sample-clearing houses, businesses that secure licensing agreements for hip-hop artists who want to legitimately release a record that incorporates elements of another aural text. The cost of licensing, especially the cost of directly sampling a performance on another record, is often quite high, and it can cost as much as $100,000 to clear a single sample. This is one primary reason why hip-hop producers often hire musicians to recreate a musical phrase in order to only pay the less expensive publishing royalty fee. It is, in part, the exorbitant cost of licensing and legal fees that has led an artistic community whose *modus operandi* hinged on the borrowing of recorded music to essentially turn its central productive practice on its head.

A contemporary example of the way intellectual property law attempts to define where a text begins and where it ends is the way songwriting credits are assigned on many hip-hop albums. Mase, the Puff Daddy protégé who later quit rap and found God, included a song on his second album that listed *nine* people on the songwriting credits—six of whom never set foot in the studio when Mase recorded the song "Stay Out of My Way."[167] The interesting thing about the Mase song is that it sampled Madonna's 1990 song "Justify My Love" (written by Madonna, Lenny Kravitz and I. Chavez), which in turn sampled Public Enemy's 1988 song "Security of the First World" (written by J. Boxley, Chuck D and Eric Sadler).

The Madonna song does not credit Public Enemy in the liner notes of the album on which "Justify My Love" appears, in part because Public Enemy did not pursue the matter, and also because this type of crediting wasn't commonplace in 1990. But the liner notes of the Mase album, released 9 years later, coassigned both songwriting credit and sampling credit to Public Enemy, despite the fact that only the Madonna song was sampled in Mase's song. Throughout the 1980s it was extremely rare for hip-hop albums to include sampling credits or to assign partial songwriting credit to an artist who was sampled, but today this clear demarcation of the boundaries within a song is common.

Copyright law emerged out of the desire of seventeenth- and eighteenth-century printing houses to prevent pirates from reprinting what the houses considered to be their property. Despite the rhetoric that surrounds copyright law, from its very inception copyright has existed primarily to protect companies that control the means of production, and in most cases copyright law facilitates a transferal of artistic property from artists to larger entities. This is very true of the contemporary music industry. Because record companies are also defined as authors, they have the power to sue artists who appropriate their property even when the songwriters are ambivalent about being sampled.

In addition, Public Enemy was forced to remove from its web site digital audio files of their own songs that their old record company, Def Jam, had refused to release commercially. Chuck D and the rest of the group felt strongly that the songs should get to their fans, so they posted them for free; but because Def Jam owned the copyrights to the songs, the company was able to exert legal pressure to get the group to remove the tracks from the Internet. This helped fuel more antagonism between Public Enemy and its longtime label, with Chuck D characterizing the group's problems as a battle to control the products of the group's labor. It is the *ownership* of the means of production that facilitates record companies' ability to assert *authorship* and therefore control the context in which its property appears.

After Chuck D made much noise, Def Jam (which began as an independent label but is now fully owned by the world's largest record company) eventually released them from their contract, after which the group released their next album in MP3 form for $6. Such radical moves are not surprising, especially coming from a man who bragged about illegally sampling on a track released 10 years earlier, titled "Caught, Can I Get a Witness," from their classic album *It Takes a Nation of Millions to Hold Us Back*. (This is the same Public Enemy album that contained "Security of the First World," the song sampled on "Justify My Love".) Chuck D raps: "Caught, now in court 'cause I stole a beat/This is a sampling sport . . . I found this mineral that I call a beat/I paid zero."[168]

This discussion of hip-hop highlights the complexities of engaging in creative endeavors while under contractual agreements with intellectual property lawyers and record executives. The musical practices that currently shape the way hip-hop was produced represent a very interesting articulation of artistic innovation, formalized bureaucratic business practices, intellectual property law and cultural traditions that grew out of African-American culture. In spite of the institutional pressures imposed on hip-hop artists, sampling has not stopped. Artists adapted, though they certainly navigated within limiting parameters completely unknown to their forebears.

Notes

1   Miller, K. D. (1993, January 20). Redefining plagiarism: Martin Luther King's use of an oral tradition. *Chronicle of Higher Education, 39, 20,* A60.

2   Scollon, R. (1995). Plagiarism and ideology: Identity in intercultural discourse. *Language in Society, 24,* 1–28.

3   Ibid., pp. 24–25.

4   Ibid., p. 3.

5   Ibid.

6   Ibid., p. 23.

7   Ong, W. (1982). *Orality and literacy.* New York: Routledge, p. 131.

8   Ibid., p. 131.

9   Bettig, R. V. (1996). *Copyrighting culture: The political economy of intellectual property.* Boulder, CO: Westview Press.

10 Scollon, R. (1995). Plagiarism and ideology: Identity in intercultural discourse. *Language in Society, 24,* 1–28.

11 Johannesen, R. L. (1995). The ethics of plagiarism reconsidered: The oratory of Martin Luther King, Jr. *Southern Communication Journal 60, 3,* 185–194.

12 Ibid.

13 Ibid., p. 186.

14 De Palma, B. (1990, November 10). Plagiarism seen by scholars in King's Ph.D. dissertation. *New York Times,* p. 1.

15 Ibid.

16 Radin, C. A. (1990, November 10). Researchers cite plagiarism by King. *Boston Globe,* p. 1.

17 De Palma, B. (1990, November 10). Plagiarism seen by scholars in King's Ph.D. dissertation. *New York Times,* p. 1.

18 Ibid., p. 1.

19 Ball, I. (1990, November 10). Luther King 'borrowed ideas.' *Daily Telegraph,* p. 11.

20 De Palma, B. (1990, November 10). Plagiarism seen by scholars in King's Ph.D. dissertation. *New York Times,* p. 1.

21   Ball, I. (1990, November 10). Luther King 'borrowed ideas.' *The Daily Telegraph,* p. 11.

22   De Palma, B. (1990, November 10). Plagiarism seen by scholars in King's Ph.D. dissertation. *New York Times,* p. 1.

23   Miller, K. D. (1993, January 20). Redefining plagiarism: Martin Luther King's use of an oral tradition. *Chronicle of Higher Education, 39, 20,* p. A60.

24   Miller, K. D. (1991, June). Martin Luther King, Jr. and the black folk pulpit. *Journal of American History, 78, 1,* 120–123.

25   Ibid.

26   Ibid.

27   Ibid., p. 121.

28   Garrow, D. J. (1991, June). King's plagiarism: Imitation, insecurity, and transformation. *Journal of American History, 78, 1,* 86–92.

29   Reagon, B. J. (1991, June). "Nobody knows the trouble I see"; or, "by and by I'm gonna lay down my heavy load." *Journal of American History, 78, 1,* 111–119.

30   Ibid., p. 117.

31   Ibid., p. 118.

32   Ibid.

33   Garrow, D. J. (1991, June). King's plagiarism: Imitation, insecurity, and transformation. *Journal of American History, 78, 1,* 86–92.

34   Miller, K. D. (1991, June). Martin Luther King, Jr. and the black folk pulpit. *Journal of American History, 78, 1,* 120–123.

35   Ibid., p. 121.

36   Reagon, B. J. (1991, June). "Nobody knows the trouble I see"; or, "by and by I'm gonna lay down my heavy load." *Journal of American History, 78, 1,* 111–119.

37   Ibid., p. 115.

38   Johannesen, R. L. (1995). The ethics of plagiarism reconsidered: The oratory of Martin Luther King, Jr. *Southern Communication Journal, 60, 3,* 185–194.

39   Miller, K. D. (1991, June). Martin Luther King, Jr. and the black folk pulpit. *Journal of American History, 78, 1,* 120–123, p. 123.

40   Miller, K. D. (1987, April). Keith Miller responds. *College English, 49,* 478–480, p. 480.

41   Ong, W. (1982). *Orality and literacy.* New York: Routledge; Rose, T. (1994). *Black noise: Hip-hop music and Black culture in contemporary America.* Hanover, CT: Wesleyan University Press.

42   Schumacher, T. G. (1995). "This is a sampling sport": Digital sampling, rap music and the law in cultural production. *Media, Culture & Society, 17,* 253–273.

43   Rose, T. (1994). *Black noise: Hip-hop music and black culture in contemporary America.* Hanover, CT: Wesleyan University Press.

44   Schumacher, T. G. (1995). "This is a sampling sport": Digital sampling, rap music and the law in cultural production. *Media, Culture & Society, 17,* 253–273.

45   Cutler, C. (1995). Plunderphonics. In R. Sakolsky & F. W. Ho (Eds.), *Sounding Off! Music as subversion/resistance/revolution* (pp. 67–86). Brooklyn: Autonomedia.

46   Fernando, S. H. Jr. (1994). *The new beats: Exploring the music, culture, and attitudes of hip-hop.* New York: Doubleday.

47   Rose, T. (1994). *Black noise: Hip-hop music and black culture in contemporary America.* Hanover, CT: Wesleyan University Press.

48   Beadle, J. J. (1993). *Will pop eat itself? Pop music in the soundbite era.* London: Faber and Faber.

49   Rose, T. (1994). *Black noise: Hip-hop music and black culture in contemporary America.* Hanover, CT: Wesleyan University Press.

50   Toop, D. (1991). *Rap attack 2: African hip-hop to global hip-hop.* London: Serpent's Tail, p. 60.

51   Kool Herc, personal correspondence, November 13, 1998.

52   George, N. (1998). *Hip-hop America.* New York: Viking.

53   Toop, D. (1991). *Rap attack 2: African hip-hop to global hip-hop.* London: Serpent's Tail, pp. 63–66.

54   Ibid., p. 65.

55   Rose, T. (1994). *Black noise: Hip-hop music and black culture in contemporary America.* Hanover, CT: Wesleyan University Press.

56   Ibid.

57   Toop, D. (1991). *Rap attack 2: African hip-hop to global hip-hop.* London: Serpent's Tail, p. 69.

58   Samuels, D. (1991, November 11). The hip-hop on hip-hop: The 'black music' that isn't either. *New Republic,* 24.

59   Fernando, S. H. Jr. (1994). *The new beats: Exploring the music, culture, and attitudes of hip-hop.* New York: Doubleday.

60   Caston, K. (1994, March 25). Hip-hop's roots: The old school. *Dallas Morning News,* p. 42.

61 Williams, S. (1994). *Message from the street: The best of Grandmaster Flash, Melle Mel & the Furious Five* [CD]. Los Angeles: Rhino.

62 Fernando, S. H. Jr. (1994). *The new beats: Exploring the music, culture, and attitudes of hip-hop.* New York: Doubleday.

63 Toop, D. (1991). *Rap attack 2: African hip-hop to global hip-hop.* London: Serpent's Tail, p. 69.

64 Fernando, S. H Jr. (1994). *The new beats: Exploring the music, culture, and attitudes of hip-hop.* New York: Doubleday.

65 Ibid.

66 Berman, E. (1993, December 23). The godfathers of hip-hop. *Rolling Stone,* 137.

67 Toop, D. (1992). *The Sugar Hill story* [CD]. New York: Sequel Records.

68 Fuchs, A. (1992, May 23). What's in a hip-hop drum beat?; Plenty if you own the original master. *Billboard,* 4.

69 Ibid.

70 Ibid.

71 Marcus, G. (1991). *Dead Elvis: A chronicle of a cultural obsession.* New York: Doubleday.

72 George, N. (1998). *Hip-hop America.* New York: Viking.

73 Brown, G. (1990). *The information game: Ethical issues in a microchip world.* New York: Humanities Press.

74 Toop, D. (1991). *Rap attack 2: African hip-hop to global hip-hop.* London: Serpent's Tail.

75 Ibid., pp. 162–163.

76 Ibid., p. 163.

77 Snowden, D. (1989, August 6). Sampling: A creative tool or license to steal? *Los Angeles Times,* Calendar, p. 61; Brown, J. H. (1990, November). "They don't make music the way they used to": The legal implications of "sampling" in contemporary music. *Wisconsin Law Review,* 1941–1990.

78 Rose, T. (1994). *Black noise: Hip-hop music and black culture in contemporary America.* Hanover, CT: Wesleyan University Press.

79 Stetsasonic. (1988). *In Full Gear.* [CD]. New York: Tommy Boy.

80 George, N. (1998). *Hip-hop America.* New York: Viking, p. 89.

81 Rose, T. (1994). *Black noise: Hip-hop music and black culture in contemporary America.* Hanover, CT: Wesleyan University Press.

82   Culture Vulture. (1992, April 26). *Newsday*, 3; Snider, E. (1992, August 23). He's back and he's proud. *St. Petersburg Times*, p. 18.

83   Hochman, S. & Phillips, C. (1992, September 13). Pop eye. *Los Angeles Times*, Calendar, p. 69.

84   Fernando, S. H Jr. (1994). *The new beats: Exploring the music, culture, and attitudes of hip-hop*. New York: Doubleday, p. 237.

85   Rose, T. (1994). *Black noise: Hip-hop music and black culture in contemporary America*. Hanover, CT: Wesleyan University Press, p. 40.

86   Toop, D. (1995). *Ocean of sound: Aether talk, ambient sound and imaginary worlds*. New York: Serpent's Tail, p. 71.

87   Berman, E. (1993, December 23). The godfathers of hip-hop. *Rolling Stone*, p. 139.

88   Toop, D. (1991). *Rap attack 2: African hip-hop to global hip-hop*. London: Serpent's Tail.

89   Norris, C. (1994, May/June). Needle phreaks: The planet's best DJs find a new groove. *Option, 56*, 53.

90   Berman, E. (1993, December 23). The godfathers of hip-hop. *Rolling Stone*, p. 142.

91   Toop, D. (1991). *Rap attack 2: African hip-hop to global hip-hop*. London: Serpent's Tail.

92   Fernando, S. H. Jr. (1994). *The new beats: Exploring the music, culture, and attitudes of hip-hop*. New York: Doubleday, p. 12.

93   Toop, D. (1991). *Rap attack 2: African hip-hop to global hip-hop*. London: Serpent's Tail, p. 78.

94   Marcus, J. (1995). Don't stop that funky beat: The essentiality of digital sampling to hip-hop music. In Negativland (Ed.), *Fair use: The story of the letter u and the numeral 2* (pp. 205–212). Concord, CA: Seeland.

95   Cox, M. (1984, December 4). Hip-hop Music. *Wall Street Journal*, p. 1.

96   Fernando, S H. Jr. (1994). The new beats: Exploring the music, culture, and attitudes of hip-hop. New York: Doubleday.

97   Simpson, J. C. (1992, May 7). The impresario of hip-hop. *Time*, 69; Rawsthorn, A. (1994, November 17). PolyGram kicks into rap groove with RAL/Def Jam move. *Financial Times*, 28; Trapp, R. (1994, November 17). PolyGram raps up hip-hop label in $33 million deal. *Independent*, p. 36.

98   Seagram reportedly buys Def Jam. (1999, February 26). SonicNet. [Online] Available: http://www.sonicnet.com

99   Lloyd, R. (1987, February 22). The Beasties' hip-hop bonanza: Selling & setting records. *Washington Post*, p. F1.

100   Silverman, E. R. (1989, May 29). Hip-hop goes the way of rock 'n' roll: Record moguls snap up labels. *Crain's New York Business*, 3.

101   Ibid.; Samuels, D. (1991, November 11). The hip-hop on hip-hop: The 'black music' that isn't either. *New Republic*, 24.

102   Vaughn, C. (1992, December). Simmons' rush for profits. *Black Enterprise*, 67; Hip-hop. [Broadcast] (1995, June 14). *CNN*.

103   McAdams, J. (1993, January 30). Clearing House: EMI Music uses sampling committee. *Billboard*, 1.

104   Snowden, D. (1989, August 6). Sampling: A creative tool or license to steal? *Los Angeles Times*, Calendar, p. 61.

105   Snider, E. (1992, August 23). He's back and he's proud. *St. Petersburg Times*, p. 18; Pop eye: Sampling wars. (1989, July 23). *Los Angeles Times*, Calendar, p. 73.

106   Garcia, G. (1990, June 3). Play it again sampler. *Time*, p. 69.

107   Ruling expands 'sampling' case law. (1998, July 10). *New York Law Journal*, p. 5; UK remixers win settlement in sample case. (1998, May 16). *Music Week*, p. S1; Russell, D. (1992, January 4). Judge clips Biz Markie on sampling issue. *Billboard*, 1.

108   Gordon, S. R. & Sanders, H. J. (1989, September 10). Stolen tunes [Letter to the Editor]. *New York Times*, p. B7.

109   Brown, G. (1990). *The information game: Ethical issues in a microchip world*. New York: Humanities Press; Marcus, J. (1995). Don't stop that funky beat: The essentiality of digital sampling to hip-hop music. In Negativland (Ed.), *Fair use: The story of the letter u and the numeral 2*, (pp. 205–212). Concord, CA: Seeland.

110   Biskupic, J. (1994, March 8). Court hands parody. *Washington Post*, p. A1.

111   (1994). *Campbell v. Acuff-Rose Music, Inc.*, 114 S. Ct. 1164 (U.S.S.C.).; Graham, G. (1994, March 8). Rappers win copyright suit. *Financial Times*, p. 6.

112   Philips, C. (1992, January 1). Songwriter wins large settlement in hip-hop suit. *Los Angeles Times*, p. F1.

113   Cox, M. (1991, December 20). Hip-hop album is ordered off shelves for lifting another record's music. *Wall Street Journal*, p. B6.

114   Landis, D. (1992, January 16). Court fights over hip-hop music. *USA Today*, p. 2D; Soocher, S. (1992, May 1). As sampling suits proliferate, legal guidelines are emerging. *New York Law Journal*, p. 5.

115   New York judge orders record recall in first-ever sampling decision. (1992, January 27). [Online] *Entertainment Litigation Reporter*. Available: Lexis-Nexus.

116   Brown, G. (1990). *The information game: Ethical issues in a microchip world.* New York: Humanities Press.

117   Sugarman, R. G. & Salvo, J.P. (1992, March 16). Sampling litigation in the limelight. *New York Law Journal,* 1; Soocher, S. (1992, May 1). As sampling suits proliferate, legal guidelines are emerging. *New York Law Journal,* 5.

118   Goldberg, D. & Bernstein, R. J. (1993, January 15). Reflections on sampling. *New York Law Journal,* 3.

119   Tomsho, R. (1990, November 5). As sampling revolutionizes recording, debate grows over aesthetics, copyrights. *Wall Street Journal,* p. B1.

120   Brown, G. (1990). *The information game: Ethical issues in a microchip world.* New York: Humanities Press.

121   Soocher, S. (1992, May 1). As sampling suits proliferate, legal guidelines are emerging. *New York Law Journal,* 5.

122   Fernando, S. H Jr. (1994). *The new beats: Exploring the music, culture, and attitudes of hip-hop.* New York: Doubleday.

123   Rule, S. (1992, April 21). Record companies are challenging 'sampling' in hip-hop. *New York Times,* p. C13.

124   Henken, J. (1988, October 16). Sounding off by the numbers: making music the MIDI way. *Los Angeles Times,* Calendar, p. 66.

125   Goldberg, D. & Bernstein, R. J. (1993, January 15). Reflections on sampling. *New York Law Journal,* 3.

126   Soocher, S. (1989, February, 13). License to sample. *National Law Journal,* 1–5; Harrington, R. (1991, December 25). The groove robbers' judgement: Order on 'sampling' songs may be rap landmark. *Washington Post,* p. D1.

127   Hochman, S. (1991, December 18). Judge raps practice of 'sampling.' *Los Angeles Times,* p. F1.

128   Brown, G. (1990). *The information game: Ethical issues in a microchip world.* New York: Humanities Press.

129   Ibid., p. 1948.

130   Rose, T. (1994). *Black noise: Hip-hop music and black culture in contemporary America.* Hanover, CT: Wesleyan University Press.

131   Documents that accompany sound masters. (1995, September). *Entertainment Law & Finance, 10, 6,* 7; Pedroso, A. I. (1994, April). Tips for music producer agreements. *Entertainment Law & Finance, 11, 1,* 3.

132   Fernando, S. H. Jr. (1994). *The new beats: Exploring the music, culture, and attitudes of hip-hop.* New York: Doubleday.

133 A new spin on music sampling: A case for fair play. (1992). *Harvard Law Review, 105,* 726–739; Finell, J. G. (1992, May 22). How a musicologist views digital sampling issue. *New York Law Journal,* 5.

134 Taraska, J. (1998, November 14). Sampling remains prevalent despite legal uncertainties. *Billboard,* 12.

135 Shiver, Jr., J. (1994, April 11). Digital double trouble: From rap music to medical formulas, little seems safe from duplication. *Los Angeles Times,* p. A1.

136 Jones, C. (1996, December 22). Haven't I heard that 'whoop' (or 'hoop') somewhere before? *New York Times,* p. B44.

137 Fernando, S. H. Jr. (1994). *The new beats: Exploring the music, culture, and attitudes of hip-hop.* New York: Doubleday.

138 Browne, D. (1992, January 24). Settling the bill: Digital sampling in the music industry. *Entertainment Weekly, 102,* 54.

139 Spero, F. (1992, December 5). Sample greed is hurting hip-hop business. *Billboard,* 7.

140 A new spin on music sampling: A case for fair play. (1992). *Harvard Law Review, 105,* 726–739.

141 Taraska, J. (1998, November 14). Sampling remains prevalent despite legal uncertainties. *Billboard,* 12.

142 Browne, D. (1992, January 24). Settling the bill: Digital sampling in the music industry. *Entertainment Weekly, 102,* 54.

143 Russell, D. (1992, January 4). Judge clips Biz Markie on sampling issue. *Billboard,* 1.

144 Ibid.

145 Hofmann, J. G. (Producer). (1999, March 12). *Beastiography.* New York: MTV.

146 Morris, C. (1992, May 23). Sampling safeguards follow suit. *Billboard,* 1.

147 Hunt, D. (1993, June 29). Liberating hip-hop with jazz sound: Freestyle Fellowship adds riffs to rhymes. *Los Angeles Times,* Calendar, p. 1; Hill, B. (1995, March 26). A grass-roots movement: Live performances build Philly band's support. *Washington Post,* p. G1; Gettelman, P. (1994, March 4). US3 breaks the sound barrier; the group's blend of hip-hop and jazz takes the blue note label to new heights. *Billboard,* p. 6; Guilliatt, R. (1993, January 31). Pop music: Jazz and hip-hop take the plunge. *Los Angeles Times,* Calendar, p. 3.

148 Landis, D. (1992, January 16). Court fights over hip-hop music. *USA Today,* 2D.

149 Treach, personal correspondence, January 30, 1998.

150 Brodeur, S. (1996, December). Seeing red: The funkadelic Redman continues to bring the outer limits back to the underground. *Source,* 85–88.

151   Redman, personal correspondence, December 5, 1997.

152   Wyclef, personal correspondence, February 27, 1998.

153   Fernando, S. H. Jr. (1994). The new beats: Exploring the music, culture, and attitudes of hip-hop. New York: Doubleday.

154   Spero, F. (1992, December 5). Sample greed is hurting hip-hop business. *Billboard,* 7.

155   Buchsbaum, H. (1993, September 17). The law in your life: Hip-hop musicians and copyright law. *Scholastic Update,* 12.

156   Landis, D. (1992, January 16). Court fights over hip-hop music. *USA Today,* 2D; Rule, S. (1992, April 24). Drumbeat heat: Record companies are challenging 'sampling' in hip-hop music. *Houston Chronicle,* p. 4.

157   Rule, S. (1992, April 24). Drumbeat heat: Record companies are challenging 'sampling' in hip-hop music. *Houston Chronicle,* p. 4.

158   Taraska, J. (1998, November 14). Sampling remains prevalent despite legal uncertainties. *Billboard,* 12.

159   DJ Muggs, personal correspondence, February 12, 1998.

160   Jones, C. (1996, December 22). Haven't I heard that 'whoop' (or 'hoop') somewhere before? *New York Times,* B44.

161   Q-Bert, personal correspondence, May 29, 1997.

162   Mike D, personal correspondence, April 13, 1998.

163   Voodo, personal correspondence, June 2, 1997.

164   Ibid.

165   DJ Spooky, personal correspondence, October 7, 1999.

166   Jones, C. (1996, December 22). Haven't I heard that 'whoop' (or 'hoop') somewhere before? *New York Times,* p. B44.

167   Mase. (1999). Stay out of my way. On *Double up* [CD]. New York: Bad Boy.

168   Public Enemy. (1988). Security of the first world. On *It takes a nation of millions to hold us back* [CD]. New York: Def Jam.

Chapter 4

Visual and Sound Collage Versus Copyright and Trademark Law

I have demonstrated how intertextuality has been a key component in a variety of areas of cultural production, from folk music, hip-hop and African-American oral folk preaching to classical music compositions, "Happy Birthday to You" and Gershwin's *Porgy and Bess*. This chapter similarly examines two more areas of cultural production in which the referencing, borrowing and incorporation of existing cultural texts into new works are commonplace. Here I look at the art world, particularly visual and sound collage, outlining brief histories of these traditions and examining the legal conflicts that have more recently emerged within these areas.

The art world has seen considerably less litigation in the area of intellectual property than, for instance, hip-hop. One significant reason is because the contemporary art world, while commercialized, rarely enters the larger realm of popular culture in which the most significant commercial exchanges take place. It is primarily when "appropriation art" enters into, and makes itself known to, the distribution network of protected cultural goods that artists find themselves embroiled in copyright or trademark lawsuits. Also, because the art world exists in a relatively marginal place when compared with other culture industries such as motion pictures, video games, music and television, artists appear to be more inclined to simply continue their practices of appropriation without concern for legal ramifications.

Sound Collage and Aural Appropriation

At the beginning of the twentieth century, visual artists began experimenting with what would come to be known as collage, a technique that recombines fragments of text and photography taken from newspapers, magazines, pamphlets and photographs to create an original work of art. The invention of photography made possible this previously unthinkable mode of cultural activity called visual collage. The invention of the phonograph by Thomas Edison in 1877 also opened up possibilities, allowing artists and musicians to "play" with "captured" sound.[1] Edison's phonograph was initially intended to be used as a stenographic device that preserved sound (in a similar manner that tape recorders are used today) rather than as a machine that would facilitate the mass distribution of music. That is, this invention was originally conceived as an object of production instead of consumption.

In 1906 the Victor Company introduced the Victrola, which allowed for a wide audience to listen to a recorded work numerous times.[2] The first documented use of the phonograph for anything other than playback occurred in 1920 when experimental composer Stefan Wolpe, during his association with Berlin Dadaism, performed a piece that used eight gramophones playing different records at a variety of speeds.[3] While this act did set a precedent, it had no real consequences because the performance did not spawn a wave of imitators (including Wolpe himself, who never again returned to this method in his career.)[4]

In the 1920s, Ernst notes, many more composers introduced new types of sounds into their works, from Antheil's *Ballet Mechanique*—which incorporated car horns, saws, hammers, anvils and airplane propellers—to Respighi's call for a performance that integrated phonograph recordings of nightingales into a symphony orchestra.[5] Between the years 1922 and 1927, French composer Darius Milhaud varied the speeds of multiple simultaneously running phonographs in order to generate a transformation in the sound of recorded works.[6] Several avant-garde composers flirted with the possibilities afforded by the phonograph. For instance, during a mid-1920s performance at the famous Bauhaus in Weimar, records were manipulated by being played backwards or by being scratched to disrupt the rhythm of the music. But, again, these experiments during the 1920s ultimately generated little meaningful impact on avant-garde music composition techniques.[7]

As consumer interest in commercially available recordings grew, artists such as Laszlo Moholy-Nagy began to advocate the manual manipulation of records to create original sounds. Dadaist Kurt Schwitters was another early artist to conceive of the phonograph as a device of production rather than one of mere consumption, and the Futurists, to be discussed later in this chapter, also prefigured later sound collage composition techniques.[8] American composer and conceptual artist John Cage was another major figure who used the phonograph as part of a composition to produce, in his words, "hitherto unheard or even unimagined sounds."[9]

Cage's *Imaginary Landscape No. 1*, first performed in 1939, utilized one Chinese cymbal, a piano, and two phonographs.[10] According to Cage's instructions, the phonograph would be played at varying speeds between 33 1/3 and 78 rpm, and the stylus would be raised and dropped to create a sense of rhythm.[11] The fourth installment of the composer's *Imaginary Landscape* series was a 4-minute piece for 12 radios, with two people "playing" each radio: one controlling the volume knob and another manipulating the tuning knob.[12] The entire performance consisted of random voices, music and static picked up from radio waves that saturated America. It became one of Cage's more well-known pieces, influencing younger avant-garde musicians such as La Monte Young.[13]

Before the invention and distribution of the magnetic tape recorder, avant-garde musicians and composers were limited to the only available methods of sound reproduction: the radio and the phonograph. After World War II, French and German composers were drawn to the new medium of tape recording, which allowed them to more freely manipulate "found sounds" that were captured from both the mass media and everyday life. Engineer and radio announcer Pierre Schaeffer began experimenting with recorded noises shortly after World War II, not because he was informed by the compositional theories of Cage and others, but because of the pleasure it gave him when he recombined sounds. Schaeffer dubbed this new technique *Musique Concrete*.[14]

Numerous musicians and composers of stature were attracted to *Musique Concrete* once tape recording technology became established at the beginning of the 1950s. John Cage felt the need to experiment with tape which resulted in his *Imaginary Landscape No. 5*, a work that was scored specifically for magnetic tape, and which called for the use of any 42 records to be "treated as sound sources, rather than being what they were."[15] Other Cage works that arranged captured sound fragments included *Williams Mix* and *Fontana Mix*, both of which used everyday sounds such as street noise, coughing, swallowing, cigarette smoking and other ephemera.[16]

This concept was taken up in the early 1960s by minimalist composer Steve Reich, whose piece *It's Gonna Rain* incorporated two recorded tracks of a street preacher shouting "It's gonna rain" that ran simultaneously, though slightly out of synch.[17] As a student in Paris, experimental composer Karlheinz Stockhausen was introduced to *Musique Concrete* during his studies with Schaeffer, and Stockhausen claimed this had a great impact upon his later work.[18] A composer who predicted in 1917 some of the strategies employed by *Musique Concrete* producers was Varese, who in 1954 was finally able to use a tape recorder to create his electronic collage masterwork *Deserts*.[19]

James Tenney, a young American musician and composer, created a piece titled *Collage #1 (Blue Suede)* in 1961. This particular work cut up and reassembled portions of Elvis's rendition of Carl Perkin's rockabilly classic "Blue Suede Shoes" by slowing it down, chopping it up and altering its tempo.[20] Also, during the late 1950s and early 1960s, Beat novelist William Burroughs and collaborator Brion Gysin created their own "cut-ups" with tape.[21] Perhaps the most widely heard example of *Musique Concrete* was "Revolution #9." A collaboration between John Lennon and Yoko Ono (an avant-garde artist well versed in *Musique Concrete* techniques), the piece used dozens of unauthorized fragments from radio, television and other mass-media sources.[22] Even though Tenney blatantly, and without permission, reused whole sections of a popular recording that was not his, no copyright difficulties arose as a result of his appropriation.[23] The same is true of "Revolution #9."

Contemporary Sound Collage

Through the 1980s, composers within the avant-garde tradition continued to use radio, turntables and tape recorders to create sound collages. In the mid-1980s, the digital sampler became commercially available, affordable and widely distributed. This quickened the process of collaging sounds, a technique that was extremely time-consuming when pieces of magnetic tape were manually spliced, moved and fixed in a new place. This new method of appropriation did not replace previous techniques, and is often used by contemporary sound-collage artists in conjunction with radio, turntable and tape collage. Three examples of this can be found in the works of 1980s and 1990s sound-collage artists Negativland, the Tape-beatles, and John Oswald.

Negativland is a West Coast-based group established in 1980 whose sound-collage endeavors initially came to the attention of the fringes of rock audiences through their association with the punk rock-oriented independent label SST. Not "popular" by any definition, they usually sell between 10,000 to 15,000 records per release.[24] The bulk of the group's collages are drawn from media sources, primarily radio and television, and are constructed using a variety of methods that include tape splicing and sampling from radio and television broadcasts.

For instance, the song "Christianity is Stupid," from their 1987 record *Escape From Noise*, features a radio preacher sarcastically shouting in a sermon "Christianity is stupid . . . Communism is good" removed from its original context, placed in one of the group's collages and replayed over and over again. Despite the fact that sound collage has a long history, the members of Negativland had little knowledge of the tradition established by avant-garde composers such as Cage, Tenney and Schaeffer. Mark Hosler, the group's informal spokesperson, told me they were not emulating a particular aesthetic style; instead, the members were simply teenagers who were reacting to a media-soaked environment. Hosler stated:

> When we were doing early Negativland recordings, which from the very beginning the television set was mixed in, we played tapes from game shows and interview talk shows, and I'd have a mike outside recording what was going on in our neighborhood. I'd run a mike into the bathroom and record the sound of water running down a tub and run it through a phase shifter. I had an old radio and had it tuned to the frequencies between stations and mixed that in. And there was no idea that we were part of anything at all; it just sort of made sense. It's not that I think that we were somehow brilliant, it's just I'm a kid, I've grown up in a media saturated environment and I'm just tuned into it. . . . I was born in 1962; I grew up watching *Captain Kangaroo*, moon landings, zillions of TV ads, the *Banana Splits*, *MASH*, and *The Mary Tyler Moore Show*, and when I started messing around with sounds and there was no conceptual pretense at all.[25]

Negativland has roughly two dozen CD releases to their name and they continue to broadcast the longest-running free-form radio show in North America, *Over the Edge*, on Berkeley-area station KPFA. Using the radio studio as an instrument, Negativland makes creative use of the studio's three reel-to-reel tape machines, two cassette decks, two CD players, two incoming phone lines, two cart machines, two mixers, a Walkman and various effects.[26] The sources for *Over the Edge* are similar to those used on Negativland's records in that they are largely drawn from the group's massive archive that covers 20 years' worth of material taken from radio, television and records.

Another sound collage group similar to Negativland is the Tape-beatles, which initially consisted of five members who formed in 1986. The Tape-beatles' full-length CDs (including *Music With Sound* and *The Grand Delusion*) are comprised of 2- to 4-minute pieces with brief interludes that incorporate sound sources from various media outlets.[27] Unlike Negativland, the Tape-beatles were well aware of the history behind audio collage when they began, though they felt that it had not been thoroughly explored as an expressive medium. Group member Lloyd Dunn[28] stated: "We were influenced by the French concrete musicians, such as Pierre

Henri and Pierre Schaeffer, and a few other modernist composers like Edgard Varese and John Cage. We were also heavily influenced by some pop music that had used tape effects and manipulation, such as the Beatles' work."[29]

Also, unlike Negativland in their early years, the Tape-beatles were quite conscious of the cultural context in which they work—specifically, the existence of copyright laws that define their activities as plagiarism. To this extent, they have adopted the phrase "Plagiarism: A Collective Vision" as their *de facto* motto. By strategically employing the word "plagiarism," they call attention to the fact that intertextual modes of cultural production are redefined by copyright law as an illegal activity. "Plagiarism: A Collective Vision" carries with it an explicit and implicit cultural and political critique that foregrounds the notion that cultural property should be a "collective," shared thing. The logo used by the Tape-beatles is a visual adaptation of that motto. Consisting of a reproduction of the AT&T "globe" trademark with Mickey Mouse ears attached, it is a bold and humorous representation of their self-described plagiarism aesthetic.[30]

Canadian composer John Oswald has taken the appropriation of popular works to an extreme. His work recalls James Tenney's *Collage #1 (Blue Suede)* in that Oswald recombines recognizable segments of well-known songs in an unapologetic manner, a method he calls "plunderphonics."[31] In defining this term, Oswald takes a scientific tone: "A plunderphone is a recognizable audio quote. Recognizable by at least a lot of people. That part is a bit vague. The piece may become less recognizable once we get through with it, but to remain 'plunderphonic' the derivation must maintain a substantial degree of its original character."[32]

The point of the plunderphonic technique is to create some sort of recognition on the part of the listener before the musical segment drops out and another brief sample is introduced, hopefully causing some sort of confusion or disorientation. In an interview with me, Oswald stated, "One can transcend the private ownership of a particular sound or image by improving upon it, and it is this way that art can progress, through a process of innovation and chameleonization."[33]

Since the mid-1980s, Oswald has released a number of plunderphonic works, with the most interesting being his 1993 release, *Plexure*. As with the Tape-beatles, the album's graphic design is a kind of visual manifesto of the plunderphonic method. *Plexure*'s artwork contains a visual collage of Bruce Springsteen's *Born in the USA*, Bobby Brown's *Bobby*, and Garth Brooks' *The Chase* album covers, cutting and pasting their various body parts together to make a sort of Pop music Frankenstein monster. The 19-minute CD consists of 12 musical movements that are titled by playfully stringing together pop star names such as "Bing Stingspreen," "Marianne Faith No Morrisey," and "Sinead O'Connick, Jr." Hundreds of 1980s and 1990s Top 40 songs have been "plundered" and squeezed into the 19 minute CD by overlapping a second, and some-times only a split second, of song fragments that are nonetheless margin-ally recognizable.

These songs are sampled, carefully constructed on a computer, and pieced together like a jigsaw puzzle in a precise manner that pays special attention to rhythm and melody to produce a jarring but flowing piece. Here, Whitney Houston bounces off Fine Young Cannibals and crashes into Peter Gabriel, rebounding into a Metallica guitar riff and off an Edie Brickell vocal, crash-landing on top of Nirvana's screeching guitars. Lis-tening to *Plexure* is like of hearing every popular song performed in the past decade during a perilous car chase while rapidly changing the chan-nels of a radio that only picks up stations playing skipping CDs, and eventually flying into a satellite dish.

At the turn of the twenty-first century, there were many other musi-cians and artists working within the sound collage medium. British ex-perimental composer John Wall does not foreground samples in a more obvious manner the way Oswald, Negativland, or the Tape-beatles do. Instead, he morphs and processes samples from obscure avant-garde and classical recordings in a way that renders the sources of his works com-pletely unrecognizable.[34] Another artist, Robin Rimbaud, who performs under the name of Scanner, uses cellular telephone conversations, short-wave radio broadcasts and other ephemera picked up from a scanner, collaging them in his music.[35]

Paul Miller—known as DJ Spooky a.k.a. That Subliminal Kid (a moni-ker derived from a William Burroughs cut-up novel)—"plays" the turntable in a way that is informed as much by the African-American hip-hop tradi-tion as it is by the European avant-garde school of *Musique Concrete*.[36] Miller studied the history of sound collage, and his influences range from his idol, hip-hop pioneer Afrika Bambaataa, to Stockhausen and Pierre Schaeffer.[37] DJ Spooky is grounded in both theory and practice, as is evidenced by the following quote culled from one of my conversations with him:

> I was in school and I did a double degree in philosophy and French Literature and I was studying a lot of 20th century theory and Cultural Studies. So I played hip-

hop mix tapes for my professors and they said, "Oh, I don't think this deconstruction stuff applies to urban youth culture." I was like, "Yo, they're taking fragments and it's no longer about the original authorial presence and it's a direct aural parallel with Literary Theory."[38]

The Letter U, The Numeral 2, Michael Jackson and Beck

All of the above-mentioned artists are part of a thread that weaves its way to the beginning of the twenty-first century. This thread connects a wide assortment of artists who use differing methods to achieve the same goal: a compelling collage of sounds emanating from everyday life and the mass media. In addition to being informed by previous intertextual practices, this type of cultural production developed as a result of artistic innovation and technological breakthroughs that allowed for new methods of creating sound collages. But by the late 1980s, the sound-collage tradition hit a major bump in the road. As has been demonstrated in the previous chapters, intellectual property-holding companies go to great lengths to secure the exclusive status of their copyrights and trademarks. It is in this environment that sound-collage artists produce their works and, in light of the numerous examples I supplied in the previous chapters, it is not surprising that some of these artists have encountered legal problems.

In 1989 Oswald produced and distributed a plunderphonics record similar in content to the *Plexure* CD described above. It contained 24 "plundered" compositions that reworked the songs of Michael Jackson, Elvis Presley, Public Enemy, Dolly Parton, Metallica and other musicians. The CD sported an eye-catching CD cover collage that skillfully placed Michael Jackson's face and jacket featured on his appropriately titled *Bad* album onto the body of a nude woman. One thousand copies were made, and sent out to libraries, radio and press on a strictly nonprofit basis.[39] A "shareright" notice, placed on the CD, stated that anyone could make a copy of it—even a digital reproduction—but that it could not be sold in any form.[40]

Roughly 2 months after the initial distribution of the plunderphonics disc, Oswald was sent a cease-and-desist order initiated by the Canadian Recording Industry Association (CRIA), which felt that the plunderphonic CD unfairly infringed on other artists' copyrights, particularly Michael Jackson's. The CRIA prohibited Oswald from distributing any more copies of the CD, forcing him to hand over all remaining copies of the CD to be promptly destroyed. When I asked Oswald about what sort of legal protection artists in his position may have, he told me: "Legal protection is not equal among everyone, but rather it is dependent on how much time and money you have to invest in establishing your eligibility for that protection. Most artists in my position do not have the deep pockets that cultural property owners have."[41]

Two years later, in 1991, Negativland released a single entitled "U2" that featured prominently on its cover a photograph of the U2 spy plane as well as the letter U and the numeral 2, with Negativland's name in smaller letters at the bottom. The CD contained two sound-collage versions of the U2 song "I Still Haven't Found What I'm Looking For" that mix in eyebrow-raising out-takes from Casey Kasem's *American Top 40* radio show. In Negativland's single, the congenial-sounding voice of Casey Kasem can be heard saying things like: "That's the letter U and the numeral 2. The four man band features Adam Clayton on bass, Larry Mullens on drums, Dave Evans—nicknamed The Edge—wait, this is bullshit. Nobody cares! These people are from England and *who gives a shit?* Just a lot of wasted names that don't mean diddley-shit!"

The collage also included 35 seconds taken from U2's original recording of "I Still Haven't Found What I'm Looking For," as well as an audio quote from U2's lead singer, Bono, that makes the vocalist sound pious and ridiculous.[42] The single was released on the small, independent record label SST with little fanfare, but within 4 days of its release SST and Negativland were sued by U2's label, Island Records, and U2's song publisher, Warner-Chappel.[43] The lawsuit required SST to cease distribution of the single; recall all promotional copies sent out to radio stations and record stores; pay Island and Warner Chappel $25,000 and half the proceeds of all copies of the single that were sold; destroy all remaining copies in stock; and, finally, deliver the master tapes and Negativland's copyrights over to Island.

By the time the lawsuit became widely publicized, only 7,000 copies of the single had been sold, many of which were probably bought because it became an instant collector's item. Recognizing that the band and their label were small fish compared to the multinational corporations they faced, the band stated, "Preferring retreat to total annihilation, Negativland and SST had no choice but to comply completely with these demands."[44] Echoing the sentiments that Oswald stated above, Negativland argue: "Companies like Island depend on this kind of economic inevitability to bully their way over all lesser forms of opposition. Thus, Island easily wipes us off the face of their earth purely on the basis of how much more money they can afford to waste than we can. We think there are issues to stand up for here, but Island can spend their way out of ever having to face them in a court of law."[45]

When the Edge, U2's guitarist, was interviewed over the phone for *Mondo 2000* magazine to promote their *Zoo TV* tour, unbeknownst to him, Negativland members Mark Hosler and Don Joyce were invited to conduct the following interview.

Mark Hosler: I wanted to ask you something more about the *Zoo TV* tour. One thing that wasn't really clear to me—you have a satellite dish so that you can take stuff down live off of various TV transmissions around the world?

The Edge: Yeah, essentially the system is, like we've got the big screens on the stage which are the final image that's created. Down by the mixing board we've got a vision mixer which mixes in, blends the images from live cameras, from optical disks, and from live satellite transmissions that are taken in from a dish outside the venue. So the combination of images can be any of those sources . . .

Don Joyce: So you can kind of sample whatever's out there on the airwaves . . .

The Edge: Yeah it's kind of like information central.

Mark Hosler: One thing I'm curious about—there's been more and more controversy over copyright issues and sampling, and I thought that one thing you're doing in the *Zoo TV* tour is that you were taking these TV broadcasts—copyrighted material that you are then rebroadcasting right there in the venue where people paid for a ticket—and I wondered what you thought about that.

Don Joyce: And whether you had any problem, whether it ever came up that that was illegal.

The Edge: No, I mean, I asked the question early on—is this going to be a problem?, and apparently it, I don't think there *is* a problem. I mean, in theory, I don't have a problem with sampling. I suppose when a sample becomes just part of another work then it's no problem. If sampling is, you know, stealing an idea and replaying the same idea, changing it very slightly, that's different. We're using the visual and images in a completely different context. If it's a live broadcast, it's like a few seconds at the most. I don't think, in spirit there's any . . .

Don Joyce: So you think the fragmentary approach is the way to go.

The Edge: Yeah. You know, like in music terms, we've sampled things, people sample us all the time, you know, I hear the odd U2 drum loop in a dance record or whatever. You know, I don't have a problem with that.

Don Joyce: Well, this is interesting because we've been involved in a similar situation along these lines . . . [46]

At this point in the interview, Joyce and Hosler revealed to the very surprised U2 guitarist that he had been discussing issues of sampling and copyright with Negativland, with whom he was familiar, though he claimed that the band had nothing to do with the lawsuit. Later in the interview, The Edge admitted that U2 had made a large cash settlement after being sued when Bono incorporated a few lines of another song into a live performance of their song that was commercially released on *Rattle and Hum*. He said, "We were actually quite shocked that the law was so stringent about it, you know, a quotation of one phrase or two phrases was a very big deal."[47]

To give the Edge the benefit of the doubt, he probably does believe that intertextual sampling practices are legitimate, but this example demonstrates how difficult it is to engage in these practices when one is caught up in a web of business and copyright relations. Even if, on the *Zoo TV* tour, his band essentially used the same techniques that Negativland did, U2 would most likely be sued if they were to do the same thing on a mass-distributed record—as is evidenced by the fact that they were sued for merely singing a few lines of another song. But because most sound-collage artists release their music within an independent distribution network (often on their own labels), the means of cultural production is located much closer to the artists, much more so than, say, U2 or the numerous hip-hop artists who sample.

Another group that has found itself in legal trouble is a collective of artists, academics and activists known as ®™ark (pronounced "art-mark"), whose name self-consciously appropriates the symbolism of trademarks.[48] This organization raises and distributes money to instigate culturally subversive, anti-corporate pranks—what the *Village Voice* describes as a "MacArthur Foundation for aesthetic anarchy." One of ®™ark's most celebrated activities included the funding of the infamous Barbie Liberation Front.[49] The BLF's confusion-inducing semiotic prank involved buying Barbie and G. I. Joe dolls, then returning them to the store shelves after switching the voice-chips in Barbie and G. I. Joe dolls so that Barbie grunted, "Dead men tell no lies" and G. I Joe gushed, "I like to go shopping with you."

In another major action funded by ®™ark, the group offered a $5,000 grant to any programmer working on a violent and sexist video game who would subvert the game's ideological message. Computer programmer Jacques Servin reprogrammed Maxis, Inc.'s combat video game SimCopter, altering an animated segment in which the heroic helicopter captain was rewarded with the image of women fawning over him. Instead, it gave the victorious video warrior an animated homoerotic sequence of two barechested men in swimsuits making out, something that went undiscovered by the company until after the game had shipped to stores.[50]

The ®™ark project that landed them in the deepest legal waters, though, was the release of a CD titled *Deconstructing Beck*, which contained 13 collages based on the music of Beck, a musician who has mixed multiple genres—from Bossa Nova and hip-hop to folk and rock—into his music. Beck has been hailed by critics and embraced by the public for his innovative use of sampling, particularly on 1996's *Odelay*, which contained hundreds of samples and which was produced by the Dust Brothers, the production team behind the Beastie Boys' *Paul's Boutique*. The other major aspect that defines Beck's musical aesthetic is his coming directly out of the folk music tradition and including folk and blues songs on his albums.

This album of compositions was released on Negativland's Seeland record label in conjunction with the ®™ark-affiliated label Illegal Art. Sold on the Internet for $5, it was a parody, according to Illegal Art's pseudonymously named Philo T. Farnsworth. "We're using Beck's techniques of making music by sampling and taking music from pre-existing records to an extreme . . . In other art forms, this is not radical at all."[51] Ray Thomas of ®™ark explained: "If I go out and steal Beck's music and say I did it, I should be prosecuted. But if I go out and hear Beck's music and am inspired by it, and I chop it up and make something new, then that should be a protected form of expression. Copyright law has evolved to cover the first case, but now it's being used, inappropriately, in the second case."[52]

One piece on *Deconstructing Beck* by Jane Dowe cuts up Beck's song "Jackass" into 2,500 segments and radically reworks the original so that it is only subliminally recognizable. While this is the most extreme deconstruction of Beck songs on the CD, many of the other collages contain only fragmentary sonic clues of the origins of the sounds. Rather than quietly distributing this CD, ®™ark fired off a massive number of e-mails and press releases announcing this work, making sure that Beck's publicist and attorney received a copy. "I was really unclear about what the repercussions might be," said Farnsworth. "That's part of what we were aiming for. We were aiming for a gray area because we wanted to stretch the boundaries of Fair Use."[53]

Beck's attorney, Brian McPhereson, immediately fired off an e-mail to ®™ark stating: "Bragging about copyright infringement is incredibly stupid. You will be hearing from me, Universal Music Group, BMG Music Publishing and Geffen Records very shortly." Despite this threat, Beck's label indicated that it would not take action at first, but Beck's publishing company, BMG, went forward and sent ®™ark a letter threatening a lawsuit. Farnsworth said that ®™ark received a "cease and desist" letter from Beck's music publishing company, but they were ignoring the letter because it was not sent to a physical address (it was e-mailed), and it was addressed to his alias (Philo Farnsworth, incidentally, is the name of the man who invented the television, among other things).[54]

At this point, Negativland stepped into the discursive fray by contacting Beck's lawyers and making themselves available to newspapers and magazines for interviews. Negativland's Mark Hosler stated:

> Our point is basically: 'Hey Beck, you make half your records out of samples and we know that you don't clear all of them—you clear the ones that are obviously recognizable.' There are way more sampled bits on his records than they are clearing—because a lot of it is obscure. . . . We're saying to him 'you're a Top-40 big-time rock star now. You come from the independent music world and it would help if you came out publicly and said: 'Hey, this *Deconstructing Beck* thing, it's just a collage. It's not ripping me off, it's not piracy—this is okay, this is exactly what I do.' So far he has said nothing and that is really unfortunate and to his detriment."[55]

Hosler told me the reason he knew that Beck only clears recognizable samples is because Beck's management told him so.[56] Beck's management, Hosler stated, "actually said that 'a lot of it is so obscure or chopped up that it doesn't matter. We don't do it.'" Soon Geffen joined BMG Publishing in a second letter, but at the time this was written, no formal legal action had been taken and it is unlikely any action will take place. Hosler said: "I then later met someone who works at Geffen Records who actually did tell me that even though no one wanted to admit it, once we stepped in and threw our name into the ring that it did have an effect. He said, 'You guys have a reputation for record labels that fuck with you look really bad, and so when you guys stepped in it did help them to decide to back off.'"[57] During this time and in the months afterward, Beck—an artist who frequently samples to create his own music—never spoke out about the actions initially taken by his record label, publishing company or his own lawyer.

Copyright Liberation Fronts
After he was sued, John Oswald wrote, "If creativity is a field, copyright is the fence."[58] He, Negativland, the Tape-beatles and others have each developed different ways to combat the monopoly that large corporations

have over the ownership of mass-produced cultural texts. The major methods of resistance include simply carrying on with what they had been doing in spite of copyright laws, lobbying to alter copyright law in a digital era, and organizing underground networks to distribute copyright-infringing sound collages that have been legally suppressed.

Oswald, Negativland and the Tape-beatles have developed similar belief systems regarding the activity of recombining elements captured from the mass media. The members of Negativland and the Tape-beatles see their actions as a life-affirming, inventive way of struggling against what they see as the highly charged ideological content of media messages. Negativland writes, "The act of appropriating from this media assault represents a kind of liberation from our status as helpless sponges, which is so desired by the advertisers who pay for it all. It is a much needed form of self-defense against the one-way, corporate-consolidated media barrage."[59] They continue: "Appropriation sees media, itself, as a telling source and subject, to be captured, rearranged, even mutilated, and injected back into the barrage by those who are subjected to it. Appropriators claim the right to create with mirrors."[60] In an interview, Lloyd Dunn echoed Negativland's sentiments, stating, "It is an empowering act to take this kind of stuff that comes out of the pipes like running water, and using it to fit our own ends."[61]

By simply continuing to produce and distribute their work, these artists make it clear that they oppose the way copyright law is currently enforced, in spite of the possibility of being sued by copyright owners. For instance, after Negativland's lawsuit involving U2, the group continued to use in their live performances the Casey Kasem out-takes and other sections of the U2 single that got them in trouble, which was in direct violation of a court order.[62] In addition to continuing to engage in cultural activities that are considered illegal, many sound-collage artists have attempted to change people's perceptions of the role of copyright law in a digital age when people can easily appropriate mass-media images and sounds.

As a group, Negativland has tried to position themselves as copyright reform activists by doing numerous interviews, writing editorials and articles for magazines and newspapers, and documenting the issues surrounding the U2 single in the form of a 270-page book, *Fair Use*. During an interview with me, Hosler said that Negativland, as a group, was trying to position themselves as experts on the topic of intellectual property law.[63] "Hopefully," he said, "this will increase our exposure in the mainstream media so that we can push and change the way these restrictive copyright laws are applied." Even though Negativland had not initially thought much about the history of sound collage or the ramifications of the type of activity in which they were engaged, the U2 incident caused them to reflect on what they were doing. Hosler told me:

> So after we got sued, we were compelled to very carefully examine what we did
> . . . how we worked on stuff, how we used stuff. What did we really think? Was
> it really defensible? Do we want to stand up for what we're doing? And of course
> you know that we all decided that what we're doing was perfectly okay and in fact
> goddamn it that we're going to scream and shout about it.[64]

In addition to writing articles and editorials for mainstream magazines like *Keyboard* and *Billboard*, members of Negativland have been involved in organized grassroots activism that aims to revamp copyright law to make it more flexible. Just as the group found itself publicly addressing issues of copyright and appropriation over the *U2* single, Negativland found itself in a similar situation in 1998, though they were not sued this time. When Negativland submitted their CD *Over the Edge Volume 3* to their long-time CD pressing plant for manufacture in mid-1998, the pressing plant refused, citing the Recording Industry Association of America's (RIAA) new guidelines regarding CDs that contain samples that are not cleared by copyright owners. The guidelines, which the RIAA maintained were aimed at curbing piracy, emphasized the fact that plants are liable if they press infringing material, which could cost the pressing plants up to $100,000 per unpaid and uncleared sample infraction.[65] Under these new guidelines, which did not distinguish between sampling and piracy, Disctronics (Negativland's pressing plant) refused to press the CD, and four other plants turned the group down as well.[66]

For a period of time, it looked as though Negativland would not be able to release the album, or any of their albums. But after they submitted their master tape anonymously to a smaller, unidentified pressing plant that was initially reluctant, their record was released.[67] Negativland responded to the RIAA's new guidelines with a terse press release and an organized e-mail campaign that aimed to persuade the RIAA that their guidelines were too limiting. In a press release that addressed this campaign and Negativland's complaints, RIAA president and CEO Hilary Rosen denied that their guidelines had anything to do with Negativland's activities. In a letter written to Rosen, Negativland called her denial "sadly disingenuous," pointing out, "We had no problem pressing any of our CDs until you issued [the guidelines]! Our records contain plenty of samples and free appropriation for which we claim 'fair use.' We do not counterfeit, pirate, or bootleg anything."[68]

After speaking with RIAA employees and pressing plants, everyone made it clear to Hosler that unlicensed samples are a violation of those guidelines, and the RIAA essentially scoffed at the idea that it would revise its guidelines for the sake of sound collage artists.[69] Commenting on the topic of copyright and sonic collage at the time of this controversy, DJ Spooky told me, "It's all about control of memory, whether you're a DJ or a rock musician practicing a guitar riff from an old record you heard when you were a kid or you are a piano player practicing a piece by Mozart from a score. If the corporations can reach into your mind and control the psychology of what you remember, then that's a pretty grim, weird *1984* scenario."[70]

In a surprising turn of events, within 2 weeks of the previous correspondence and, importantly, after a month of intense lobbying organized by Negativland, the RIAA revised its guidelines. This was quite an impressive victory considering the David and Goliath scenario pitting a band that sells no more than 10,000 copies of its recent releases against the organization that represents every major company within the music industry. The amended guidelines state:

> Some recordings presented for manufacture may contain—as part of an artist's work—identifiable "samples" or small pieces of other artists' well-known songs. In some instances this sampling may qualify as "fair use" under copyright law, and in other instances it may constitute infringement. There are no hard and fast rules in this area and judgments on both "fair use" and indemnification must be made on a case-by-case basis.[71]

In an RIAA press release, Rosen made it clear that these new guidelines were written as a response to Negativland's grassroots campaign when she stated, "Hopefully, this step will give bands like Negativland the fair shake they deserve with CD pressing plants."[72] The new guidelines were "a very positive and extraordinary concession on the part of the RIAA," said Negativland, cautiously adding, "though it remains to be seen as to how this will play itself out in the real world and how much this will actually help." Nevertheless, Negativland stated, "On the plus side, this is the first time EVER that an organization who represents the interests of the mainstream corporate music world . . . has actually acknowledged that a gray area exists in copyright law and that collage is a legitimate and valid form of music."[73]

Unfortunately, this story does not have as happy an ending as it could, because, despite the amendment to the guidelines, Negativland has continued to have difficulty finding pressing plants that will manufacture their CDs. For a 1999 release, *The ABC's of Anarchism* (with Chumbawumba),

Hosler said: "We found a pressing plant for that, but we didn't tell them who we were. We were very secretive, and they did press it. But after they pressed it they called us up in a panic and asked, 'What did we just press?'"[74] They found a plant that knows what Negativland is about and will press their records only if they sign an indemnification agreement that puts all the legal and financial responsibility on the group if there was ever a suit. It does not mean they will print every CD Negativland brings to them, but for now that plant has pressed the group's other CDs that were "freaking out" other lawsuit-leery pressing plants.

Although Hosler acknowledges that what they have done is a type of lobbying, he insists that the entire reason Negativland exists is to make records and open up copyright law through the act of releasing these records that appropriate "found" sounds. Hosler therefore states, "You hear by example that it is nothing to be threatened by. It's not ripping off anybody or taking any revenue stream that somebody else deserved." But, Hosler points out: "The problem now is, of course, we are trying to get them manufactured. Back in the 1980s and early 1990s when we doing recordings that had all sorts of stuff on them, nothing happened. The pressing plants weren't concerned. The pressing plant that pressed the U2 CD and LP never said a darn thing."[75]

Even though Negativland's U2 single was suppressed, it remains in distribution through a number of ways. First, it has been widely boot-legged and sold in stores. Second, it has been passed on by friends to other friends on mix tapes. Third, the single remained in circulation through the efforts of the Copyright Violation Squad (CVS). The CVS was initially formed by the Tape-beatles in response to the lawsuit brought against John Oswald, but the group remained active when other groups like Negativland suffered the same fate.[76] Further, physical tape trading has been complemented with the distribution of free digital audio files on the Internet.

Other artists have resisted intellectual property laws in different ways, for instance, by openly and publicly mocking the copyright system. Well aware of sound collage's history, the KLF (Kopyright Liberation Front) employed intertextual avant-garde production techniques and parlayed them into a briefly successful pop career. Under the moniker The Timelords, they had a number-one British hit, which was subsequently used as a vehicle for a satirical book titled *The Manual (How To Have a Number One Hit the Easy Way)*.[77] The KLF's debut album, *1987 (What the Fuck's Going On?)*, made extensive and provocative use of samples from the Monkees, the Beatles, and ABBA, with the album's liner notes claiming that all sounds were "liberated . . . from all copyright restrictions."[78]

After ABBA's song publishers (Polar Music) demanded that the samples be removed, the KLF quickly released—almost as if the whole affair was planned from the beginning—an edited version of the album that deleted all offending samples and included instructions for how consumers could recreate the original version of *1987* using their old records.[79] In response to Polar Music's role in suppressing their album, the members of the KLF took a trip to Sweden where they had a prostitute dressed as one of the women in ABBA receive a fake gold album that contained the inscription "for sales in excess of zero" outside the headquarters of Polar Music—all while *The Queen and I* played in the background.[80]

Visual Collage and Appropriation Art

Unlike the above-mentioned forms of sound collage, which could only be facilitated by recording technology, the mode of cultural production at the core of visual collage—essentially a cut-and-paste technique—has been around for centuries. Wescher documents that "it is certain that collage, montage, and assemblages of various materials had innumerable predecessors in past centuries, but only an insignificant number of these can be related in any way to what is done today."[81]

The tradition of text collages can trace an origin to twelfth-century Japan, where calligraphers began to copy poems onto paper that they pasted together from irregularly cut pieces of tinted paper. The artists then sprinkled the paper with stars, birds or flower patterns, then brushed with ink in ways to suggest mountains, rivers or the sky.[82] There are many examples throughout the centuries of this kind of folk art in Europe as well, where collaged fragments of images, cloth, text, or all of the above were used for religious purposes, among other things. But these techniques had virtually no influence on the evolution of the visual arts and thus remained on the sidelines of artistic development. It was not until the twentieth century that collage became influential and was recognized as a legitimate means of artistic expression.

Cubist Collage
In 1912, Pablo Picasso glued an object onto one of his Cubist paintings, an act that created what is considered to be the first deliberately executed collage within the modern art world. The object was an oil cloth that contained a design of a chair (on which Picasso painted wooden strips to

further the illusion of a piece of furniture), and it was prominently placed upon a typically cubist painting of objects crammed together.[83] Picasso framed the painting with a coarse rope to further draw attention to its status as an object and this created the first work of fine art to appropriate materials from everyday life.[84] Poggi wrote of this work, and the collage aesthetic in general, "The invention of collage put into question prevailing notions of how and what works of art represent, of what unifies a work of art, of what materials artists may use; it also opened to debate the more recent Romantic definition of what constitutes originality and authenticity in the work of art."[85]

Newspaper fragments were the most frequently used materials in Picasso's earliest collages. Picasso used these to give shape to musical instruments or bottles and wineglasses in his paintings *Violin* and *Siphon, Glass, Newspaper, Violin*. This use of newspapers is important because it negates the idea of an original, unique object. Poggi argues, "Moreover, with a life span of only a day or perhaps a week, it quickly assumes the status of refuse, thereby exemplifying the principle of obsolescence inscribed in the very nature of the commodity."[86]

While Picasso has received most of the credit for inventing the collage technique, Georges Braque and Juan Gris also executed collages in the fall of 1912, with Gris being the first to publicly exhibit a collage.[87] Who was the first to deliberately paste an object onto a painting is of little importance, because this art-making approach quickly spread throughout European art communities as if it had been fermenting for years. Many artists began adhering wallpaper patterns, newspaper scraps, bottle labels and the like to their paintings, creating a complex interplay between illusion and reality, while at the same time further blurring the lines between the "high" and the "low" culture.[88]

Futurism, Dadaism and Surrealism

These three movements have very obvious connections, though they are quite different in many ways. But because this is not intended as a history of art I will keep the discussion of the specifics of these movements to a minimum and instead will focus on their relationship with collage. The Italian Futurists preceded the Dadaists, with the former's aesthetic and cultural anarchism (though not with their pro-war ideology) serving as a prototype for Dada's goofball stunts and artistic innovations.[89]

While much is known about collage in the history of Cubism, and in the subsequent development of modern art more generally, less is known of Futurism's role in the development of collage: "Few realize how many adherents the new medium found in that movement too, and yet Boccioni, Balla, Severini, Carra, and Russolo, the artists who signed the First Manifesto of Futurist Painting, all practiced cutting and pasting, and some of them produced truly fundamental works with that technique."[90] Umberto Boccioni and Gino Severini were the first to include a variety of materials in their Futurist sculptures, and after visiting Picasso's and Braque's studios in early 1912, Severini became obsessed with types of sculpture that incorporated a melange of modern materials that pushed sculpture beyond what he referred to as the mummified homogeneity of marble and bronze.[91]

By the fall of 1914, Picasso had almost completely stopped making collages, but the Futurists reinvigorated their interest in its possibilities, particularly in its potential for delivering their pro-war propaganda, which partially explains their increased use of words and letters in their collages at the time.[92] As I implied earlier, even though there were aesthetic similarities between the Dadaists and the Futurists, the former did not share the latter's worldview, which was perhaps best summarized in the *Futurist Manifesto:* "We will glorify war—the world's only hygiene—militarism, patriotism, the destructive gesture of freedom-bringers, beautiful ideas worth dying for, and . . . will fight moralilism, feminism, every opportunistic or utilitarian cowardice."[93]

Whereas the Futurists amounted to, essentially, a bunch of artsy, chest-beating libertarian rednecks with paintbrushes *and* guns, the Dadaists were reacting against the ravages of World War I that the Futurists promoted, as well as what the Dadaists saw as a Western civilization that generated it.[94] Like the Futurists, the Dadaists used collage and photomontage because they believed these techniques to be important polemical and political tools.[95] German artist Kurt Schwitters stated, "The artists in this group were united in their belief that traditional, hierarchical Western culture and capitalist political systems had brought about the disastrous political conflict, and they banded together to develop new, oppositional languages to undermine those traditions."[96]

It is the language of fragmentation that provided the framework for collage's capacity for social and political critique taken up by Zurich and Berlin Dadaists such as Schwitters, Raoul Housmann, Jean Arp, Francis Picabia and others.[97] In an example of the cut-and-paste method the Dadaists helped pioneer, Tristan Tzara gave instructions on how "to make a Dadaist poem" that entailed taking a newspaper, cutting out an article's individual words, placing them in a bag and randomly pulling them out.[98] He wrote: "The poem will resemble you./And there you are—an infinitely original author of charming sensibility/even though unappreciated by the vulgar herd."[99]

The final line that sarcastically referred to the "infinitely original author" highlights Dada's suspicion (and that of many of the other early twentieth-century avant-garde movements) of Western notions of originality and authorship. Collage, which was taken up by the Dadaists with gusto, was perhaps the ultimate attack on that concept (though, it was also an attack on other central tenets of art as well). Dada wound down by the early 1920s, and many of the artists associated with that movement moved into the Surrealist fold. The emergence of Surrealism as an organized movement can be marked by the debut in 1924 of *La Revolution Surrealiste,* published by Surrealist figurehead André Breton.[100] Like the Futurists and the Dadaists, the Surrealists also printed their own manifesto, or a series of them, with the first *Surrealist Manifesto* also being published in 1924.[101] Written by Breton, this manifesto emphasized the "revolutionary" potential of the Surrealist-pioneered method of "automatic writing," which highlighted the importance of opening up the subconscious through the act of letting writing flow automatically from one's head.[102]

With the emergence of Surrealism came a new interest in collage; Breton claimed Picasso and Braque as the Surrealists' own, in part because he saw their collages as opening up new sources of "unreal reality" for art.[103] Max Ernst, who was associated with both Dadaism and Surrealism, began producing a series of influential collages in the 1920s, gaining a significant amount of influence in the 1930s when many Surrealist and non-Surrealist imitators followed his lead. Sometimes creating purely collaged works derived from his massive supply of old mail-order catalogs, sometimes combining collaged fragments with painting, and sometimes applying the collage aesthetic to the design of sets for ballets, Ernst further expanded the scope of collage.[104]

Pop Art

Robert Rauschenberg and Jasper Johns epitomized the Neo-Dada movement that soon transformed into Pop Art, and they were among the two earliest and most well-known artists who made collage a significant part of their work in the 1950s. Rauschenberg's "combine paintings" and his other works tended to incorporate eclectic and disparate objects into his art, overlaying with paint such things as news photos, pieces of cloth and pictures torn from an art history book.[105] Rauschenberg's statement that he hoped to blur the line between art and life—acting within the gap between the two—echoed one of the original motivations underpinning the collage method, which intended to bring an end to the long-standing demarcation between art and "real life" material objects.[106]

This drive brought about Pop Art, a movement which included Rauschenberg, Roy Liechtenstein and Andy Warhol, among others—artists who incorporated commercial imagery into their own paintings and collages. The images produced by television, comics, motion pictures and other forms of media naturally seeped into the consciousness of the artists associated with Pop Art, providing a language or a vocabulary with layers of meaning with which contemporary artists could communicate.[107] But, as some artists who practiced collage and other forms of appropriation began to find, much of the syntax and words of that language were privately owned, protected by copyright and trademark law.

Interestingly, many of the early intellectual property infringement lawsuits involving visual artists resulted from one artist's appropriation of another's work, particularly the work of photographers who felt their copyrighted work was being exploited. Because Andy Warhol's work is so heavily based on the appropriation of images found in the popular media, it is not surprising that he was sued a number of times for the unauthorized use of privately owned images. In one example of this, Warhol was convinced by his painting mentor, Henry Geldzahler, to stop dwelling on death during his mid-1960s period (e.g., his series of auto-accident silkscreens, for instance) and, instead, look at "life." In explaining what Geldzahler meant, he opened up an issue of a magazine and showed Warhol a centerfold of flowers.[108]

Running with this idea, Warhol had a number of pieces made that were based on a photograph of four poppies by Patricia Caulfield; the series of Warhol's paintings was called, simply, *Flowers*.[109] Caulfield's photographic image, which appeared in *Modern Photography*, was enlarged and professionally silk-screened onto canvas. The flowers were then painted in bright colors by Warhol's friends and associates at his Factory, with nearly 1,000 *Flowers* being produced. They were shown in the Leo Castelli gallery and eventually licensed as posters, which was how Caulfield eventually found out about Warhol's appropriation (she discovered the posters in a New York City bookstore).[110]

Warhol settled with Caulfield and her attorney, handing over two of his paintings and agreeing to pay her a royalty in the form of artwork or monetary compensation whenever he used the paintings in the future. Despite the settlement, Caulfield remained unsatisfied because Warhol's appropriations disturbed her on a more fundamental level. She said: "The reason there's a legal issue here is because there's a moral one . . .

What's irritating is to have someone like an image enough to use it, but then denigrate the original intent."[111] Even though her work was not hijacked wholesale—her photos merely provided a template on which a variety of bright, sometimes unnatural, colors were painted—Caulfield remained upset because she was a real person at the receiving end of an appropriation method that is most often discussed in abstract, theoretical terms.

Caulfield did not believe that Warhol had transformed her work to any significant degree, and no matter how much he actually may have, the fact that Warhol clipped out Caulfield's photograph and used it in his work was, to her, inherently problematic and "morally" wrong. This is undoubtedly how many musicians who have been sampled feel, as is evidenced by the sentiments quoted in chapter 3, and Caulfield's use of the term "original" in conjunction with her other statements underscores the resonance that Romantic notions of originality still have. These ideas are, to a certain extent, precisely what Pop Art and other movements that used appropriation practices were trying to undermine. As Buchloh states:

> When Robert Rauschenberg and Andy Warhol introduced mechanically produced, "found" imagery into the high-art discourse of painting by technological procedures of reproduction such as the dye transfer process and silkscreen printing, gestural identity and originality of expression were repudiated. The procedures that had concretized notions of creative invention and individual productivity in the preceding decade were negated in the mechanical construction of the painting.[112]

Photojournalist Charles Moore found out that Warhol had used in a series called "Red Race Riot" his pictures (published in *Life* magazine) of three men who were attacked by police dogs in Birmingham. The works were produced in a similar manner as the *Flower* paintings, but despite the transformation in the medium, context and composition, Moore was extremely angry and he arranged a meeting with the artist. Moore claims he told Warhol, "I want it settled so you know, and other artists know, you can't just rip off a photographer's work."[113] The case was settled out of court, with Warhol handing over to Moore a number of prints from the *Flowers* series, somewhat of an irony considering the appropriative history of that series.

Photographer Fred Ward's photo of Jacqueline Kennedy for *Life* magazine, which was shot soon after the assassination of her husband, was used by Warhol and he, again, settled the dispute with Ward by giving the photographer (and Ward's agent) one of his works. Similarly, when Rauschenberg used a photograph from *Newsweek* taken by Dennis Brack of a man lying in a pool of blood during the 1968 Detroit riots, Brack protested. Again, the dispute was settled when Rauschenberg gave a copy of the work that incorporated the photo to both Brack and his agent.[114]

Rauschenberg also found himself in legal hot waters when he incorporated into a print named *Pull* a photograph taken by Morton Bebe of a man diving into a pool, something that was widely reprinted in the early 1970s and used in an ad campaign for the Nikon camera company.[115] This print is considered to be one of Rauschenberg's most important pieces, consisting of "two pieces of fabric, cheesecloth glued to silk taffeta, with the image of a man in a swan dive silk-screened in the center. Around the edges, forming a border, are other offset-printed images, and there is a small paper bag glued to the fabric near the top of the print."[116] Bebe, who was extremely displeased, sent Rauschenberg a letter, to which Rauschenberg replied and expressed surprise at Bebe's reaction. Rauschenberg replied back, "I have received many letters from people expressing their happiness and pride in seeing their images incorporated and transformed in my work."[117] Rauschenberg continued:

> Having used collage in my work since 1949, I have never felt that I was infringing on anyone's rights as I have consistently transformed these images sympathetically with the use of solvent transfer, collage and reversal as ingredients in the compositions which are dependent on reportage of current events and elements in our current environment, hopefully to give the work the possibility of being reconsidered and viewed in a totally new context.[118]

In mid-1977 Bebe retained a lawyer, suing Rauschenberg for copyright infringement and asking for a minimum of $10,000 in damages plus attorney and court fees, and profits from the sale of *Pull*. In 1980, Bebe and Rauschenberg settled, with Bebe receiving a copy of *Pull*, $3,000, and a promise that Bebe would be attributed whenever the work was displayed in the future. Bebe claimed that he settled for less than he was seeking primarily because his legal costs were mounting and he did not want to lose the court case on a technicality, adding yet another example of a case of a copyright infringement lawsuit to the art world that never set a legal precedent.[119] Rauschenberg's attorney argued that his client admitted no wrongdoing in the settlement, adding:

> It is the position of Mr. Rauschenberg and Gemini G. E. L. that an artist working in the medium of collage has the right to make fair use of prior printed and published materials in the creation of an original collage including such preexisting elements as a part thereof and that such right is guaranteed to the artist as a fundamental right of freedom of expression under the First Amendment of the Constitution.[120]

It is interesting that a number of the cases involving one artist suing, or threatening to sue, another for copyright infringement have been settled, in part, by the infringing artist giving the other artist (and, often, the artist's lawyer or agent) a piece of his or her work. While the art world most certainly has been long involved in the sphere of commercial exchange, lawyers and people from the world of business are often surprised at the extent to which the art world continues to function on the basis of a series of unwritten understandings and agreements.[121] The art world, states Buskirk,[122] functions "to a large degree on the basis of generally understood but not legally codified rules that must be observed by those who wish to play the game."[123] Infringement cases have been settled by using artwork in exchange for cash, which indicates the existence of social relations that aren't heavily contractual and the degree to which important practices of the art world and the larger corporate world have yet to be drawn into each other.

Situationism

The next art movement to use methods of appropriation was Situationism, which gained notoriety in part because its members played an instrumental role in sparking the May 1968 uprising in Paris.[124] One of the movement's most known figures who epitomized the political nature of this movement was Guy Debord, a man who articulated the Situationists' critique of consumer society in his book *Society of the Spectacle*.[125] Situationism is significant because it contributed to the field of art the concept of "detournement," which is, as Greil Marcus defines it, "the theft of aesthetic artifacts from their contexts and their diversion into contexts of one's own devise."[126]

One example of this is the alteration of popular comic strips by changing the words in speech balloons to offer a covert or an overt critique of consumer culture, such as, "In our spectacular society where all you can see is things and their price . . . the only free choice is the refusal to pay."[127] Situationist detournement went one step further than Pop Art (which usually opted for an unaltered representation of cultural products) by modifying cultural images presented by the mass media in a way in which they commented on themselves.[128]

The art associated with the British punk rock movement of the late 1970s was a melding of the traditions of Situationist detournement and Dadaist collage, and its art was often very primitive and shocking in nature. For instance, a Sex Pistols flyer that advertised their 7-inch single, "God Save the Queen" (a tirade against the queen of England released at the time of the queen's Silver Jubilee celebration in 1977) contained a photomontage of a picture of the queen with a safety pin through her lips, a quintessential symbol of punk culture.[129] The cover of one of their singles was a detournement of, as Marcus describes:

> . . . a borrowed travel club comic strip, depicting happy tourists on the beach, in a nightclub, cruising the Mediterranean, celebrating their vacations in speech balloons Jamie Reid [the group's art director and a former Situationist] had emptied of advertising copy and filled with the words Johnny Rotten was singing on the plastic—"a cheap holiday in other people's misery!"[130]

The travel company sued because it claimed the cover art infringed on their copyrights and also because, in part, the company could not have been pleased about being associated with the most controversial punk rock group of the time. This use of comic art is another early example of litigation surrounding a piece of appropriation art, but, again, while it resulted in the withdrawal of the single from the marketplace, it did not set any legal precedents.[131]

Contemporary Appropriation Art

Appropriation Art refers not to an art movement *per se* but to an approach to creating art that puts at its center the practice of incorporating existing images into a work of art. The term *Appropriation Art* has recently come into more common usage to describe a disparate group of contemporary artists who share a common fundamental approach, though they may differ in radical ways, stylistically or politically. Most of the artists discussed in this chapter can be said to have engaged in Appropriation Art, generally, and Dadaist Marcel Duchamp has been labeled as the father of Appropriation Art with his "ready-mades."[132]

For his 1915 ready-made piece, *Fountain*, Duchamp simply bought a mass-produced urinal, signed the name "R. Mutt" on its white porcelain surface, and exhibited it, essentially, as both a humorous prank on the art world and a critique of the Romanticist and Enlightenment notions of originality and authorship that Dada was rebelling against. Another Duchamp prank/critique that used this appropriation technique was his *LHOOQ,* in which he took a reproduction of Da Vinci's famous *Mona Lisa* and drew a mustache and a goatee on that famous face.[133] In both cases, Duchamp borrowed wholesale various existing cultural texts in a way that made those texts essential to his critiques, and through those critiques he was able to transcend the original meanings of the signs he appropriated.

One of the earliest contemporary practitioners of Appropriation Art who borrowed in extreme ways—beyond the fragmentary borrowings of

collage—was Elaine Sturtevant. In the 1960s, she began producing paintings identical to Warhol's that were explicitly displayed as such. Considering Warhol's appropriations in his own work, using Warhol's paintings as
a subject was fitting, and Sturtevant was applauded by such Pop artists as
Claes Oldenburg who, in a somewhat humorous and ironic turn of events,
turned nasty when she began producing replicas of *his* work. During the
1980s, this technique became a more prominent mode of artistic production, as artists consciously challenged the very notion of creative
originality.

Sherrie Levine is one of the artists who has most radically challenged
these beliefs by rephotographing famous photographs and painting identical copies of works in the public domain by Piet Mondrian, Jean Miro
and Henri Matisse, among others. Levine's emphasis on the brushstrokes
and other technical aspects of a painting undercut the celebrated "originality" of the masters' works, and her work had political and feminist
undercurrents because she chose to solely recreate the work of "seminal"
male artists whose styles have been associated with the male aesthetic.[134] Mike Bidlo, who created his own versions of Picasso, Pollock
and De Chirico, employed a similar strategy, though without the same
philosophical underpinnings.[135]

A contemporary and controversial artist who follows the
Appropriationist trajectory initiated by Duchamp, but in the context of an
omnipresent mass media and marketplace, is Jeff Koons. Buskirk writes,
"Koons is one of a number of artists who have responded to an increasingly image saturated society by taking pictures directly from the media,
advertising or elsewhere and repositioning them within their own
work."[136] Koons's credibility and integrity as an artist has been challenged
because of his showboating and his very public marriage to Italian ex-
porn star and politician Ilona Stoller (a.k.a. La Cicciolina).

Koons's wedding of art and commerce has been hailed and vilified in
the art world in much the same way Madonna's work has been in the
music world. For instance, whereas noted art critic Martha Buskirk[137] writes
favorably of Koons, Yve-Alain Bois (Harvard University professor of modern art) states: "His work is totally trivial and a pure product of the market. He's considered to be an heir to Duchamp, but I think it's a trivialization
of all that. I think he's kind of a commercial artist."[138] Koons first came to
notoriety with an exhibit that included a display containing a series of
ordinary, brand-new vacuum cleaners that were neatly arranged and presented within shiny, clear Plexiglas cases. Although it was not the target
of the scandal provoked by Duchamp's ready-mades, it was something
that nevertheless caused quite a bit of outrage.[139]

In 1988, Koons presented his "Banality" show (an all-out exploration of the remoter regions of bad taste and American kitsch), which was similarly controversial and financially successful. "Banality" contained a work called *String of Puppies*, a carved wooden statue (in an edition of three) depicting a middle-aged couple holding a string of German shepherd dogs. This work was based on a cutesy, mildly amusing mass-produced postcard that Koons bought at a store and which was part of a portfolio of similar images from popular culture that Koons had been collecting for over 2 years.[140] Koons had simply taken the postcard and sent it to his Italian studio to be made into a painted sculpture by hired craftsmen, resulting in the 42" × 62" × 37" work *String of Puppies*.[141]

Aside from being rendered in three dimensions and having a few new details incorporated, the sculpture added color to the black-and-white photograph—for example, the puppies were rendered an unnatural bright blue.[142] Overall, Buskirk argues, the postcard photograph and Koons's work differ dramatically "in terms of medium, scale, color, detail and context in which they would be appreciated."[143] Nevertheless, the sculpture obviously derived from the postcard photo, something Koons never tried to hide. And, given the context of the "Banality" show of which it was a part, it was most likely easy for the people who viewed and who bought the sculptures (the three sold for a total of $367,000) to figure out that it referred, generally or specifically, to a piece of kitsch.[144]

In 1989, the photographer who took the picture on the postcard sued Koons. (Koons has also been sued for his appropriation of the trademarked and copyrighted cartoon characters the Pink Panther and Odie from the comic strip *Garfield*).[145] The photographer, Art Rogers, discovered Koons's work when he opened a copy of the *Los Angeles Times* and saw a photograph of *String of Puppies* as part of a story about how "Manhattan millionaire Jeff Koons has once again shocked the world with the extremity of his kitsch vision."[146] Rogers was angered because first, his work had been appropriated without permission; second, Koons made a significant amount of money from the sales of his derivative work; and third, his "heart-warming snap was apparently viewed by swanky Manhattan as a hilarious piece of crud."[147]

A federal court ruled in 1991 that Koons was guilty of copyright infringement, and in 1992 the U.S. Court of Appeals in New York upheld the lower court's ruling. Further setting a precedent, later in 1992 the Supreme Court refused to hear Koons's appeal, upholding the original ruling.[148] Buskirk argued, "In the absence of other decisions, then, the Koons case will establish a key legal precedent," especially because it was affirmed by both a court of appeals and the Supreme Court.[149] Koons's attorney, John Koegel, claimed that *String of Puppies* was protected by the "fair use" provision of the copyright statute, but Koons's form of appropriation was not obvious enough for a court to rule that it was used as parody or critique.

Interestingly, the term "appropriation" is used as widely in legal context as it is in the art world; in legal circles, appropriation means theft or piracy. In fact, Koegel does not even like to use the word in court. The judge who made the initial ruling did not believe that Koons's appropriation could be considered "fair use," stating, "No copier may defend the act of plagiarism by pointing out how much of the copy he has not pirated." He added, "There is no case here."[150] Discussing the concepts of parody and critique in relation to Koons's work, the judge stated:

> The problem in the instant case is that given that "String of Puppies" is a satirical critique of our materialistic society, it is difficult to discern any parody of the photograph "Puppies" itself. . . . The circumstances of this case indicate that Koons' copying of the photograph "Puppies" was done in bad faith, primarily for profit making motives, and did not constitute a parody of the original work.[151]

Even though the 1994 *Campbell v. Acuff-Rose Music, Inc.* Supreme Court decision established that a work's commercial nature did not keep it from being considered "fair use," it did so within relatively narrow parameters. The 2 Live Crew version of Roy Orbison's "Pretty Woman" was unambiguously a parody of the original song, and the Supreme Court's loosening of the commercial presumption within the "fair use" statute was limited to works that explicitly convey a purpose of parody. But in cases when a parody, satire or critique may be more nuanced, the precedent that the same Supreme Court set in their upholding of the *Rogers v. Koons* decision makes it less likely a court would rule that a piece of Appropriation Art (or any cultural text that borrows in more subtle ways) is a "fair use."

In addition, in 1997 the Supreme Court complicated matters when it ruled that "fair use" provisions do not apply to *satire* when a copyrighted work is not the target of, but is instead merely invoked to facilitate, the satire.[152] In this case, lawyers representing Dr. Seuss Enterprises successfully argued that *The Cat NOT in the Hat!*—a Penguin Books published, Dr. Seuss-like retelling of the O. J. Simpson murder trial that used the same rhyming and illustration style—did not constitute "fair use."[153]

Because the referencing of the copyrighted Dr. Seuss character was not used to directly parody *The Cat in the Hat* itself, the Supreme Court ruled that it was not protected expression.[154] In the Koons case, which did not employ obvious satire, it did not matter to the court that, as Greenberg argues, "those aspects of Rogers' piece which the court viewed as 'original' are no longer apparent in Koons' sculpture. Gone is the 'charming' and cuddly warmth of Rogers' photograph, and in its place is a garish, perhaps horrifying, perhaps hilarious image."

Other artists being sued for infringing on intellectual property owners' rights include Dennis Oppenheim, who created a commissioned sculpture that included the images of Mickey Mouse and Donald Duck for a Santa Monica development. The work, which resembles a jungle gym and features 34 fiberglass figures of Mickey Mouse and Donald Duck skewered with bronze rods, was designed to "contrast an ominous disease with childhood innocence."[155] Oppenheim cast the figures from 60-year-old plastic toys from Japan, which were most likely pirated, making them appear even further removed from the Disney-sanctioned-and-licensed versions with which most of us are familiar. Moreover, he transformed them into fiberglass and colored them dull shades of green, orange and yellow. The artist commented: "You go to a flea market, you buy a bunch of figures, two of them turn out to be Mickey Mouse and Donald Duck, and you put them in a sculpture or a collage. Artists do this all the time. That's appropriation."[156]

But Disney has no sympathy for any unlicensed reproduction or transformation of their intellectual property, and Disney's vice president of intellectual property law, Claire Robinson, said about the case, "We have a legal responsibility to defend our copyrights, and we do so aggressively."[157] Disney Productions, a major producer of what Harris[158] calls "postindustrial folklore," has invested a considerable amount of capital in the promotion and marketing of its cartoon characters.[159]

Among other things, Disney Productions has sued artists for including Disney characters in their work as well as the producers of the Academy Awards for using Snow White in an opening musical number of a broadcast.[160] Oppenheim said that his attempts to negotiate a license agreement with Disney failed. At one point Disney offered him a license for $15,000 but Oppenheim could not afford it. Disney rejected Oppenheim's offer to trade his artwork for a license; obviously, Disney does not operate within the same quasi-covenantal framework that the art world does. The better-known artists who have incorporated Disney characters into their works of art—such as Roy Lichtenstein, Andy Warhol, Keith Haring and Wayne Thiebaud—bought licenses from Disney. Their move demonstrates how impossible it is to get away with appropriating Disney characters without doing so.[161] In arguing for the legitimacy of Appropriation Art's productive and creative practices, Badin states:

> Art is fundamental to society precisely because of its ability to challenge old understandings, what Marcie Hamilton has called a "reorientation experiment." Thus, appropriation should not be mistaken for plagiarism. By recontextualizing the image, the artist has, in fact, transformed and altered it in an attempt to force viewers to see the original work and its significance differently. In turn, the audience is reoriented to view not only the object, but to observe anew the positioning of boundaries between the piece and the space that surrounds it.[162]

This echoes one of the underlying arguments contained in chapters 2, 3 and 4—that the intertextual borrowing of preexisting cultural elements lies at the heart of many, if not most, creative cultural practices.

Conclusion

Hopkins emphasizes that collage is not just a technique, but rather "a philosophical attitude, an aesthetic position that can suffuse virtually any expressive medium."[163] The collage aesthetic crosses disciplinary boundaries, playing an essential role in the works of not just the visual and sound-collage artists discussed here, but also in such works as T. S. Elliot's *The Waste Land*, William Burroughs' *Naked Lunch*, James Joyce's *Ulysses* and Igor Stravinsky's music. *The Waste Land*, for instance, is very much a collage of a wide variety of elements, integrating bits of near-movie dialogue with "enough quotes from Tristan und Isolde, Ovid, Verlaine, and so on, to require six pages of footnotes."[164] Furthermore, it contains numerous other verbatim and bastardized quotations from Shakespeare, Dante, Greek myth, Arthurian legend, the French Symbolists and many other sources.[165]

Hopkins writes of *The Waste Land*, "Though the author's voice is present from time to time, weaving the disparate elements together and lecturing us like a docent in a museum of literature, the final effect of his poem is more that of a vast historical collage than an intimate conversation with a familiar companion."[166] Cultural producers across media and disciplines have explicitly acknowledged the centrality of intertextuality to their creative practices. Echoing Stravinsky's comment, "A good composer does not imitate, he steals," T. S. Elliot succinctly stated in a famous line, "Good writers borrow; great writers steal."[167]

Intertextuality is central to many different practices of cultural production, but various intertextual modes of cultural production directly conflict with the logic(s) of intellectual property law (with its situated notion of authorship and ownership). Sound-collage artists have engaged in specific and very pointed criticisms of intellectual property law—such as Oswald's statement, "If creativity is a field, then copyright is the fence" as well as the Tape-beatles' de facto motto, "Plagiarism: A Collective Vision" and their more general attacks on individual creativity and originality.

Similar criticisms of this notion of originality were lobbed by visual collage artists at the beginning of the twentieth century. Tristan Tzara's set of instructions for writing a Dadaist poem made fun of Romantic notions of creativity. After telling the reader to randomly cut and paste text from a newspaper, he concluded by stating "And there you are—an infinitely original author of charming sensibility, even though unappreciated by the vulgar herd."[168] The final line that very sarcastically referred to the "infinitely original author" highlights Dada's suspicion of these notions of originality and authorship, which were taken up with gusto by the nineteenth-century Romanticist movement. Collage, which was used by the Dadaists, was perhaps the ultimate attack on that concept.

Although the fundamental intertextual practice of borrowing and reconfiguring existing cultural texts has not changed, some of the methods used to create music and visual art have been altered. That is, artists can more literally reference fragments of cultural texts with the advent of the VCR, the recording studio (and, later, portable analog tape recorders, digital audio recorders, etc.) and the camera (and, later, silk-screen machines, photocopiers, digital scanners, etc.). While digital sampling and scanning (or more primitive "cut-and-paste" methods) differ significantly from the methods used by more "traditional" musicians and visual artists, there are distinct similarities.

In the same way musicians can borrow riffs and songs wholesale, so can those who sample, and the same is true of painters, photographers and collage artists. But sound- and visual-collage artists can also work in more subtle ways, just as traditional musicians do. Even though the same basic premise is in operation, that of borrowing, it is complicated by the fact that today's artists may now *exactly* "capture" and replicate an image or sound rather than paint or perform something that appropriates, but which is necessarily an interpretation. I am not arguing these two ways of producing culture are exactly the same, but it is important to note that there are substantial links between earlier modes of cultural production and contemporary practices.

At the beginning of the twentieth century, avant-garde strategies such as collage and ready-mades employed by Duchamp posed more of a threat to the strictures of the art world than to the world market, more generally. But as artists increasingly employ methods of reproduction similar to those used by mass media, when significant aspects of these two worlds become articulated, intellectual property owners are more likely to feel threatened.[169] Furthermore, when artists such as Warhol and Koons become more visible to the world of popular culture from which they borrow, they increase the chances of drawing the attention of intellectual property owners.

By looking at these different areas of culture within the framework of articulation theory, we can understand how areas of cultural production that had previously been (relatively) untouched by intellectual property law become entangled, connected—articulated—in these new relations. To map the intersections and contradictions, one must identify the primary characteristics of the areas of cultural production that are affected. I briefly did this in the above discussion of sound and visual collage, demonstrating that both share certain similarities but differences as well— particularly in regard to the economic positions of the artists. In addition, we must identify the way in which notions of authorship and ownership operate within an area of cultural production, and how those notions do or do not clash with those that ground intellectual property law.

As the *Koons* case demonstrated, many judges do not carve out much legal room for the intertextual practices that lie at the heart of these kinds of artistic activities, instead preferring to interpret them as an infringement on one's exclusively owned property. Of course, this is an unrealistic view of how art, music and other creative cultural practices have been produced for years. But because the notion of private property is so powerful within U.S. jurisprudence, many judges have not been sympathetic toward such practices. These particular judicial conceptions of who constitutes an author (and therefore an owner) increase and consolidate the power of intellectual property owners—who are overwhelmingly corporate owners.

Moreover, the differing economic positions and overall profile of, say, Jeff Koons and Negativland create very differently articulated relationships between of the law, these two cultural producers and intellectual property owners. Koons is a well-known multimillionaire artist and Negativland occupy a much more marginal position within the economy, but both engage in intertextual methods of appropriation (though in very different media). The *differences* in the basic social positions of Koons and Negativland help explain why Negativland (and other sound-collage artists) continue to engage in the practices that originally got them into legal trouble, while Koons's overt appropriations have been significantly curtailed. Of course, the *similarities* between the two's overall mode of cultural production explains why they both were sued in the first place.

Although avant-garde sound collage and hip-hop often share a similar intertextual mode of cultural production, they differ in one significant way. Unlike most hip-hop artists, many sound-collage artists have rebelled outright against the system of intellectual property law not by simply continuing to engage in their productive practices, but, as Beck's lawyer put it, by "bragging" about it. In regard to hip-hop and sound collage, one key element clearly explains the way intellectual property law has been differently articulated with these two areas of cultural production: the nature of the distribution system in which they are immersed and the artists' economic ties to that system.

Because of their decidedly avant-garde, noncommercial tactics, sound-collage artists simply do not make themselves very well known within the mainstream of the popular culture from which they sample. Overwhelmingly, sound-collage artists do not reenter into the commercial distribution network that informs their work. And when they do run into legal difficulty from their sampling, there are no institutional imperatives from within the avant-garde sound-collage community to encourage artists to capitulate to the demands of copyright law. That is, there are few pressures to develop the licensing clearance system that has evolved within hip-hop.

Unlike avant-garde sound collage, hip-hop has become a billion-dollar industry whose artists largely release albums on the same major labels that own many of the songs from which they sample. This coexistence and symbiosis does not occur within the avant-garde sound-collage community, because these artists release their works almost entirely through a distribution network of independent labels and, increasingly, on the Internet. Therefore, hip-hop is implicated within the larger political economy of the music industry in a way that sound-collage art, in its more rarefied form, is not. Sound-collage and hip-hop artists are positioned similarly within a copyright law regime that only acknowledges a particular form of authorship and ownership. This particular regime does not recognize intertextual modes of cultural production as legitimate.

I want to be careful not to use the language of articulation theory as merely a fancy way of saying "because of varying circumstances, different things happen." By paying attention to the way in which differing notions of authorship and ownership are at play in these areas of cultural production, and to the location of the cultural producers in relation to the means of production, we can generate a rough map that helps explain the varying reactions of different types of cultural producers. By mapping the different notions of authorship and ownership, we can understand why the norm in the area of the visual arts is *artists* suing *artists*—instead of intellectual property-holding corporations suing other companies or individuals, which is more typical.

In almost all cases, within the visual arts, it has been photographers suing artists who appropriate, as in the examples of the woman who sued Andy Warhol and the man whose lawsuit against Jeff Koons reached a verdict stage (one of the only cases of that nature to do so). Photographers and appropriation artists are articulated differently with intellectual property law and mass media; moreover, there seems to be two competing definitions of what constitutes authorship. Photographers such as Caulfield, Bebe and Moore felt that the incorporation of their photographs into another's artwork was very much a moral issue, and they expressed it as such. Again, as Caulfield stated, "The reason there's a legal issue here is because there's a moral one . . . What's irritating is to have someone like an image enough to use it, but then denigrate the original intent."[170]

Interestingly, the appropriation artists also made moral claims by framing their borrowings as something that is necessary and essential for them to carry on with what they do and, importantly, as something that was fundamentally related to freedom of expression®. In regard to Rauschenberg, his attorney argued that "an artist working in the medium of collage has the right to make fair use of prior printed and published materials in the creation of an original collage including such preexisting elements as a part thereof and that such right is guaranteed to the artist as a fundamental right of freedom of expression under the First Amendment of the Constitution."[171] The moral claims made by cultural producers across the variety of areas discussed throughout this book are *extremely* rich with meaning and cultural significance.

Photographers are situated differently than fine artists to mass media and copyright law because professional photographers often make a living from selling or licensing their copyrighted photographs to mass-media outlets, whereas fine artists usually hawk their goods within the less formalized networks of the art world. More famous appropriation artists may make additional income by licensing their copyrights to mass-media outlets (Warhol is a good example), but this is not their primary source of revenue, nor is it a sphere of culture in which they typically do business. In addition, the relationship between appropriation artists and mass me-

dia is different from that between photographers and mass media because, rather than the media serving as a site for business transactions, it
is more of a site of an *artistic* transaction where media texts are borrowed and used in new contexts. The contradiction that occurs revolves
around the fact that those media texts may often be the labor product of
a photographer who has carefully considered such issues as composition,
lighting and other technicalities.

Throughout photography's history, photographers have had to fight
against a perception that what they are doing is unoriginal, that they are
simply capturing nature "as it exists." Because of this, photographers
have felt the need to emphasize the unique authorial nature of their work.
This need to position themselves as the original, individualistic authors of
their work has certainly played a part in their desire to protect their "property" from being appropriated by others. The discourses within Appropriation Art that repudiate these notions of authorship and ownership
certainly do not sit well with photographers, especially when their work is
implicitly characterized as cultural detritus stripped of authorial intent and
potentially used by other artists at will in any context. The fact that photographers have had strong reactions when their work is recontextualized,
and that they have legally acted on those feelings, is an illustration of how
these two types of artists are differently articulated with intellectual property law.

Through articulation theory, we can see how hip-hop, folk music, sound
collage and visual collage are interconnected and, further, how relations
fostered by intellectual property law connect these practices to things as
seemingly different as the appropriation of indigenous knowledge about
local plants. To summarize from my discussion in chapter 1, articulation
allows us to understand particular connections in three ways. First, it is
important to remember that intellectual property law is comprised of
multiple laws with very different histories that evolved out of particular
forms of commerce. Nevertheless, they are all connected by the same
basic internal logic: a culturally bound notion of *authorship* and *ownership*. Second, we can understand how particular areas of *cultural production* and *intellectual property* law are articulated with *each other*.
Third, articulation creates a framework that makes sense of the connections between all of the areas of cultural production described and analyzed in this book *as being linked to each other through intellectual
property law*.

Cultural producers most definitely have agency in the face of the expanding sphere of intellectual property law. They can and do resist rela-

tions fostered by the law as they enter into new areas of cultural activity in a number of different ways. But they engage in resistive activities within the context of a hegemonic struggle that places the power of the state (both its judicial and policing arms) on the side of wealthy individuals and corporations. While there may be an infinite number of *potential* articulations that may exist, the gravitational pull of legal and economic systems that people and groups must operate against severely limits the options of artists and others. For instance, Negativland may continue to attempt to make copyright law less restrictive by releasing collage CDs that demonstrate they are of no economic threat to intellectual property owners. But if they cannot get their CDs pressed, this presents a serious obstacle to their art (even in an age of online digital distribution).

By maintaining an equal focus on institutional pressures and on sites where culture is produced, chapters 2, 3 and 4 have examined creative practices that exist primarily within North American and Western European cultures. In chapter 5, I widen the lens of analysis to look at how Western intellectual property laws interact with non-Western, Third World cultures. Specifically, I examine how multinational pharmaceutical and agribusiness companies appropriate indigenous knowledge about plants and other organic materials and employ patent law to make and market profitable, proprietary medicines. In examining this form of cultural appropriation I also wish to complicate the argument of "free appropriation" espoused by many appropriation artists discussed in chapter 4. As was the case with my relatively brief discussion of "world music" in chapter 2, free appropriation has particularly negative consequences when unequal power relations are involved.

Notes

1   Chanan, M. (1995). *Repeated takes: A short history of recording and its effects on music.* New York: Verso.

2   Korn, A. (1995). Renaming that tune: Audio collage, parody and fair use. In Negativland (Ed.), *Fair use: The story of the letter u and the numeral 2* (pp. 221–234). Concord, CA: Seeland.

3   Cutler, C. (1995). Plunderphonics. In R. Sakolsky & F. W. Ho (Eds.), *Sounding off!: Music as subversion/resistance/revolution* (pp. 67–86). Brooklyn: Autonomedia; Clarkson, A. (1981). *Stefan Wolpe: A brief catalogue of published works.* Islington: Sound Way Press.

4   Ibid.; Ibid.

5   Ernst, D. (1972). *Musique concrete.* Boston: Crescendo Publishing.

6   Ibid.

7   Russcol, H. (1972). *The liberation of sound: An introduction to electronic music.* Englewood Cliffs, NJ: Prentice-Hall.

8   Korn, A. (1995). Renaming that tune: Audio collage, parody and fair use. In Negativland (Ed.), *Fair use: The story of the letter u and the numeral 2* (pp. 221–234). Concord, CA: Seeland.

9   Dyson, F. (1992). The ear that would hear sounds in themselves: John Cage 1935–65. In D. Kahn and G. Whitehead (Eds.), *Wireless imagination: Sound, radio, and the avant-garde* (pp. 373–407). Cambridge, MA: MIT Press, p. 379.

10 Russcol, H. (1972). *The liberation of sound: An introduction to electronic music.* Englewood Cliffs, NJ: Prentice-Hall.

11 Dyson, F. (1992). The ear that would hear sounds in themselves: John Cage 1935–65. In D. Kahn and G. Whitehead (Eds.), *Wireless imagination: Sound, radio, and the avant-garde* (pp. 373–407). Cambridge, MA: MIT Press.

12 Revill, D. (1992). *The roaring silence: John Cage—a life.* New York: Arcade Publishing; Toop, D. (1995). *Ocean of sound: Aether talk, ambient sound and imaginary worlds.* New York: Serpent's Tail.

13 Young, L. M. (1993). Ruminations on radio. In N. Strauss (Ed.), *Radiotext(e).* (pp.181–187). New York: Semiotext(e).

14 Russcol, H. (1972). *The liberation of sound: An introduction to electronic music.* Englewood Cliffs, NJ: Prentice-Hall.

15 Revill, D. (1992). *The roaring silence: John Cage—a life.* New York: Arcade Publishing.

16   Kun, J. (1997, March/April). A select history of found sound. *Option,* pp. 65–68; Ewen, D. (1971). *Composers of tomorrow's music: A non-technical introduction to the musical avant-garde Movement.* New York: Dodd, Mead & Company.

17   Russcol, H. (1972). *The liberation of sound: An introduction to electronic music.* Englewood Cliffs, NJ: Prentice-Hall.

18   Witherden, B. (1996, December). The primer. *Wire,* 40–43; Ewen, D. (1971). *Composers of tomorrow's music: A non-technical introduction to the musical avant-garde movement.* New York: Dodd, Mead & Company.

19   Russcol, H. (1972). *The liberation of sound: An introduction to electronic music.* Englewood Cliffs, NJ: Prentice-Hall.

20   Polansky, L. (1984). The early works of James Tenney. In Peter Garland (Ed.), *The music of James Tenney* (pp. 119–294). Santa Fe: Soundings Press.

21   Lydenberg, R. (1992). Sound identity fading out: William Burroughs' tape experiments. In D. Kahn and G. Whitehead (Eds.), *Wireless imagination: sound, radio, and the avant-garde* (pp. 409–437). Cambridge, MA: MIT Press.

22   Korn, A. (1995). Renaming that tune: Audio collage, parody and fair use. In Negativland (Ed.), *Fair use: The story of the letter u and the numeral 2* (pp. 221–234). Concord, CA: Seeland.

23   Cutler, C. (1995). Plunderphonics. In R. Sakolsky & F. W. Ho (Eds.), *Sounding off!: Music as subversion/resistance/revolution* (pp. 67–86). Brooklyn: Autonomedia.

24   Negativland. (1992, March). The case from our side. *RetroFuturism,* 1750–1757.

25   Mark Hosler, personal correspondence, August 8, 1994.

26   England, P. (1996, May). Signals from the edge. *The Wire,* p. 32.

27   Tape-beatle News. (1990, January). *RetroFuturism,* 1531; Tape-beatle News (1991, January). *RetroFuturism,* 1644.

28   Dunn, L. (1993, February). News & Commentary. *CVS Bulletin,* 1815.

29   Ibid., p. 217.

30   The Tape-beatles undergo severe trauma, depression. (1990, July). *RetroFuturism,* 1596–1597.

31   Oswald, J. (1995). Creatigality. In R. Sakolsky and F. Wei-Han Ho (Eds.), *Sounding off!: Music as subversion/resistance/revolution* (pp. 87–90). Brooklyn: Autonomedia.

32   Oswald, J. (1995). Interview with Norman Igma. In Negativland (Ed.), *Fair use: The story of the letter u and the numeral 2,* (pp. 218–220). Concord, CA: Seeland.

33   Oswald, J. personal correspondence, November 13, 1993.

34   Harrington, R. (1995, May 17). The saga of Negativland's sued success. *Washington Post,* p. C7.

35   Toop, D. (1995). *Ocean of sound: Aether talk, ambient sound and imaginary worlds.* New York: Serpent's Tail.

36   Shapiro, P. (1996, December). The illbient alliance. *Wire,* pp. 24–30.

37   Kun, J. (1996, September/October). I am who I play: DJ Spooky's art of noises. *Option,* 54–; Norris, C. (1994, May/June). Needle phreaks: The planet's best DJs find a new groove. *Option,* 52–57.

38   DJ Spooky, personal correspondence, October 7, 1998.

39   Korn, A. (1995). Renaming that tune: Audio collage, parody and fair use. In Negativland (Ed.), *Fair use: The story of the letter u and the numeral 2* (pp. 221–234). Concord, CA: Seeland.

40   Oswald, J. (1995). Interview with Norman Igma. In Negativland (Ed.), *Fair use: The story of the letter u and the numeral 2* (pp. 218–220). Concord, CA: Seeland.

41   Oswald, personal correspondence, November 13, 1993.

42   Negativland. (1991). *U2.* [CD] Los Angeles, SST.

43   Harrington, R. (1995, May 17). The saga of Negativland's sued success. *Washington Post,* p. C7.

44   Negativland. (1992, March). The case from our side. *RetroFuturism,* 1750–1757.

45   Ibid., p. 1752.

46   Ibid., p. 72.

47   Ibid., p. 86.

48   Needham, K. (1998, March 21). One hack of a fight. *Sydney Morning Herald.* [Online]. Available: *www.smh.com.au/icon/content/980321/hack.html*

49   Bunn, A. (1998, February 25). Machine Age. *Village Voice.* [Online]. Available: *www.villagevoice.com/columns/9809/bunn.shtml*

50   Anderson, M. (1998, April 23). Where Beck and anti-Beck Collide. *Valley Advocate,* p. 23.

51   Anderson, M. (1998b, May 21). Fables of the deconstruction. *Valley Advocate,* p. 12.

52   Ibid.

53   Strauss, N. (1998, May 6). Tweaking Beck with piracy. *New York Times,* p. E3.

54   Cook, M. (1998, May 5). I'll name that tune in court. *Independent,* pp. 6–7.

55   Ibid., p. 7.

56   Mark Hosler, personal correspondence, August 7, 1999.

57   Ibid.

58   Oswald, J. (1995). Creatigality. In R. Sakolsky and F. Wei-Han Ho (Eds.), *Sounding off!: Music as subversion/resistance/revolution* (pp. 87–90). Brooklyn: Autonomedia.

59   Negativland. (1995). Fair use. In R. Sakolsky and F. Wei-Han Ho (Eds.), *Sounding off!: Music as subversion/resistance/revolution* (pp. 91–96). Brooklyn: Autonomedia, p. 92.

60   Ibid.

61   Dunn, L. (1993, February). News & Commentary. *CVS Bulletin,* 1815.

62   Silfer, K. (1993, Spring). Recontextualizing captured fragments. *Reign of Toads,* 20–33.

63   Mark Hosler, personal correspondence, October 17, 1993.

64   McLeod, K. (1994, October). Interview with Negativland. *Nine Times,* 62.

65   Negativland. (1998, September 2). Do we really have to sue the RIAA???? [Online]. Available: *www.negativland.com/riaa/dowesue.html*

66   Kaufman, G. (1998, September 1). Negativland CD rejected by four more pressing plants. *SonicNet.* [Online]. Available: *www.sonicnet.com*; Verna, P. (1998, September 19). RIAA adjusts CD plant anti-piracy guidelines. *Billboard, 110, 38,* 1.

67   Jenkins, M. (1998, September 20). In Negativland's plus column. *Washington Post,* p. G4.

68   Rosen, H. (1998, August 20). Statement by the Recording Industry Association of America. [Online]. Available: *www.negativland.com/riaa/riaaastatement082298.html*; Negativland. (1998, August 23). From: Negativland. To: Hilary Rosen. [Online]. Available: *www.negativland.com/riaa/nland_statement_082298.html*

69   Ibid.

70   DJ Spooky, personal correspondence, October 7, 1999.

71   Negativland. (1998c, September 2). RIAA responds positively to Negativland. [Online]. Available: *www.negativland.com/riaa/positiv.html*

72   Ibid.

73   Negativland. (1998, September 2). RIAA responds positively to Negativland. [Online]. Available: *www.negativland.com/riaa/positiv.html*

74   Mark Hosler, personal correspondence, August 7, 1999.

75   Ibid.

76   Dunn, L. (1993, February). News & Commentary. *CVS Bulletin,* 1815.

77   Boyd, B. (1993, November 26). Who has hidden the agenda. *Irish Times,* p. 12; Watson, B. (1997, March). King boy d. *Wire,* pp. 32–37; Strauss, N. (1995). KLF. In E. Weisbard (Ed.), *SPIN Alternative Record Guide* (pp. 213–214). New York: Vintage Books.

78   Strauss, N. (1995). KLF. In E. Weisbard (Ed.), *SPIN Alternative Record Guide* (pp. 213–214). New York: Vintage Books, p. 213.

79   Ibid.; Beadle, J. J. (1993). *Will pop eat itself? Pop music in the soundbite era.* London: Faber & Faber.

80   Ibid., p. 12.

81   Wescher, H. (1968). *Collage.* (R. E. Wolf, Trans.) New York: Harry N. Abrams, p. 19.

82   Ibid.

83   Ibid.

84   Poggi, C. (1992). *In defiance of painting: Cubism, futurism, and the invention of collage.* New Haven: Yale University Press.

85   Ibid., p. 1.

86   Poggi, C. (1989). Mallarme, Picasso, and the newpaper as commodity. In K. Hoffman (Ed.), *Collage: Critical views* (pp. 171–192). Ann Arbor, MI: University of Michigan University Research Press, p. 184.

87   Poggi, C. (1992). *In defiance of painting: Cubism, futurism, and the invention of collage.* New Haven: Yale University Press.; Greenberg, C. (1989). *Collage.* In K. Hoffman (Ed.), *Collage: Critical views* (pp. 67–77). Ann Arbor, MI: University of Michigan University Research Press.

88   Hoffman, K. (1989). Collage in the twentieth century: An Overview. In K. Hoffman (Ed.), *Collage: Critical views* (pp. 1–37). Ann Arbor, MI: University of Michigan University Research Press.

89   Tisdall, C. & Bozzolla, A. (1978). *Futurism.* New York: Oxford University Press.

90   Wescher, H. (1968). *Collage.* (R. E. Wolf, Trans.) New York: Harry N. Abrams, p. 53.

91   Wescher, H. (1968). *Collage.* (R. E. Wolf, Trans.) New York: Harry N. Abrams.

92   Poggi, C. (1992). *In defiance of painting: Cubism, futurism, and the invention of collage.* New Haven: Yale University Press.

93   Marinetti, F. T. (1989). *The Futurist cookbook.* (S. Brill, Trans.). San Francisco: Bedford Arts.

94   Huelsenbeck, R. (1974). *Memoirs of a Dada drummer* (J. Neugroschel, Trans.). Berkeley: University of California Press (original work published in 1969).

95   Richter, H. (1965). *Dada: Art and anti-art* (D. Britt, Trans.). New York: Oxford University Press (original work published in 1964).

96   Dietrich, D. (1993). *The collages of Kurt Schwitters: Tradition and innovation.* New York: Cambridge University Press, p. 9.

97   Ibid.; Freeman, J. (1989). The Dada & Surrealist word-image. Cambridge, MA: MIT Press; Hoffman, K. (1989). Collage in the twentieth century: An Overview. In K. Hoffman (Ed.), *Collage: Critical views* (pp. 1–37). Ann Arbor, MI: University of Michigan University Research Press.

98   Tzara, T. (1977). *Seven Dada manifestos and lampisteries* (B. Wright, Trans). New York: Calder Publications.

99   Ibid., p. 39.

100 Breton, A. (1978). *What is Surrealism? Selected writings.* New York: Monad Press.

101 Pierre, J. (1979). *An illustrated dictionary of Surrealism* (W. J. Strachan, Trans.). Woodbury, NY: Barron's.

102 Nadeau, M. (1965). *The history of Surrealism* (R. Howard, Trans.). New York: Macmillan.

103 Wescher, H. (1968). *Collage.* (R. E. Wolf, Trans.). New York: Harry N. Abrams., p. 185.

104 Ibid.

105 *Twelve Americans: Masters of collage.* (1977). [Exhibit catalog]. New York: Andrew Crispo Gallery; UK remixers win settlement in sample case. (1998, May 16). *Music Week,* p. S1; Wescher, H. (1968). *Collage.* (R. E. Wolf, Trans.). New York: Harry N. Abrams.

106 Hoffman, K. (1989). Collage in the twentieth century: An Overview. In K. Hoffman (Ed.), *Collage: Critical views* (pp. 1–37). Ann Arbor, MI: University of Michigan University Research Press; Rosenberg, H. (1989). Collage: Philosophy of put-togethers. In K. Hoffman (Ed.), *Collage: Critical views* (pp. 59–66). Ann Arbor, MI: University of Michigan University Research Press.

107 Cathcart, L. L. (1982). *The Americans: The collage.* Houston, TX: Contemporary Arts Museum.

108 Bockris, V. (1989). *The life and death of Andy Warhol.* New York: Bantam Books.

109 Ibid.

110 Morris, G. (1981, January). When artists use photographs. *ARTnews, 80,* 1,102–106.

111   Ibid., p. 105.

112   Buchloh, B. (1982). Parody and appropriation in Francis Picabia, Pop and Sigmar Polke. *Artforum, 20, 7,* 28–34, p. 29.

113   Morris, G. (1981, January). When artists use photographs. *ARTnews, 80, 1,* 105.

114   Ibid.

115   Morris, G. (1980, April 19). "Diver" v. "Pull" goes to court. *Peninsula Times Tribune,* p. A1.

116   Morris, G. (1981, January). When artists use photographs. *ARTnews, 80, 1,* 103.

117   Ibid.

118   Ibid., p. 104.

119   Morris, G. (1981, January). When artists use photographs. *ARTnews, 80, 1,* 102–106.

120   Ibid., p. 104.

121   Buskirk, M. (1992). Commodification as censor: Copyrights and fair use. *October 60,* 82–109.

122   Buskirk, M. (1992, Spring). Appropriation under the gun. *Art in America, 80,* 37–40.

123   Buskirk, M. (1992). Commodification as censor: Copyrights and fair use. *October 60,* 106.

124   Bracken, L. (1997). *Guy Debord: Revolutionary.* Venice, CA: Feral House; Vienet, R. (1968). *Enrages and Situationists in the Occupation Movement, France, May '68.* Brooklyn: Autonomedia.

125   Debord, G. (1983). *Society of the spectacle* (Rev. Ed.). Detroit, MI: Black & Red; Home, S. (1991). *The assault on culture: Utopian currents from Lettrisme to Class War.* Stirling, Scotland: AK Press.

126   Marcus, G. (1991) *Dead Elvis: A chronicle of a cultural obsession.* New York: Doubleday, p. 168.

127   Blazwick, I. (Ed.) (1989). *An endless passion . . . an endless banquet: A Situationist scrapbook.* London: Verso.

128   Plant, S. (1992). *The most radical gesture: The Situationist International in a postmodern age.* New York: Routledge.

129   Marcus, G. (1991) *Dead Elvis: A chronicle of a cultural obsession.* New York: Doubleday.

130   Ibid., p. 14.

131   Ibid.

132   Hugnet, G. (1989). The Dada spirit in painting. In R. Motherwell (Ed.), *The Dada painters and poets* (pp. 101–120). Cambridge, MA: The Belknap Press of Harvard University Press.

133   Ribemont-Dessaignes, G. (1989). History of Dada. In R. Motherwell (Ed.), *The Dada painters and poets* (pp. 101–120). Cambridge, MA: The Belknap Press of Harvard University Press.

134   Greenberg, L. A. (1992). The art of appropriation: Puppies, piracy, and post-modernism. *Cardozo Arts & Entertainment Law Journal, 11,* 1–.

135   Dannat, A. (1992, March 23). The 'mine' field. *Independent,* p. 20.

136   Buskirk, M. (1992, Spring). Appropriation under the gun. *Art in America, 80,* 37–40, p. 37.

137   Buskirk, M. (1992). Commodification as censor: copyrights and fair use. *October 60,* 82–109.

138   Hays, C. L. (1991, September 19). A picture, a sculpture and a lawsuit. *New York Times,* p. B2.

139   Gayford, M. (1992, July 26). What's yours is mine. *Sunday Telegraph,* p. 113.

140   Hays, C. L. (1991, September 19). A picture, a sculpture and a lawsuit. *New York Times,* p. B2.

141   Dannat, A. (1992, March 23). The 'mine' field. *Independent,* p. 20.

142   Hays, C. L. (1991, September 19). A picture, a sculpture and a lawsuit. *New York Times,* p. B2.

143   Buskirk, M. (1992, Spring). Appropriation under the gun. *Art in America, 80,* 37–40, 39.

144   Streitfeld, D. (1993, March 5). Copyright Controversy. *Washington Post,* p. C2.

145   It's art, but is it theft as well? (1991, September 22). *New York Times,* D7.

146   Dannat, A. (1992, March 23). The 'mine' field. *Independent,* p. 20.

147   Ibid.

148   Moore, T. (1992, October 15). Photographer wins lawsuit against Koons. *San Francisco Chronicle,* p. E2.

149   Buskirk, M. (1992, Spring). Appropriation under the gun. *Art in America, 80,* 37–40, 37.

150   Rogers v. Koons. (1992). 960 F.2d 301 (2d Cir.), cert denied, 113 S. Ct. 365.

151   Ibid.

152   Anderson, M. (1998b, May 21). Fables of the deconstruction. *Valley Advocate,* p. 12.

153   Penguin Books seeks lifting of injunction against Dr. Seuss Satire. (1997, October). *Sports & Entertainment Litigation Reporter,* 4.

154   Anderson, M. (1998b, May 21). Fables of the deconstruction. *Valley Advocate,* p. 12.

155   Muchnic, S. (1992, Oct. 16). Disney demands removal of sculpture. *Los Angeles Times,* pp. B1–.

156   Ibid.

157   Ibid.

158   Harris, N. (1985, Summer). Who owns our myths? Heroism and copyright in an age of mass culture. *Social Research,* 241–267.

159   Buskirk, M. (1992, Spring). Appropriation under the gun. *Art in America, 80,* 37–40.

160   Easton, N. J. (1989, April 7). Disney sues over use of Snow White at Oscars. *Los Angeles Times,* p. F5; Cartoon figure run afoul of law. (1989, April 27). *Chicago Tribune,* p. 1A; Johnson, P. (1989, April 26). Disney gets grumpy with preschool. *USA Today,* p. D1.

161   Keane, J. (1992, February 13). Going over the top with Mickey Mouse. *Guardian,* p. 25; Muchnic, S. (1992, Oct. 16). Disney demands removal of sculpture. *Los Angeles Times,* pp. B1–.

162   Badin, R. (1995, Winter). An appropriate(d) place in transformative value: Appropriation art's exclusion from Campbell v. Acuff-Rose Museic, Inc. *Brooklyn Law Review, 60,* 1653–.

163   Hopkins, B. (1997). Modernism and the collage aesthetic. *New England Review, 18, 2,* 5–12.

164   Ibid., p. 8.

165   Ibid.

166   Hopkins, B. (1997). *Modernism and the collage aesthetic.* New England Review, 18, 2, pp. 5–12, p. 8.

167   Oswald, J. (1995). Creatigality. In R. Sakolsky and F. Wei-Han Ho (Eds.), *Sounding off!: Music as subversion/resistance/revolution* (pp. 87–90). Brooklyn: Autonomedia, p. 89; Gaines, J. (1988, November 27). Of copyrights and copycats. *Boston Globe,* p. A21.

168   Tzara, T. (1977). *Seven Dada manifestos and lampisteries* (B. Wright, Trans). New York: Calder Publications.

169   Buskirk, M. (1992). Commodification as censor: copyrights and fair use. *October, 60,* 82–109.

170 Morris, G. (1981, January). When artists use photographs. *ARTnews, 80, 1,* 105.

171 Ibid.

Chapter 5

Patent Law and the Appropriation of Third-World Indigenous Knowledge

The watershed event that more fully brought the scientific fields that dealt with living matter into the sphere of intellectual property law was the 1980 *Diamond v. Chakrabarty* Supreme Court decision. In this case, a five-to-four majority decided that a living, genetically altered microorganism could be patented under U.S. law. Microbiologist Ananda M. Chakrabarty had invented a genetically altered bacterium that hadn't been seen in nature, an organism that demonstrated the promise of breaking down crude oil and was therefore a useful and potentially profitable product for cleaning up oil spills. The U.S. Patent and Trademark Office (PTO) ruled that Chakrabarty's bacterium did not qualify for a utility patent, but the Supreme Court ruled otherwise, stating, "Anything under the sun that is made by man can be patented."[1]

I demonstrate in chapters 5 and 6 that biotech companies and scientists have taken these words as gospel, paving the way for the patenting of numerous things pertaining to human and plant life. It is important to note that, when discussing "plant patenting" or "gene patenting," what is being referred to is the patenting of the active ingredients of a plant, or a gene isolated from its natural surroundings—not the thing itself. But, in practice, holding such a patent allows the owner to control the uses of plant extracts or genes as they relate to various industrial, agricultural or medical uses. It allows the patent holder *de facto* ownership of such genes or plant extracts.

Authorship, Ownership and Patent Law

More generally, this chapter is concerned with issues surrounding patent law, globalization and indigenous communities. In discussing these points,

Vandana Shiva asks: "When indigenous systems of knowledge and production interact with dominant systems of knowledge and production, it
is important to anticipate whether the future options of the indigenous
system or the dominant system will grow. Whose knowledge and values
will shape the future options of diverse communities?"[2] This is a question
of articulation and hegemony (though Shiva does not refer to these concepts specifically), and it goes to the heart of all of the cases discussed in
this book—whether they be folk music, African-American folk preaching,
sound collage or the useful knowledge of local plants held by indigenous
people.

As has been argued in the previous chapters, intellectual property law
assumes a particular conception of authorship and ownership. I have
demonstrated that copyright and trademark share these underlying assumptions, despite the very different contexts from which these laws developed. The same is true of patent law. Yes, patent law arose from legal
philosophies markedly different from copyright and trademark and, yes,
patent law does have a very clear understanding of innovation as incre-
mental, cumulative and developed in a community context in which only
what is not "obvious" can be patented. Nevertheless, *in practice*, it is an
individual or a corporation that is the sole owner of a patent.

Furthermore, I believe there is a parallel between the way, for instance,
a piece of art or writing can be considered *copyrightable* and the way
products of scientific knowledge can be considered *patentable*. Although
a "new" work of art is viewed as coming out of a particular tradition and
is impacted by influences, its ability to gain copyright protection is determined by the fact that it is original and has at least a degree of creativity.[3]
Similarly, a patented invention must be determined by the Patent and
Trademark Office (PTO) as being "novel," and not too heavily steeped in
"prior art."[4] It is assumed in patent law that new inventions are based on
earlier knowledge, just as it is assumed that artists or writers don't create
work from a cultural vacuum. But in practice—in the way each type of
protection is registered—neither law is currently open to recognizing cultural production as being the result of a collective effort.

Roht-Arriaza writes: "the individual nature of patent law is reinforced
in the trade-related intellectual property rights (TRIPs) agreement . . .
which recognizes intellectual property rights only as private rights. Rights
belonging to the public, or a sector of it, do not fit easily."[5] Coombe
argues that "such rights preclude consideration of collectively managed,
long-evolving genotypic shifts in plant resources."[6] For instance, the Director General of the World Intellectual Property Association (WIPO) stated
in a letter to the United Nations Human Rights Centre that the organiza-

tion did not recognize the standing of indigenous peoples in intellectual property matters. The Director General wrote that "intellectual property is distinguished by the type of intellectual creation and not by the groups responsible for its creation. This position reflects WIPO's insistence on *individual authorship* as a prerequisite for protection" [emphasis mine].[7]

Gudeman argues:

> Built upon the Cartesian duality of mind and body, intellectual property rights are aligned with practices of rationality and planning. The expression "intellectual property rights" makes it appear as if the property and rights are products of individual minds. This is part of a Western epistemology that separates mind from body, subject from object, observer from observed, and that accords priority, control, and power to the first half of the duality. The term "intellectual" connotes as well the knowledge side and suggests that context of use is unimportant. . . . In contrast to this modernist construction, in a community economy innovations are cultural properties in the sense that they are the product and property of a group.[8]

Western science has typically dismissed or denigrated indigenous systems of knowledge and transmission by characterizing the natural materials that communities have preserved, improved and developed as simply being "wild species" or, at most, "primitive species." Far from being the result of luck and happenstance, the existence of these plant varieties in developing areas is the result of indigenous people transmitting the medicinal (and other) uses of plants through oral methods, often through stories or songs. This non-Western, oral-based cultivation of knowledge has helped lead to conceptual and legal categories that exclude from patent protection the contributions and knowledge of local communities, farmers and indigenous peoples.[9]

Whereas the knowledge developed in scientific laboratories is protected as "property," the more informal, traditional systems are open to appropriation because they are the "common heritage of humanity" and are therefore open to plundering. Although these biological materials brought into Western seed banks, gene banks and laboratories are freely collected, these materials can be extracted, "improved" and designated as private property.[10] Naomi Roht-Arriaza writes, "The problem is not with the free use and exchange of resources per se but with the designation of only some resources as common, while others are protected as private."[11]

Farming

Seeds are a product that have provided quite a conundrum for businesses that sell them because they are a renewable resource—unlike other industry products, farmers can collect the seeds at the end of a season, save them, and then replant them for the next season. Despite the existence of a growing seed industry that focused on small family farming concerns, before the 1920s, seed transactions were primarily carried out by farmers themselves. But during the 1920s scientists developed techniques for developing hybrid corn that could produce more edible varieties, using seeds that were dissimilar from the first generation hybrid and, therefore, couldn't be replanted.

During this time, seed companies had been lobbying for protection of the crop varieties they were developing, which resulted in the passage of the Plant Patent Act (PPA) in 1930. This was the first intellectual property rights regime for plants in the world, and in 1970, the Plant Variety Protection Act (PVPA) was passed. From the vantage point of private industry, this protection was still inadequate, but it nevertheless established the principle that plant breeders should have legal monopoly rights for the fruits of their labor. Finally, the *Diamond v. Chakrabarty* decision—and the series of patents granted in its wake—expanded the protections that the PPA and PVPA allowed and provided a level of protection that was agreeable for private industry.[12]

Policing Farming

When proprietary protection of certain hybrid crops was not as strong, large biotech and chemical companies had little interest in this aspect of the agriculture industry. But because patent protection has expanded to protect crops, companies like DuPont and Monsanto now have the incentive to invest billions of dollars in this field of commerce. Monsanto currently owns many patents on widely sold crops and has filed for patents on a number of other crops such as cotton. Gary Barton, Monsanto's director of public affairs, stated in 1998: "More than 30 input and output products are in our R&D pipeline. We are working on products in corn, maize, potatoes, soyabeans, oil crops, tea and almost every crop."[13]

In the early 1980s, few patents on crops were sought, the trading of seed by farmers was commonplace and, importantly, much of the research on crop development was in the public sector. But this research was increasingly passed to the private sector, and corporations became more interested in this area of commerce. Because these patented crops still produce new seeds at the end of each season, seed companies enforce contracts with farmers that ensure they do not replant the seeds. The American Seed Trade Association's executive director, David Lambert, argues that "patenting seeds is no different than patenting any other kind of product."[14]

Monsanto shares this conception of seeds as industrial products that are the same as other inventions, and it has prosecuted numerous farmers for violating its intellectual property rights. Monsanto also regularly publishes polite but threatening advertisements in farming trade magazines, referring to the company's prohibition against saving patented seeds as "contractual sterility."[15] By 1998, the company made out-of-court settlements with over 100 farmers, settlements whose terms included payment of penalties (upwards of $35,000), the destruction of crops grown from saved seeds, and an agreement that allows Monsanto to inspect a farmer's property in the future.[16]

Monsanto has taken such steps as hiring Pinkerton agency detectives to track down offenders, as well as creating and advertising the existence of hotlines for neighbors to report farmers who save seeds.[17] Pinkerton detectives were hired to investigate tips on the illegal "brown bag" sales of Roundup Ready soybean seed, with Monsanto spokesperson Karen Marshall openly stating, "We investigate all reports of suspected piracy of our biotech traits. . . . We have followed up on hundreds of leads in more than 20 of the 29 soybean-producing states."[18]

Moreover, the contract for Monsanto's brand of Roundup Ready soybeans allowed the company to search a customer's farmland for signs of saved seeds, with Monsanto's soybean marketing manager, Douglas J. Dorsey, emphasizing, "We intend to enforce the grower agreement against saved seeds."[19] To nab offenders, the company can track purchase records and check with seed dealers, and it has also developed a kit that uses a principle similar to a pregnancy test that can determine from leaf tissue whether or not a plant was derived from saved, patented seeds.[20]

Monsanto holds the patent for the active ingredient in its Roundup Ready soybeans, which allows them to prevent other companies even from distributing or testing *herbicides* that contain the same active ingredient. For instance, Zeneca's Touchdown herbicide, which Roundup Ready soybeans can also tolerate, has been prevented from entering the market because Monsanto told regional dealers and university researchers that testing its privately owned soybeans with Touchdown herbicide would constitute intellectual property infringement. The contract that Roundup Ready soybean consumers must sign clearly prohibits the use of "a herbicide containing the same active ingredient as Roundup Ultra herbicide (or one with a similar mode of action.)"[21] Further, Monsanto rewards dealers who sell Roundup exclusively, which helps to maintain the strong grip over the soybean market it already has.[22]

This company, like other large seed-owning companies, similarly offers incentives for seed distributors to carry their patented seeds (rather than public domain seeds) to promote a cycle of dependence between the seed companies and farmers who must purchase seeds every year. And the fact that traditional seed varieties don't yield enough to compete with genetically modified crops ensures that the farmers who still use traditional seeds will likely abandon them in favor of patented, modified crops. Patent-holding seed companies that are concerned about seed saving and that cannot easily monitor the activities of smaller farmers are more reluctant to deal with these farmers, instead favoring larger corporate farms. This reluctance will likely grow in the future as farming grows more standardized and corporatized.[23]

The following case is representative of this new trend in seed policing. In 1990, a small-time farming couple from Iowa, Denny and Becky Winterboer, were served with legal papers notifying them they were being sued by Asgrow Seed Company, a subsidiary of Upjohn, for selling some of the soybean seeds collected from their harvest to their neighbors. They had participated in a time-honored practice of "brown bag" sales, in which farmers sell a portion of their crop to their neighbors for seed—something the Winterboer's family, as well as most other farmers, have done for decades. (Moreover, seed sharing has been at the heart of farming since staple food crops became domesticated 11,000 years ago, and it continues to be an important part of subsistence farming in Third World countries.)[24]

The Winterboers sold to their neighbors the seed for about half the price that the company charged, which, to the company, constituted a blatant violation of their intellectual property rights over the patented soybean strains, A1937 and A2234. When the company suspected their infringement, it then dispatched Mike Ness—a neighboring farmer and friend of Denny's father—to buy seeds from the Winterboers, which Ness promptly handed over to Asgrow.[25] The Winterboers fought this lawsuit all the way to the Supreme Court, resting their case on the strength of a part of the 1970 Plant Variety Protection Act, which is known as the "farmer's exemption."

This piece of legislation allowed farmers to save proprietary seed, replant it and/or sell to their neighbors as long as both parties were farmers whose primary occupation was growing and selling crops "for other than reproductive purposes."[26] This exemption acknowledged farmers' involvement in developing new varieties of crops and maintaining the genetic diversity of the crops they planted, and was based on the logic that, as long as seed companies recoup their investment and continue to develop new, marketable hybrids, farmers should be allowed to continue to engage in the time-honored practice of seed saving, selling and trading.

But this conventional wisdom was strained in the 1980s when such biological matter came to be seen as information that could be protected under intellectual property law and, during this time, the "farmer's exemption" became reinterpreted as the "farmer's *privilege*," with those who exercised this privilege being labeled as "pirates." This articulation of seed selling, seed growing and the law allowed for Asgrow to refer to itself as "a developer, producer and marketer of genetics"—a claim that would have made no sense a few decades ago if it were made by a seed company.[27]

The Supreme Court ruled against the Winterboers, reinterpreting the wording of the farmer's exemption and maintaining that the Winterboers' "brown bag" sales *did* infringe on the intellectual property rights of the Asgrow Seed Company. In addition to this judicial attack on the traditional practice of seed saving, around the same time the case was heard by the Supreme Court, the U.S. Congress amended the Plant Variety Protection Act to remove the farmers' exemption altogether. The combined judicial and legislative blows against farmers greatly sped up the way farming has come under the rule of intellectual property law and the level at which farming has become further corporatized.[28]

In one of the broadest patents ever awarded, the European Patent Office (EPO) assigned a patent to the U.S-based Agracetus for *all future* genetic alterations of soybeans created using the company's method or *any other method that might be developed*.[29] Agracetus was merely the first to perfect the genetic alteration process with a soybean, and it was granted the patent in spite of the fact that, like most other scientific discoveries, the company's researchers drew on previous contributions by other scientists.[30] In protesting the award of this patent, Monsanto joined forces with other public interest groups such as the Rural Advancement Fund International (RAFI), a remarkable move considering the fact that they share absolutely no common ground and have constantly butted heads with each other (imagine arch-conservative Pat Buchanan and gay congressman Barney Frank wrestling for world peace in a vat of Jell-O).

Monsanto filed its opposition to the patent in 1994 and, at the time, spokesperson Karen K. Marshall stated, "The claims are simply too broad given what was going on in genetic engineering at the time they filed for the patent."[31] The strongly worded 292 page patent opposition document that Monsanto filed took to task virtually every aspect of the patent, claiming that it should be "revoked in its entirety. . . . It is not . . . novel. . . . It lacks an inventive step. . . . A sufficient disclosure [of scientific method] is woefully lacking."[32]

Then, in 1996, Monsanto quietly withdrew its protest after it bought Agracetus for $150 million. It changed its public position, hypocritically stating, "Monsanto will defend it."[33] RAFI has continued with its formal opposition to the European patent, but as the organization recognized, "We're tiny almost to the point of being insignificant on a world scale and we're often swimming against a strong tide."[34] In addition to the European soybean patent, there are many other similarly broad patents that have been issued by the EPO and the U.S. PTO, including an incredibly lucrative patent on *all fruits and vegetables* that are engineered to produce proteins that make them more sweet.[35]

At the same time Monsanto and other companies fought to police the age-old practice of saving seeds, a new technology emerged that makes such practical concerns obsolete.[36] The "Technology Protection System," or "terminator technology" as it is more commonly known, enables seed companies to genetically alter a seed to make it sterile after one planting.[37] This process was developed by the U.S.-based Delta & Pine Land, whose president stated, "We expect the new technology to have global implications."[38] Delta & Pine Land claimed that the terminator seed would be targeted primarily in the southern hemisphere to prevent farmers from saving, trading and/or replanting seeds that are sold by U.S. corporations.[39]

While sterile seeds may be an inconvenience for U.S. farmers who, for various reasons (including being riddled with debt), want to continue to save seeds, this may prove devastating for poorer Third World countries that rely on subsistence farming. U.S. Department of Agriculture (USDA) spokesperson Willard Phelps stated that the goal of the terminator technology is "to increase the value of proprietary seed owned by U.S. seed companies and to open new markets in second and Third World countries."[40] Terminator seed primary creator Melvin J. Oliver made clear his invention's purpose: "Our system is a way of self-policing the unauthorized use of American technology. . . . It's similar to copyright protection."[41]

Among other things, this technology holds the potential to further concentrate in the hands of a few corporations control over the supply of the world's food crops.[42] This is particularly disturbing considering the fact that, only *five years* after their introduction, 40% to 45% of corn and soybeans grown in the U.S. (and 50% in Canada) are genetically altered and patented.[43] The planting of altered (and patented) soybeans, corn, potatoes and canola in the United States and Canada has exploded, and the market for such crops is expected to grow from $30 billion in the late

1990s to as much as $500 billion in the next few decades.[44] The dramatic, and continued, rise in the use of patented crops in North America is likely to be eventually followed by other countries throughout the world, despite opposition from European countries.

In mid-1998, Monsanto made moves to purchase terminator seed patent holders Delta & Pine Land.[45] But this technology met with sizable worldwide opposition, and after intense protests, in early 1999 Monsanto (which had previously spiritedly defended the technology) stepped back in "recognition that we need some level of public acceptance to do our business."[46] Later, Monsanto backed out of the merger, but Delta & Pine—which still holds the patent with the USDA—has continued to commercially develop the technology.[47] Delta & Pine official Harry Collins stated in January 2000, "We've continued right on with work on the Technology Protection System. We never really slowed down. We're on target, moving ahead to commercialize it. We never really backed off."[48]

Even though Monsanto and AstraZeneca publicly vowed not to commercialize the technology, with both companies planning mergers with other agribusiness and pharmaceutical companies, there are no assurances company policy will not change. For instance, AstraZeneca stated in 2000 that these issues "cannot even be considered until after completion [of the merger]."[49] In addition, in 1999, seven new terminator technology patents were awarded to Delta & Pine (with the USDA), Novartis, Pioneer Hi-Bred, Cornell Research Foundation, Purdue Research Foundation and ExSeed Genetics (in conjunction with Iowa State University). And the USDA, which co-owns all of Delta & Pine's terminator patents, has repeatedly refused to nullify its holding in the patent and, further, twice denied in 1999 that any more terminator-related patents were in the works—which, as it turns out, was not true at all.[50]

Defenders of the terminator technology (and patenting, in general) argue that without the protection patents allow in the safeguarding of their research and development investments, there would be no incentive to develop new, innovative products—an argument I will examine in chapter 5, in my discussion of human gene patenting. Companies like Monsanto (whose motto is "Food—Health—Hope") insist that its motivations for developing the terminator technology are grounded in a desire to create more pest-resistant plants so that they can prevent world hunger.[51] But if you believe that selfless line of reasoning, then I have a genetically altered monkey-boy I want to sell you.

Aside from the potentially disastrous effects on the world's subsistence farmers, there are numerous potential environmental dilemmas that the

terminator technology poses. First, there is a potential that the steriliza-
tion process might spread to indigenous crops when insects pollinate
both the "terminator" plants and other local plants.[52] In addition to these
other potential environmental problems, the terminator technology—and
seed patenting more generally—will decrease the world's biodiversity by
ensuring that only one type of plant variety can come from a seed, rather
than the multiple varieties that have been developed and cultivated by
farmers over the centuries.[53]

Patenting and Reduced Biological Diversity
Significantly, 97% of the vegetable varieties sold by commercial seed houses
in the United States at the beginning of the century are now extinct, and
86% of the fruit varieties have been lost. These numbers are actually quite
conservative because there were surely more varieties in use that the
USDA could not collect in the nineteenth century.[54] Roughly 75% of the
genetic diversity of the world's 20 most important food crops has disappeared and has been lost forever. Much of this has to do with the proliferation of the unvaried, genetically altered high-yield crops that have been
introduced by large multinational corporations.[55]

The U.S. Plant Patent Act (PPA), which was introduced in the 1930s
to stimulate species development and diversity, has not achieved those
goals under an intellectual property regime. According to a study critical
of the PPA: "Despite hard-won 'protection' in place for 65 years, plant
breeders and nursery men are on a statistical decline in the U.S. . . . So is
the diversity of the plants with which they work. The PPA hasn't been a
boon to plant breeding—it looks more like a bust."[56]

The overwhelming trend around the world has been, at the insistence
of multinational agribusiness companies, the displacement of local biological diversity with patented and uniform varieties. The biological diversity contained in what once was a commons is now being enclosed and
redefined as private property, a trend that has been globalized with the
increased numbers of developing countries that have signed intellectual
property treaties backed by Western governments and businesses.

Without lapsing into hyperbole, I should reiterate that biological diversity is of the utmost importance if life on Earth as we know it is to survive.
The erosion of biodiversity begins as a chain reaction, with the death of
one species being linked to the death of numerous others, which in turn
alters interconnected food chains and ecosystems around the world. Because biodiversity has been key in plants' ability to adapt to changing
conditions (and therefore humans' ability to do the same), reduced
biodiversity threatens the ecological support systems of millions of people

on the planet. Before this becomes a crisis in the First World, dwindling biodiversity will first affect Third World inhabitants who will become more dependent on the multinational corporations for patented seeds when global, uniform intellectual property systems become the norm around the world.

Corporate Consolidation in the Agribusiness Industry

As in other industries, during the 1990s there has been a massive consolidation of ownership in the seed industry, with chemical and plastics companies such as Monsanto, DuPont and Dow heavily investing in the development and patenting of lucrative crops. In 1997, Monsanto's $7.5 billion in sales were derived primarily from its agricultural- and pharmaceutical-related products, and the company continued to grow, buying numerous seed companies and patents. For instance, Monsanto bought Plant Breeding International for $524 million, a massive merger that is typical of the agribusiness industry in the late 1990s. The company then went on a 2-month spree of buying seed companies to dramatically enlarge their overseas market share.[57]

In addition, DuPont invested over $3 billion in acquiring numerous seed companies, food patents and biotechnology ventures, and in 1999 it announced that it was paying $7.7 billion to acquire the world's largest seed company, Pioneer Hi-Bred International.[58] When they are not merging, these big companies are engaging in high-stakes patent lawsuits that keep smaller players out of the arena completely. For instance, French agribusiness company Rhone Poulenc Agro was awarded $65 million in damages by a U.S. jury when Monsanto was found guilty of violating its patent on genetically altered corn.[59] With the quick pace of mergers, the composition of big players will undoubtedly continue to rapidly change, but what is certain is that fewer companies will control more of the agribusiness markets.

In 1999, the top three seed companies (DuPont, Monsanto, Novartis) accounted for 20% of the global seed trade, and the top five "gene giants" (those companies that specialize in genetic patents, including AstraZeneca, DuPont, Monsanto, Novartis and Aventis) monopolize nearly two-thirds of the global pesticide market (60%).[60] The top three seed companies (DuPont, Monsanto and Novartis) account for virtually 100% of the transgenic seed market.[61] Such control over the market allows these companies to pressure distributors that sell seeds to farmers to carry their patented seeds instead of public domain seeds that farmers have cultivated, saved and replanted for years.

A farmer's choice to continue to plant these nonproprietary seeds becomes increasingly difficult or impossible in an environment where near-monopolies exist within the agribusiness industries.[62] University of Indiana seed geneticist Martha Crouch commented on the situation surrounding the distribution of seeds, stating, "Free choice is a nice idea, but it doesn't seem to operate in the real world."[63]

The declining number of agribusiness companies allows these businesses to increase their control over farming, and the existence of patented seeds that must be purchased every year speeds up the corporatization of farming that has already taken place in North America. For instance, smaller farmers have been forced to spend more on costly supplies (proprietary pesticides, seeds, etc.) than what they get back when they sell their crops in the world market. Capital-intensive, corporate-controlled agriculture is spreading into poorer countries through the process of globalization, which makes it impossible for smaller farmers to compete and survive.[64]

Biotech and agribusiness companies claim that the purpose of seed patenting is to increase agricultural production to feed the world's poor, but such increased production would only facilitate large corporate farmers who could afford these expensive products.[65] Of course, the companies are not really concerned with helping the world's farmers because, to satisfy their stockholders they must maximize their profits (which obviously isn't done by being generous).[66] Because developing countries have been forced to adopt patent laws, this affects the ability of researchers in those countries to deliver patented agricultural technology to farmers who could benefit from it but who can't afford it.[67]

The Appropriation of Third-World Indigenous Knowledge and Resources

Much of the world's biodiversity—that which holds the keys to developing successful cures for many diseases—is contained in the biological material found in Third World countries, and the existence of which has set off a modern-day prospecting rush for what has been called "green gold." Researchers have used indigenous knowledge about the medicinal uses of plants, herbs and insects to allow companies to sort out from the vast array of "useless" biological material what can be used as ingredients for patented medicines. Of the 120 active compounds derived from plants that are widely used in contemporary medicines, 75% of them were already known within traditional indigenous knowledge systems.

Using those knowledge systems increases *four hundred fold* a scientist's ability to locate which plants have specific kinds of medicinal uses.[68] McGirk[69] points out that "finding the right gene or chemical sequence can be like looking for a needle in an Everest-sized haystack. One shortcut researchers rely on, increasingly, is the knowledge of tribal shamans and medicine men."[70] In another estimate, by consulting with the local communities, "bioprospectors can increase the success ratio in trials for useful substances from one in ten thousand samples to one in two."[71]

For example, the U.S.-Pharmagenisis brings to the global market medicines that are directly based on the knowledge of Asian native healers. This phenomenon is not new, and the appropriation of Third World indigenous knowledge has a long-standing colonialist history that entails taking without giving any compensation. For instance, the medicinal knowledge of the drug curare, which was used by the Makushi Indians of Guyana to incapacitate their prey, was taken from these people by British explorers in the 1800s and used to develop an extremely lucrative drug that was used as an anesthetic and muscle relaxant—a drug that still makes millions of dollars a year for Western companies. In addition, quinine, a substance used to treat malaria, was derived from the South American Cinchona Officinalis tree. It had been used by the Amazonian people to treat fever for centuries before the Europeans came.[72]

Using an active ingredient extracted from an indigenous plant in northeastern Brazil, the U.S.-based MGI Pharma more recently developed a drug to allay symptoms of xerostomia, or "dry mouth syndrome." The drug's development capitalized on the local knowledge about the properties of the *jaborandi* plant (which means "slobber mouth plant"), knowledge that had been passed down for generations by the tribespeople of northeastern Brazil. The company, of course, did not compensate in any way the native Brazilians who knew about the plant's therapeutic properties, despite the fact that it was the local wisdom that specifically led the U.S. researchers to a drug discovery in the first place.[73]

The patented research on hyper-sweet vegetable proteins (mentioned earlier) was derived from local knowledge about West African plants called katempfe and the serendipity berry, both which contain thaumatin. The thaumatin plant protein is 100,000 times sweeter than sugar, and the genetically modified and patented version of the protein will likely prove to be extremely valuable considering that the market for low-calorie sweeteners approached $1 billion in the U.S. market alone in the late 1990s.[74] Unsurprisingly, there have been no arrangements to return any of the benefits to the local communities that have long used these plants as sweeteners.

In another similar example, researcher Sally Fox received a patent in 1990 on colored cotton. This product is very important for companies seeking environmentally friendly fabrics that do not use dye processes that can harm the environment. The seed for colored cotton, drawn from a USDA database and collected by Gus Hyer in his travels to Latin America, was the product of numerous years of traditional, collective development by groups in Latin America.[75] The active ingredients of the African Pygeum tree, used by indigenous healers to cure what translates as "old men's disease," have been patented by a Frenchman to treat the enlargement of the prostate—an ailment common to older men. Sales from the product derived from the tree's active ingredient total over $220 million a year, and the tree now may be on the verge of extinction as the result of the hundreds of tons of its bark that have been harvested.

In 1997, seven of the world's biggest-selling drugs were derived from natural products.[76] In addition, more than half of the drugs most frequently prescribed throughout the world have been derived from plants, plant genes or plant extracts. These drugs are a standard part of medical treatment for lymphatic cancer, glaucoma, leukemia and various heart conditions, and they account for over $40 billion a year.[77] This trend will most certainly continue, as will the use of indigenous knowledge to help create new medicines. Stenson and Gray write:

> Since the time of early colonialism the North has recognized the value of the South's genetic resources; this has included the indigenous peoples' traditional crop varieties as much as the tropics' wild germplasm. The germplasm from both sources has contributed, and continues to contribute, a colossal amount to the economies of the North, and is partly responsible for the structure of the modern global economy and the developing world's disadvantaged place within it. Yet, as should be clear by now, the indigenous and rural communities of the developing world have never been compensated for the removal of this germplasm.[78]

The concept of "collective development" is important because over the centuries indigenous communities have significantly contributed to the diversity of the germ plasms that forms the basis of the production of crops. Roht-Arriaza writes, "This genetic diversity is developed and maintained by community-based innovation systems through which farmers breed varieties suited to their specific local needs and microenvironments."[79] It is this contribution to the genetic diversity within Southern Hemisphere countries that has preserved and developed the plant varieties that Northern companies find so lucrative. It is a form of labor, and it is no mere accident.

But because the global intellectual property laws pushed by the U.S. do not recognize collective innovation, indigenous communities cannot benefit through existing patent law from the sale of products derived from their own knowledge of plants. At the same time, the Eurocentric concept of individual authorship that is embodied in intellectual property law enables corporate researchers to file patents under their own name or the company that employs them.

Gudeman writes: "Through the concept of intellectual property rights we deploy widely accepted Western assumptions. We assume that innovations as products or processes have a technical essence that can be identified; once distinguished, this core can be abstracted from its context of use, converted to a written form, transported home, and tested in a laboratory."[80] Biotech companies argue that naturally occurring biological products may provide the basis for their innovations, but they only become valuable after the firms invest considerable time and money. By applying this line of reasoning that rests on traditional, conservative assumptions about how the economy works, the time and labor of indigenous farmers is rendered worthless and is devalued as being merely "nature." Therefore, under this patent system, intellectual property can only be produced within laboratories by people in white lab coats employed by companies with huge amounts of capital at their disposal.[81]

The United Nations estimated that the Third World loses at least $5 *billion* annually in unpaid royalties to multinational corporations that appropriate from the knowledge systems of indigenous peoples. It is even more important to note the total amount that companies make from knowledge and resources largely proffered from the Southern Hemisphere: $32 *billion annually*. Multinational corporations hold the vast amount of patents on naturally occurring biological materials found in the Southern Hemisphere, with these companies owning 79% of all utility patents on plants and Northern universities and research institutions controlling 14%; parties in Third World countries, comparatively, have almost no holdings.[82]

Virtually no profits from these products trickle back down South, while the wealth is accrued in the hands of the patent holders. A specific example that illustrates this disparity is the case of the rosy periwinkle, a native plant found in Madagascar that contains alkaloids that are indigenously used to treat diabetes. Alerted to the medicinal values of this plant by the people in the region, the Lilly Company developed a compound now used in chemotherapy that has also yielded a drug (worth $100 million annually) that can treat Hodgkin's disease. Commenting on this, The World Wide Fund for Nature claimed:

If Madagascar had received a significant part of this income, it would have been one of the country's largest (if not the single largest) source of income. . . . Madagascar is the unique home of perhaps 5 percent of the world's species. It is the biological equivalent of an Arab oil sheikdom. Yet, without an income from its huge biological wealth, it has chopped down most of its forests to feed its people.[83]

International Treaties and Intellectual Property Law

Intellectual property laws, which are first and foremost *property* laws, do nothing but exacerbate the unequal distribution of wealth between rich and poor nations by ensuring that those who already own property are able to use that power to increase their proprietary holdings. North American and European countries, particularly the United States, have led an unrelenting battle against developing countries to force them to adopt an intellectual property system that is advantageous to these already wealthy countries. The Trade-Related Aspects of Intellectual Property Rights (TRIPS), which came into effect in 1995 under the World Trade Organization (WTO), has been an instrumental element in forcing WTO member countries to adopt U.S.-backed intellectual property laws.[84]

TRIPS imposes minimum standards on copyright, patent, trademarks and trade secrets standards that are much more stringent than the legislation in developing countries, and which often run counter to their national interests.[85] Significantly, multinational pharmaceutical and agribusiness companies, represented by Western governments, helped to develop aspects of this global intellectual property code.[86] The general public in the First and Third World had no say in TRIPS; rather, this treaty was largely shaped and written by three organizations—the Union of Industrial and Employees Confederations (UNICE), Keidanren, and the Intellectual Property Committee (IPC). The IPC is a coalition of 12 corporations, including Bristol Myers, DuPont, Hewlett Packard, IBM, Johnson & Johnson, Monsanto and Warner.[87]

All of these companies have a material interest in the expansion of intellectual property law into new markets, with some of them holding major patents on biomaterials originating in the Third World for which the companies are not receiving royalties.[88] Speaking extremely candidly about the crafting of TRIPS and other global intellectual property treaties, James Enyart of Monsanto stated, "Industry has identified a major problem for international trade. It crafted a solution, reduced it to a concrete proposal and sold it to our own and other governments. . . . The industries and traders of world commerce have played simultaneously the role of patients, the diagnosticians and the prescribing physicians."[89] In other words, the industries played the role of judge, jury and executioner, because the implementation of these intellectual property laws threaten to be extremely detrimental to developing countries.

Numerous countries (such as Brazil) that had previously resisted TRIPS-imposed intellectual property standards have recently moved to comply with this trade agreement.[90] Such capitulation is the result of the power the U.S. wields over the world economy, and it has threatened with economic blackmail the countries that don't comply, claiming that they must strengthen their patent laws if they want access to U.S. markets.[91] The United States' insistence is prompted by a desire to protect the $10+ billion worth of patents on products such as insect-resistant crops and drugs developed from plants that grow in the same countries whose patent laws the U.S. is trying to influence.[92] PTO commissioner Bruce A. Lehman stated, "The United States is the fountain of innovation in this industry, and there's not any question that we favor strong intellectual property laws in this area. . . . We're [U.S. government] very aggressive about this."[93]

Before TRIPS, countries like Egypt, India and China did not impose strong patent restrictions on its domestic industries, which supported the development of its drug industries by allowing them to use different methods to produce mainly generic drugs developed by Western companies. These drugs were similar to, but far cheaper than, the brand-name drugs that most of those countries' citizens could not even remotely afford.[94]

Developing countries—whether they were Switzerland and the United States in the nineteenth century or Brazil and Thailand in this century—have developed most quickly when there were no extensively enforced patent monopolies that hindered access to human knowledge. The United States, in fact, had extremely lax intellectual property laws at the turn of the twentieth century, which allowed it to gain a competitive advantage in technology, much more so than if imported technology had been heavily protected against copying by law.[95] Therefore, the strict enforcement of intellectual property law ensures that developing countries remain non-competitive and subservient within the world economy.

> Historically, countries that have not been leaders in the development of new technologies have either emphasized the right of their citizens to have free access to inventions without patents or have granted preferential treatment so that their access to foreign technology is unfettered. Once these same countries establish their own technology base, they often turn around and demand of less-developed countries the restrictions that would have made their own progress impossible.[96]

At the same time knowledge of indigenous peoples is rendered unpatentable, these same people are expected under TRIPS to pay for the

Western "knowledge" (in the form of information, entertainment, etc.) that is increasingly entering their countries. Boyle observes, "Curare, batik, myths, and the dance 'lambada' flow out of developing countries, unprotected by intellectual property rights, while Prozac, Levis, Grisham, and the movie *Lambada!* flow in—protected by a suite of intellectual property laws, which in turn are backed by the threat of trade sanctions."[97]

Even more importantly, most patented biotechnology is aimed at those who can pay for the higher prices these products carry. Cosmetic drugs and fancy, slow-ripening tomatoes are favored over a vaccine for malaria or drought-resistant crops for people who live in dry climates. Also, stronger intellectual property provisions threaten to block the transfer of information by raising prices for technology beyond what developing countries can afford, thus freezing them out of the production of computer software and generic drugs.[98]

Worldwide Opposition to Patenting

Just because governments are capitulating to demands by the United States for stronger intellectual property laws, this does not mean that this is a popular course of action for many of those governments' citizens. Terminator technology, for example, has been met with a great amount of antagonism and protest around the world, particularly in India, which I will discuss later in this chapter. In Britain, the Ethical Consumers Organization physically slashed hundreds of plants that were believed to be Monsanto's, and the protest became so fevered that a British judge issued an injunction warning that any protesters who destroy Monsanto's property would be sent to jail.

In addition to anti-terminator rallies in Zimbabwe and Bangladesh, protesters from around the world marched on Monsanto's St. Louis, Missouri headquarters and, in a creatively humorous bit of performance art, Monsanto CEO Robert B. Shapiro was hit in the face with a pie during a public speech in San Francisco (the "Biotic Baking Brigade" took credit).[99] Further, the Indian government legislated a ban on the import and production of all terminator seeds, and the UN funded Consultative Group on International Research—the world's largest agricultural research organization—recommended the ban of all technologies that produce sterile seeds.[100]

Citing the terminator seed as the primary reason, the Dutch Parliament renewed its opposition to the approval of the 1998 Patent Directive by the European Parliament, which brought the European patent system in line with that of the United States.[101] The protests, however, are not isolated to the terminator seed. There has been opposition in Europe to genetically modified food, leading the European Union to suspend the licensing of transgenic crops for planting or importing in its member states. In Britain, from the laboratories to the supermarkets a temporary moratorium on genetically modified crops has been imposed and there has been a more general consumer backlash against such practices throughout Europe, something that did not occur simultaneously in North America.

Organized opposition to the ways in which the knowledge of indigenous peoples has been appropriated in drug patenting has also increased. For example, a U.S.-based company patented the active properties of a hallucinogenic drug that is of extreme religious importance to Amazon tribes.[102] The patenting of the drug was seen by Ecuadorian activist Valerio Grefa as "a true affront to the culture of our peoples," and the issue was taken by Ecuadorian activists as an opportunity to galvanize opposition to the U.S.-Ecuador intellectual property treaty that would allow U.S. companies to locally enforce patents on indigenous plants found in Ecuador.[103] Grefa organized demonstrations, generated popular dissent and lobbied heavily against the passage of the treaty. "Ecuadorian and U.S. officials, as well as activists for indigenous people around the world watched, astounded, as Grefa's tactics played a key role in scuttling a trade accord between Ecuador and the United States that had been in the works for more than three years."[104]

In addition to nongovernmental organizations, some governments have joined the fray, with countries such as the Philippines filing charges against U.S. firms within the World Trade Organization's judicial system for their patenting of local herbal and medicinal plant extracts for commercial purposes.[105] Despite the fact that it agreed to the terms of TRIPS, the Brazilian government has prosecuted people and organizations (such as Selva Viva, or "Living Rainforest") for selling indigenous knowledge about roots, shells and seeds to multinational pharmaceutical corporations such as Johnson & Johnson, Sandoz and Lilly.

The charges pressed against Selva Viva followed the passing of a Brazilian law that protects the nation's biodiversity and imposes stiff penalties against foreigners (and the citizens who help them) who attempt to lay claims on the biological materials found in rain forests. According to the author of the bill, the biodiversity law sought to end "neo-colonialism—the invasion which in no way benefits our region."[106] It should be noted that while Brazil, India and the Philippines have opposed the patenting of indigenous life forms and the U.S.-imposed intellectual property system in general, other governments have capitulated to the demands of the U.S. government and have been less than antagonistic.

Countries that have actively opposed certain patents have found it to be an expensive process. In 1999, the owner of an American-based seed company, Larry Proctor, won a U.S. patent and a U.S. Plant Variety Protection Certificate that allowed him control over a yellow strain of Mexican beans that are especially popular in the Northwest region of that country. He had bought a bag of commercial seeds in Mexico, isolated the yellow beans and allowed them to grow and self-pollinate. With this legal protection, Proctor initiated a lawsuit against two companies that import that strain of beans to the U.S.—Tutuli Produce and Productos Verde Valle.[107]

The president of Tutuli Produce, Rebecca Gilliland, stated: "In the beginning, I thought it was a joke. How could he [Proctor] invent something that Mexicans have been growing for centuries?" Proctor's company, POD-NERS, demanded a royalty of 6 cents per pound on the import of these yellow beans, which prompted U.S. customs officials to inspect shipments and take samples of Mexican beans at the border, at an additional cost to Gilliland's company. Because of the lawsuit, she says, her company lost customers, who are an important source of income to Mexican farmers. Soon after, the Mexican government announced that it would challenge the U.S. patent on this bean variety, but the process would be long and costly, running at least $200,000 in U.S. dollars in legal fees.[108]

The cost of such a battle is important, because poorer countries typically don't have the resources to regularly battle these types of patents, especially when there are more pressing domestic concerns. Just as many artists don't have the capital to defend themselves against copyright infringement charges when their fragmentary borrowings may very well be "fair use," the cost and time that goes into opposing patents that are unfair or not legitimate makes it unrealistic for governments around the world to police this kind of appropriation.

In addition to the issue of high legal costs, to attempt to repeal a patent a claim must be backed by written evidence of "prior art." In one case, two U.S. researchers were granted a patent on extracts from tumeric, an herb native to India that has been used to heal wounds. An ancient Sanskrit text was eventually presented as evidence and the U.S. PTO subsequently withdrew the patent. Although some patents have been revoked, the imposition of the standards of print cultures on largely oral cultures put an unfair burden on the natives of developing countries, who are also charged with the task of monitoring uses of their knowledge around the world, something that is nearly impossible for them to do.[109]

India

In regard to what is occurring throughout the world with the patenting of biological materials, India is both typical and atypical. It is typical because the active ingredients found in the country's indigenously cultivated biological materials have been patented or targeted to be patented by primarily U.S.-based companies. India is atypical in this regard because there has been a widespread resistance to this phenomenon on both a governmental and grassroots level. It is unfortunately again typical, however, in that the country has recently given in to U.S. demands that it conform to international intellectual property law agreements. For many reasons, India represents a microcosm of many of the trends relating to the patenting of life around the world.

In 1992, a U.S. patent on an extract from the neem tree was granted to W. R. Grace (the company that later received a European patent on all future genetic modifications of soybeans). The tree, known as the "blessed tree" and the "curer of all ailments" in its native country of India, has for centuries been used as a medicine, a spermicide and a fuel, among other things.[110] Its oil can be used as a pesticide that repels over 200 species of insects, and the bark, leaves and seeds have been used to treat a variety of illnesses including leprosy, diabetes, ulcers and skin disorders. Other indigenous uses of its extracts include dental hygiene, soap, facial cream, nail polish and cooking oil.[111]

The patent grants the company exclusive rights over a version of a pesticide extracted from the neem that has an extended shelf-life.[112] The company argued that the process it developed was "novel" and an advance on Indian techniques, but Shiva argues that this novelty

> . . . exists mainly in the context of the ignorance of the West. Over the 2,000 years in India, many complex processes were developed to make them available for specific use, though the active ingredients were not given Latinized scientific names. Common knowledge and use of neem were the primary reasons given by the Indian Central Insecticide Board for not registering neem products under the Insecticides Act of 1968.[113]

Claiming that Grace did not "invent" the product and that it was based on "prior art," the Foundation for Economic Trends (FET) filed a legal challenge against the patent with the U.S. PTO, a challenge that was supported by 200 organizations from 35 countries.[114] Despite its challenge, the FET lost the battle, and from 1985 to 1995, over 37 patents were granted in the United States and in Europe for neem-derived products.[115] With its patents secure, Grace began establishing a base in India, approaching Indian-owned manufacturers with proposals for them to stop selling their own products and to instead supply Grace with raw materials, to buy local technologies from the companies outright and take over local production.[116]

Indians were further incensed by a U.S. firm's patenting of a particular strain of basmati rice, a type of rice grown exclusively in India. Drawing from India's basmati rice, Rice Tech Inc. claims to have developed a superior version of the Indian rice—a rice with characteristics very similar to basmati—marketing it under the names Texmati and Kasmati.[117] Because Indian farmers export $250 million worth of basmati rice annually, with the U.S. being a target market, many Indians felt that this was a legally sanctioned and technologically sophisticated way of appropriating the country's resources. Granted, the Rice-Tech patents do not cover basmati and jasmine rice *as they exist in nature*. But because genetically altered and patented strains of *already existing crops* have proliferated so quickly, these patented rice strains actually pose a real long-term threat to Indian farmers.

Extracts from the plants dudhi, black nightshade and chottagokhuru—which have been used by Indians to treat worm infestation, stomach irritation, menstrual pain and urinary infections—were also patented for use in various applications. U.S. companies such as Proctor & Gamble registered patent claims over various uses of these extracts, including "pharmaceutical compositions for the treatment of skin disorders" and for "gastro-protection"—uses that include ways in which Indians already apply them.[118] After U.S. firms patented antidiabetic formulations based on brinjal, bitter gourd and jamun extract, India's Council for Scientific and Industrial Research (CSIR) decided not to oppose the patent. Despite the fact that there is much in the native folklore that suggests that bitter gourd is a useful element of a diet therapy for diabetics, the CSIR decided that it would not be logistically possible to formally oppose each and every one of the numerous patents on Indian plant-derived products.[119]

As I stated previously in this chapter, many countries have succumbed to economic pressure, signing trade treaties that force them to adopt intellectual property laws that conform to those in North America and Western Europe. In its government's longtime refusal to adopt these patent laws, India significantly resisted Western intellectual property regimes and the patent-assisted appropriation of the country's biological resources. In refusing to adopt such laws, the country allowed its own pharmaceutical companies to copy the drugs created by Western firms, rationalizing that they are appropriating from the multinational corporations that in turn make their profits by pillaging the world's indigenous knowledge and biological diversity.

After a decade of pressuring India to adopt intellectual property laws that conformed to those of the United States, particularly its patent law, in 1990 the Bush Administration singled out India as an "unfair trading partner" and imposed harsh tariffs on the country. The president of Pharmaceutical Manufacturers Association (PMA), Gerald J. Mossinghoff, endorsed the move, stating: "This decision demonstrates the Bush Administration's continuing and encouraging commitment to strong worldwide intellectual property protection. These countries have been put on notice that it is time to initiate reforms so that patents can be properly protected."[120] Claiming that it loses $5 billion annually to patent piracy, the PMA has been instrumental in lobbying the U.S. government to crack down on this activity. Because of its economic muscle, the United States has been able to greatly influence the intellectual property policies of other developing countries—even when those policies do not necessarily benefit them.

Although India joined the World Trade Organization, by the mid-1990s it had still not passed the necessary intellectual property laws to ratify the country's membership. In 1995, India's prime minister, Narasimha Rao, attempted to make the necessary change to the country's patent law (as an exporter of software and film, it already had tough copyright laws). India's Parliament refused to pass this law because of widespread concern over how this would affect Indian pharmaceutical production and farming, because stricter plant variety protection would increase the price of seeds in ways that Indian farmers could not afford.[121]

In 1997, prompted by complaints filed by the United States, the World Trade Organization ruled that India failed to set up the necessary intermediary legislative steps to create pharmaceutical, crop and chemical patent protections, and it increased its economic pressure on India to change its patent laws.[122] In a move that a newspaper editor at *The Hindu* accused of being "clandestine," the Narasimha Rao administration was able to push the Patents Amendment Bill through the Indian Parliament with some backroom deals and other forms of manipulation.[123] In 1999, the Parliament passed the Patents Amendment Act, which for the first time allowed exclusive marketing rights for agrochemical and pharmaceutical products.[124]

Despite the slow, creeping implementation of patent law in India, some members of the country's police and the judicial system have joined the backlash against what many perceive as multinational corporations dictating the policies of their sovereign nation—a nation that has a relatively recent history of colonialism. Many police agencies have indicated that enforcing intellectual property law is not among their priorities, and in some areas, police have been known to tip off infringers about planned raids.

Moreover, even when people are arrested and charged with such infringements, groups of judges have subverted these prosecutions by throwing out cases on technical grounds, asserting lack of jurisdiction or failure to pay court fees, even when such assertions are not legitimate. In addition, up until early 1999, the Indian Patent Office (IPO) created numerous obstacles to registering patents, imposing stricter limits than what the then-current patent statute required. Nevertheless, all of these forms of resistance within the government's infrastructure will likely dissipate as India becomes immersed in U.S.-backed intellectual property regimes.[125]

Resistance has also cropped up on a more grassroots level. The first major demonstration against the appropriation of India's biological diversity occurred in 1993 on its Independence Day, August 15, when farmers declared that their local knowledge was protected by "Samuhik Gyan Sanad," or "collective intellectual rights."[126] As the head of the Farmer's Association, an Indian farmer's advocacy group, M. D. Nanjundaswamy has led direct actions against multinational corporations that he believes are engaged in "biopiracy" (a term for the type of appropriation discussed throughout this chapter). In 1992, members of the Farmer's Association raided the offices of the U.S.-based seed company Cargill and attacked its seed cleaning and packaging plant.

In regard to this measure, Nanjundaswamy stated, "What the multinationals are doing is international piracy, and, in view of the mischief they do, we are justified in taking this action."[127] Five years later, to protest the terminator technology, Nanjundaswamy's indigenous farmer organization launched what they dubbed "Operation Cremate Monsanto," which was aimed at "burning" the company out of their country. In 1998, 200 farmers descended on Monsanto-owned property that contained genetically modified crops and burned fields, with Nanjundaswamy stating, "We are making a call for direct action against Monsanto and the rest of the biotech gang."[128]

Anticipating the coming patent law changes within India, in 1997 the Indian government-funded Council of Scientific and Industrial Research (CSIR) embarked on a program that attempted to prevent multinational corporations from patenting research derived from the knowledge of indigenous peoples by heading those companies off at the proverbial pass. CSIR director-general Raghunath Mashelkar explained:

We aim to develop a standardization and documentation of the traditional knowledge so that they are protected from bio-piracy in the future and we will develop new combinations to market at the global level. . . . India is endowed with rich medicinal plants. The knowledge till now was essentially spread through word of mouth. But if left unprotected in the new patent regime, there is the danger of losing our knowledge to global competitors.[129]

Conclusion

To protect its indigenous knowledge, India's government has resorted to patenting the indigenous knowledge developed by the citizens of its country and by their ancestors. By attempting to protect the further appropriation of India's material and intellectual resources by patenting them, the country is further pulled into the social relations of intellectual property law it has for so many years tried to resist. A comparable example was discussed in chapter 2, in which blues singer Willie Dixon was compelled to sue Led Zeppelin for "borrowing" large chunks of his songs. In doing so, he was forced to implicitly buy into notions of authorship and originality that are relatively foreign to the blues tradition.

This is also similar to the situation in which members of Negativland found themselves when they were forced to counter-sue their former label, SST, after the group was sued by that label during the legal fallout over the U2 single. When SST sued them for trademark infringement when they parodied the label's motto and logo, Negativland counter-sued with a number of charges, including copyright infringement (because SST released their music without permission). Despite the fact that Negativland resisted the continued expansion of intellectual property law into their area of cultural production, to protect themselves and gain some leverage in this legal game, they needed to use legal tactics similar to those used against them. India's patenting of its own native knowledge about local plants echoes this contradiction.

My discussions of plant patenting and world music demonstrate that "free appropriation" within these areas of cultural production can have detrimental effects—effects that seem quite removed from the world of the sound- and visual-collage artists who advocate such a position. In these circles, "free appropriation" is equated with artistic freedom and is seen as a necessary part of keeping collage art traditions alive. My purpose in raising this point is not to lambaste these Western artists for holding a position that, applied in other contexts, has negative consequences for other cultures. It is, rather, to point out important contradictions that surface as we try to apply one solution to the problems posed by the expansion of intellectual property law as it is applied simultaneously across areas of cultural production.

Despite the fact that patent and copyright law have quite different histories, their shared, individualistic assumptions of authorship and ownership (in the way musical or scientific texts are determined to be copyrightable or patentable) are relatively similar. Because, under current patent law, the collective development of resources cannot be defined as a type of authorship, the people whose communities have labored for centuries cannot be designated even as co-owners of the patented products their indigenous knowledge helped generate. Despite the fact that a patent may cover a modified version of the active agents in an indigenous plant, it was the *labor and knowledge produced by the community that led companies to the development of the patented product in the first place.*

Again, greater analytical focus can be provided by specifically asking *who* is defined as an author, *what* is being authored, *how* a thing is authored and *where* the means of production is located. The process of "authoring" seeds in these cultures is similar to what I described above in my discussion of folk music—it is a communal effort, with the knowledge required to maintain (and credit for maintaining) the plants being shared. Therefore, the knowledge is understood to be "owned" by the entire community. But Western science and patent law construct authorship in a way that does not recognize such cultural practices as being legitimate and further holds very narrow notions of what types of knowledge can be recognized as a form of authorship.

Patented products that are derived from indigenous plants are identified (or "written") using scientific equipment that allows for the isolation and identification of chemicals and genes. This is how these products of scientific knowledge are authored, making it possible only for those who have the capital to invest in the software, hardware and specialized labor power required for its production to engage in this activity. In other words, only those with control of the means of production can be considered authors and, therefore, owners.

Of course, this situation is not limited to the Third World, and it is indicative of trends occurring in farming over the past two decades. Within the United States, agriculture's movement in the twentieth century from a system dominated by small farmers to one dominated by corporate farming has been essentially a movement in the *means of production* from individuals and families to corporations. This shift has intensified with the rise of crop patenting, which produces new sources of wealth for corporations that hold large amounts of capital and which thus assists the increased corporate consolidation in this sector. Inventions such as the terminator seed, by definition, ensure that control of the means of production is maintained by corporations.

The perception that valuable knowledge can only be created in corporate or university laboratories thus enables powerful companies to legally appropriate the resources of developing countries. The fact that these companies are largely located in the First World further contributes to the unequal distribution of resources throughout the world, especially given the fact that the Third World loses an estimated $5 billion annually in potential royalties from patents relating to indigenous knowledge of plants. And the United States' pressure on developing countries to pass TRIPs compliant intellectual property legislation ensures that these countries will be able to gain a monopoly over the production of these products not only in the First World but in developing countries as well. Such a scenario provides a concrete answer to Shiva's question posed at the beginning of this chapter: "Whose knowledge and values will shape the future options of diverse communities?"[130]

Notes

1   Shulman, S. (1999). *Owning the future.* New York: Houghton Mifflin.

2   Shiva, V. (1997). *Biopiracy: The plunder of nature and knowledge.* Boston: South End Press.

3   Elias, S. (1996). *Patent, copyright & trademark: A desk reference to intellectual property law.* Berkeley: Nolo Press.

4   Ibid.

5   Roht-Arriaza, N. (1997). Of seeds and shamans: The appropriation of the scientific and technical knowledge of indigenous and local communities. In B. Ziff & P. V. Rao (Eds.), *Borrowed power: Essays on cultural appropriation* (pp. 255–287). New Brunswick, NJ: Rutgers University Press, p. 263.

6   Coombe, R. J. (1998). Intellectual property, human rights & sovereignty: New dilemmas in international law posed by the recognition of indigenous knowledge and the conservation of biodiversity. *Indiana Journal of Global Legal Studies, 6,* 59–, p. 87.

7   Coombe, R. J. (1998). Intellectual property, human rights & sovereignty: New dilemmas in international law posed by the recognition of indigenous knowledge and the conservation of biodiversity. *Indiana Journal of Global Legal Studies, 6,* pp. 86–87.

8   Gudeman, S. (1996). Sketches, qualms, and other thoughts on intellectual property rights. In S. B. Brush & D. Stabinsky (Eds.), *Indigenous people and intellectual property rights* (pp. 102–121). Washington, DC: Island Press, p. 103.

9   Roht-Arriaza, N. (1997). Of seeds and shamans: The appropriation of the scientific and technical knowledge of indigenous and local communities. In B. Ziff & P. V. Rao (Eds.), *Borrowed power: Essays on cultural appropriation* (pp. 255–287). New Brunswick, NJ: Rutgers University Press.

10   Ibid.

11   Ibid., p. 266.

12   Stenson, A. J. & Gray, T. S. (1999). *The politics of genetic resource control.* New York: St. Martin's Press.

13   Plenty in a name: History & geography of patents. (1998, March 28). [Online]. *Statesman.* Available: Lexis-Nexis.

14   Shulman, S. (1999). *Owning the Future.* New York: Houghton Mifflin, p. 146.

15   Berland, J. & Lewontin, R. C. (1999, February 22). Genetically modified food: It's business as usual. *Guardian,* p. A14.

16   Burns, J. (1998, May 15). Seed-saver blitz. *Farmers Weekly*, p. 10; Steyer, R. (1998. May 3). Seed warnings are getting through: Opposition wanes to Monsanto policy. *St. Louis Post-Dispatch*, p. E1.

17   Steyer, R. (1998, October 1). Monsanto gets tough on seed pirates: Publicly identifies farmers who break the rules. *St. Louis Post-Dispatch*, p. B1.

18   Hord, B. (1998, April 9). Of seeds, patents and piracy: Conflicts flare over sales, planting. *Omaha World-Herald*, p. A1.

19   Steyer, R. (1996, February 25). Farmers fret over challenge to seed-saving tradition. *St. Louis Post-Dispatch*, p. 1E.

20   Feder, B. J. (1996, March 3). Out of the lab: A revolution on the farm. *New York Times*, p. 3C.; Steyer, R. (1996, February 25). Farmers fret over challenge to seed-saving tradition. *St. Louis Post-Dispatch*, p. 1E.

21   Fairley, P. (1998, August 12). Zeneca claims Monsanto is "monopolizing" herbicides market. *Chemical Week*, p. 8.

22   Ibid.

23   Stenson, A. J. & Gray, T. S. (1999). *The politics of genetic resource control*. New York: St. Martin's Press.

24   O'Sullivan, K. (1999, March 8). GM food advocates playing dumb on root causes of famine, environmentalist asserts. *Irish Times*, p. 7.

25   Shulman, S. (1999). *Owning the future*. New York: Houghton Mifflin.

26   Ibid., p. 85.

27   Ibid.

28   Ibid.

29   Ibid.; Rubenstein, B. (1995a, May). W. R. Grace's cotton, soybean patents spur controversy. *Corporate Legal Times*, p. 26.

30   Kilman, S. (1994, November 25). W. R. Grace sprouts new controversy. *Wall Street Journal*, p. B4; Tansey, G. (1994, December 1). Soyabean patent breeds discontent. *Financial Times* [Online]. Available: Lexis-Nexis.

31   Riordan, T. (1994, December 1). Grace unit's European biotech patent on soybeans meets opposition. *New York Times*, p. D8.

32   Soybean species patent: Full speed backwards at Monsanto. (1996, October). *Intellectual Property Today*, p. 29.

33   Ibid.

34   Shulman, S. (1999). *Owning the future*. New York: Houghton Mifflin, p. 101.

35   Fritz, M. (1994, December 1). Biotechnologists reap what they patent. *Ottawa Citizen*, p. F12.

36   Brittenden, W. (1998, March 22). "Terminator" seeds threaten a barren future for farmers. *Independent* [Online]. Available: Lexis-Nexis.

37   Weiss, R. (1999, February 8). Sowing dependency or uprooting hunger? *Washington Post,* p. A9.

38   Vidal, J. (1998, April 15). Mr. Terminator ploughs in. *Guardian,* p. 4.

39   America's seeds of destruction. (1998, November 3). *Statesman* [Online]. Available: Lexis-Nexis.

41   Edwards, R. (1998, October 10). Devilish seed. *New Scientist,* p. 21.

42   Collett, G. (1998, December 1). Terminator seed gene "frightening." *Nelson Mail* [Online]. Available: Lexis-Nexis.

43   Mittal, A. (1999, March 1). Seeds sow controversy. *San Francisco Chronicle,* p. A21; Roughton, B., Jr. (1999, September 26). Americans' genetically modified foods face disdain in Europe. *Times-Picayune,* p. A33.

44   Chemical companies bet on the farm. (1998, February 27). *Globe & Mail* [Online]. Available: Lexis-Nexis.

45   Webster, J. (1998, December 14). Monsanto's terminator leaves seed buyers no hasta la vista. *Scotsman,* p. 16.

46   Lambrecht, B. (1999, April 23). Monsanto will wait for studies of disputed new gene technology. *St. Louis Post-Dispatch,* p. A4.

47   Mitchell, S. (1995, February). When clusters get personal: The latest cluster system uses individual instead of census data. *American Demographics,* p. 42.

48   RAFI. (2000, May). Terminator two years late. *RAFI Communiqué* [Online]. Available: http://www.rafi.org.

49   Ibid.

50   Ibid.

51   Kneen, B. (1999, July 5). Genetic "life control" means something down on the farm: The seeds of discontent. *Ottawa Citizen,* p. A13.

52   Menon, S. (1998, August 3). Terminator seed. *India Today,* p. 57.

53   Mittal, A. (1999, March 1). Seeds sow controversy. *San Francisco Chronicle,* p. A21; Roughton, B., Jr. (1999, September 26). Americans' genetically modified foods face disdain in Europe. *Times-Picayune,* p. A33.

54   Roht-Arriaza, N. (1997). Of seeds and shamans: The appropriation of the scientific and technical knowledge of indigenous and local communities. In B. Ziff & P. V. Rao (Eds.), *Borrowed power: Essays on cultural appropriation* (pp. 255–287). New Brunswick, NJ: Rutgers University Press.

55   Duffy, A. (1998, December 16). Biodiversity "crackpot" wins Pearson medal. *Ottawa Citizen,* p. A10.

56   New study discounts "benefits" of patenting plants. (1996, April). *Intellectual Property Today*, p. 16.

57   Howard, H. (1998, November). High-tech killers at the gate. *News & Views, 12, 3*, 6; McDonald, D. B. (1999, April). Who owns nature? *Entertainment Design* [Online]. Available: Lexis-Nexis.

58   Chemical companies bet on the farm. (1998, February 27). *Globe & Mail*. Available: Lexis-Nexis; RAFI. (1999a). Traitor technology: "Damaged goods" from the gene giants. *Rural Advancement Fund International* [Online]. Available: http://www.rafi.org/ pr/release30.html.

59   Allen, S. & Hsu, K. (1999, July 11). In seed business, growing pressure. *Boston Globe*, p. A12.

60   RAFI. (1999). World seed conference: Shrinking club of industry giants [14 paragraphs]. RAFI News Release [Online]. Available: http://www.rafi.org.

61   Ibid.

62   Schmickle, S. (1998, July 22). Genetic engineers are getting patents on code of life. *Star Tribune*, p. 1A.

63   Service, R. F. (1998, October 30). Seed-sterilizing "terminator technology" sows discord. *Science, 282,* 850.

64   Shiva, V. (2000, May 11). How big business starves the poor. *Daily Telegraph*, p. 22.

65   O'Sullivan, K. (2000, January 17). More malnutrition with genetic farming forecast. *Irish Times*, p. 5.

66   Erlichman, J. (1999, October 12). GM foods: Fighting for the future of our food. *Independent*. [Online]. Available: Lexis-Nexis.

67   Tam, P. (2000, January 3). First in a series: Genetically modified foods. *Ottawa Citizen*, p. A1.

68   Shiva, V. (1997). *Biopiracy: The plunder of nature and knowledge.* Boston: South End Press.

69   McGirk, T. (1998, November 9). Gene piracy. *Time (international edition, Asia),* 34.

70   Ibid., p. 34.

71   Roht-Arriaza, N. (1997). Of seeds and shamans: The appropriation of the scientific and technical knowledge of indigenous and local communities. In B. Ziff & P. V. Rao (Eds.), *Borrowed power: Essays on cultural appropriation* (pp. 255–287). New Brunswick, NJ: Rutgers University Press, p. 259.

72   Shulman, S. (1999). *Owning the future.* New York: Houghton Mifflin.

73   Ibid.

74   Rifkin, J. (1998, October 28). Beware of the bio-century. *Guardian,* p. 4.

75   Roht-Arriaza, N. (1997). Of seeds and shamans: The appropriation of the scientific and technical knowledge of indigenous and local communities. In B. Ziff & P. V. Rao (Eds.), *Borrowed power: Essays on cultural appropriation* (pp. 255–287). New Brunswick, NJ: Rutgers University Press.

76   Biotech, Third World style. (1999, December 12). *Los Angeles Times,* p. M4.

77   *1999 Human Development Report.* (1999). Oxford: Oxford University Press.

78   Stenson, A. J. & Gray, T. S. (1999). *The politics of genetic resource control.* New York: St. Martin's Press, p. 75.

79   Roht-Arriaza, N. (1997). Of seeds and shamans: The appropriation of the scientific and technical knowledge of indigenous and local communities. In B. Ziff & P. V. Rao (Eds.), *Borrowed power: Essays on cultural appropriation* (pp. 255–287). New Brunswick, NJ: Rutgers University Press, p. 260.

80   Gudeman, S. (1996). Sketches, qualms, and other thoughts on intellectual property rights. In S. B. Brush & D. Stabinsky (Eds.), *Indigenous people and intellectual property rights* (pp. 102–121). Washington DC: Island Press, p. 112.

81   Shiva, V. (1997). *Biopiracy: The plunder of nature and knowledge.* Boston: South End Press, p. 52.

82   Shulman, S. (1999). *Owning the future.* New York: Houghton Mifflin.

83   Boyle, J. (1996). *Shamans, software, & spleens: Law and the construction of the information society.* Cambridge, MA: Harvard University Press, p. 128.

84   Emmott, S. (1994, September 17). Genes, share them or lose them. *New Scientist,* p. 41; TRIPS & its negative consequences. (1999, July 20). *Hindu* [Online]. Available: Lexis-Nexis.

85   Shiva, V. (1997). *Biopiracy: The plunder of nature and knowledge.* Boston: South End Press, p. 52; TRIPS & its negative consequences. (1999, July 20). *Hindu* [Online]. Available: Lexis-Nexis.

86   Watkins, K. (1995, November 20). Whose property is life? *Independent,* p. 20.

87   Shiva, V. (1997). *Biopiracy: The plunder of nature and knowledge.* Boston: South End Press.

88   Ibid.

89   Ibid., p. 83.

90   Merrylees, D. (1998, May/June). Brazil's IP revolution: A plethora of new rights. *IP Worldwide* [Online]. Available: Lexis-Nexis.

91   Kiely, T. (1991, February). Life patents go global. *Technology Review, 94, 2,* 21.

92   Green. P. L. (1997, September 11). Patents for plants, animals a ticklish topic for Geneva. *Journal of Commerce,* 4A.

93   Ibid.

94   Ibid.

95   Stenson, A. J. & Gray, T. S. (1999). *The politics of genetic resource control.* New York: St. Martin's Press.

96   Crucible Group. (1994). *People, plants, and patents.* Ottawa: International Development Research Centre.

97   Boyle, J. (1996). *Shamans, software, & spleens: Law and the construction of the information society.* Cambridge, MA: Harvard University Press, p. 125.

98   *1999 Human Development Report.* (1999). Oxford: Oxford University Press.

99   A watershed in biotechnology's global march. (1998, December 27). *St. Louis Post-Dispatch,* p. A9.

100 Edwards, R. (1998, March 28). Farmers may soon be entirely reliant on seed companies. *New Scientist,* p. 22; Hawkes, N. (1998, November 4). War on killer seed. *Times* [Online]. Available: Lexis-Nexis; Lambrecht, B. (1998, April 19). "Terminator" genes renders seeds sterile: Farmers no longer could save them for next year. *St. Louis Post-Dispatch,* p. A1.

101 Howard, H. (1998, November). High-tech killers at the gate. *News & Views, 12, 3,* 6; McDonald, D. B. (1999, April). Who owns nature? *Entertainment Design* [Online]. Available: Lexis-Nexis.

102 Amazon tribal leaders want drug patent pulled. (1999, March 31). *St. Louis Post-Dispatch,* p. A1.

103 Shulman, S. (1999). *Owning the future.* New York: Houghton Mifflin, p. 127.

104 Ibid., p. 135.

105 Amazon tribal leaders want drug patent pulled. (1999, March 31). *St. Louis Post-Dispatch,* p. A1.

106 Osava, M. (1997, August 14). Biodiversity: Crackdown on eco-pirates. *Interpress Service* [Online]. Available: Lexis-Nexis.

107 RAFI. (2000). Mexican bean biopiracy. *Rural Advancement Fund International* [Online]. Available: http://www.rafi.org/pr/release39.html.

108 Ibid.

109 *1999 Human Development Report.* (1999). Oxford: Oxford University Press.

110 Shiva, V. & Holla-Bhar, R. (1993, November/December). Intellectual piracy and the neem tree. *Ecologist, 23, 6,* 223–227.; Wolfgang, L. (1995, September 15). Patents on native technology challenged. *Science, 269,* 1506.

111 Hoversten, P. (1995, October 18). Legal battle takes root over "miracle tree." *USA Today,* p. 8A; Pearce, F. (1993, October 9). Pesticide patent angers Indian farmers. *New Scientist, 140, 1894,* 7.

112   Lemonick, M. D. (1995, September 25). Seeds of conflict: Critics say company's patent on a pesticide from an Indian tree is "genetic colonialism." *Time*, 50; Saltus, R. (1995, September 13). US firm is accused of "usurping" patent. *Boston Globe*, p. A6.

113   Shiva, V. (1997). *Biopiracy: The plunder of nature and knowledge*. Boston: South End Press, p. 71.

114   Kleiner, K. (1995, September 16). Pesticide tree ends up in court. *New Scientist*, 7.

115   Agarwal, A. (1996, October 26). Pirates in the garden of India. *New Scientist*, 14; US patent being examined. (1999, July 23). *Statesman*. Available: Lexis-Nexis.

116   Shiva, V. (1997). *Biopiracy: The plunder of nature and knowledge*. Boston: South End Press.

117   Kamal, S. & Saran, R. (1998, March 7). Economy & Policy. *Business Today*, p. 23.

118   Arthur, C. (1998, May 8). Row over patent plan for medicinal plants. *Independent*, p. 5.

119   Warring over karela. (1999, July 21). *Hindu* [Online]. Available: Lexis-Nexis.

120   Drug patents divide India and the US. (1990, May 14). *Chemical Marketing Reporter, 237, 20*, 7.

121   Kazmin, A. L. (1997, March 24). Now these copycats have to discover new drugs. *Business Week (international edition), 3519*, 114.

122   Chakravarti, S. & Aiyar, S. (1997, November 17). WTO negotiations: Playing hardball. *India Today*, p. 52; Debroy, B. (1998, September 22). Patently pragmatic. *Business Today*, 34; Patent ruling against India. (1997, August 20). *Chemical Week*, 4.

123   A monopoly for foreigners now [Editorial]. (1994, December 4). *Hindu* [Online]. Available: Lexis-Nexis.

124   Corporate muscle flexing gets its way. (1999, March 24). *Toronto Star* [Online]. Available: Lexis-Nexis.

125   Ahuja, S. D. (1999, January/February). IP treaties show little effect in India. *IP Worldwide* [Online]. Available: Lexis-Nexis.

126   Shiva, V. (1997). *Biopiracy: The plunder of nature and knowledge*. Boston: South End Press, p. 81.

127   Webb, S. (1993, September 30). Survey of India. *Financial Times*, p. XXI.

128   Woolf, M. & Lean, G. (1999, February 14). The seeds of destruction. *Independent*, p. 26.

129   Srinivasan, A. (1997, October 13). India to patent traditional knowledge of herbal cures. *Business Times,* p. 9.

130   Shiva, V. (1997). *Biopiracy: The plunder of nature and knowledge.* Boston: South End Press, p. 72.

Chapter 6

The Private Ownership of People: Genetics, Consumer Databases and Celebrities

There are three very different ways that humans can be privately owned in contemporary times: first, through patenting human genes and other biological materials; second, through collecting consumer profiles in proprietary databases; and, third, through "right of publicity" law, which protects celebrity images from commercial appropriation. Human gene patenting gives pharmaceutical firms with equipment that can analyze genetic structures the ability to *own* a human gene as it is isolated from its natural environment or as it exists in pharmaceutical products. This ownership gives those firms a unique power to set the terms for, and reap the benefits from, other *independent* research on diseases connected with the genes or cell lines they own.

In the case of the consumer, the privatization of one's image is facilitated by corporations that use massive databases to collect personal information such as credit histories, medical histories, debit and credit card purchases, mail orders, and other transactions. The contents of these proprietary databases piece together bits of one's behavior in the marketplace to create a profile of a consumer, resulting in what Lyon labels one's "data image."[1] Finally, the celebrity's proprietary control over his or her image is secured and maintained through a complex series of case law and legislation that has come to be known as the "right of publicity," which allows the celebrity to control his or her image within a commercial context.

The Private Ownership of Genes and Cells

In the 1990s, large biotech and pharmaceutical companies began investing millions of dollars into wide-scale DNA surveying, something that has been advocated by anthropologists for years—albeit for quite different reasons. As I demonstrated in chapter 5, beginning in the 1980s, the valuable knowledge about biological matter found primarily in Third World countries was sought out. Most recently, it is information about human genes that is being hunted, captured and patented for use in scientific studies that lead to the development and sale of commercial medical products. For instance, the nomadic Bedouin people of the Middle East are being studied for medical clues relating to obesity and deafness, and people from small towns in Quebec have been the focus of genetic studies that center on manic depression.[2] Researchers are studying the Arhuacan Indians of the Colombian Santa Marta Mountains—who play host to a type of virus associated with leukemia and AIDS—for possible cures for those diseases.

One of a few projects that aims to collect and catalog, for scientific purposes, the genetic makeup of the thousands of cultures from around the world is the Human Genome Diversity Project.[3] Another is the International Histocompatibility Workshop Anthropology for Component (IHWAC), whose database contains detailed information on roughly 130 populations submitted by 83 laboratories. The largely academic organizations that are engaged in the collection and preservation of the earth's diverse human genetic legacy have largely altruistic aims, but they can nevertheless unintentionally contribute to the privatization of the genetic commons. Despite the benevolent aims of the organization, several IHWAC researchers have filed for and received patents on human cells, cell products, or genes contained in the database—many of which have important medical uses and will be likely valuable.[4]

As was stated in the previous chapter, the discovered gene itself is *technically* not patented; the patent supposedly grants ownership over the way the gene exists in isolation from its natural environment and as it exists in various kinds of products. When corporations patent medical processes that are directly related to the existence of certain genes (for instance, genes that are thought to cause a particular disease), they argue that they do not own the gene itself. Nevertheless, the patent gives them *de facto* control over the practical uses of that gene (diagnostic tests, drugs, treatments, etc.), which is what is meant when the phrase "gene patenting" is used in this book.

U.S. citizens are also subject to this sort of genetic appropriation. In the United States, the Pennsylvania Amish community—whose gene pool has remained relatively unmixed for the past three centuries because of religious strictures against out-marriage—has also been studied, and their

DNA has been acquired by several biotech firms to uncover clues having to do with Alzheimer's disease and diabetes. Rebecca Huyard, an Amish medical administrator in Strasburg, Pa., remembers how researchers from John Hopkins University came to their community and collected hundreds of genetic samples from Amish farming people during the 1970s and 1980s. She said, "They came, they took blood, they made promises and they never reappeared."[5]

The case of the Pima Indians of Arizona, who have a high incidence of hypertension and obesity, provides another example of the genes of U.S. citizens being appropriated by private companies. The interest in the Pima followed the discovery of the "tubby" gene associated with chronic obesity, which was patented by Jeffrey Friedman at Rockefeller University, who then licensed it to Amgen for an initial fee of $20 million. The company that was interested in studying the genetic roots of obesity among Pima Indians patented genes found in these groups, and stands to profit handsomely from their research—a sort of sci-fi extension of the manifest destiny.[6]

The first major case of this kind of appropriation came about in the 1970s when U.S. citizen John Moore's spleen was removed to treat a rare form of leukemia. Unbeknownst to Moore, his doctor developed a cell line from that spleen and assigned the patent on it to the University of California.[7] The long-term market value of the patent has been estimated at roughly $3 billion, and Moore's doctor received $3 million in stocks from Genetics Institute, the firm that marketed and developed a drug from the patent.[8] Moore sued, but despite two appeals in the California court system, he lost, receiving no compensation or right to control the use of his own genetic material.[9]

The California Supreme Court claimed that to give Moore any rights would open the floodgates of commercialization and lead to the commodification of the human body. In a dissenting opinion, Judge Broussard wrote,

> . . . the majority's rejections of plaintiff's conversion cause of action does *not* mean that body parts may not be bought or sold for research or commercial purpose or that no private individual or entity may benefit economically from the fortuitous value of plaintiff's diseased cells. Far from elevating these biological materials above the marketplace, the majority's holding simply bars *plaintiff*, the source of the cells, from obtaining the benefit of the cell's value, but permits the *defendants*, who allegedly obtained the cells from plaintiff by improper means, to retain and exploit the full economic value of their ill-gotten gains free of . . . liability.[10]

Patenting the genes of people from Third World countries is becoming a widespread and deeply contested practice. In 1992 the U.S. Department of Commerce applied for a patent on a cell line derived from the blood of a Guayami Indian (a tribe that is indigenous to Panama). The illiterate Guayami woman whose blood was taken had apparently been given "informed consent" in Spanish, a language she neither spoke nor understood. The Commerce Department's stated reason for pursuing the patent was "to protect the CDC research and to *attract private investors*" [my emphasis].[11] After much controversy and severe criticism from many nongovernmental organizations, the U.S. dropped its bid on the patent.[12] "We are pleased that the claim was withdrawn," said Rodrigo Contreras of the World Council of Indigenous People, though he points out that it was pulled only after pressure from the Guayami's supporters and "not from the generosity of U.S. firms."[13]

Around the same time that U.S. researchers initiated the Guayami patent application, others applied for a patent on a cell line derived from the people of the Solomon Islands, who protested this claim.[14] In a letter to the Ambassador to the Solomon Islands, Ron Brown, the U.S. Secretary of Commerce in 1994, explained matter-of-factly: "Under our laws, as well as those of many other countries, subject matter relating to human cells is patentable and there is no provision for considerations relating to the source of the cells that may be the subject of a patent application."[15]

In a similar, earlier case, residents of Tristan da Cunha, a remote island in the South Atlantic, unsuccessfully fought over control of their own genetic material after researchers took blood samples from virtually every island resident. The island's residents suffer from unusually high rates of asthma, and they were targeted by Canadian researchers who hoped to isolate the gene that predisposes people to develop asthma.[16] Those researchers then sold the information to a U.S.-based genomic company, Sequana Therapeutics, which used that genetic material to secure a $70 million deal with the German pharmaceutical company Boehringer Ingelheim.[17]

Boehringer, in turn, got exclusive worldwide rights to develop and commercialize therapies based on the asthma genes. What did the islanders get? They received equipment to diagnose asthma, but—in a slap in the face—nothing to help treat the disease.[18] Kevin Kinsella, president of Sequana, represents the attitude of many pharmaceutical and biotech firms when he stated: "Gene discovery is just the first step in a 1,000-mile journey to find a therapy. It's a process that costs us millions and takes years of work. So how much does somebody who gets his arm pricked deserve?"[19] A quick answer to his rhetorical question might be, say, the right to not be exploited through high-tech methods that enable the First World to engage in further logical extensions of colonialism.

The Race to Map the Human Genome

The research on genetic diversity is done within the context of one of the most important races in recent memory, certainly more important than the competition to reach the moon in the 1960s. During the 1990s, particularly in the second half of the decade, billions of dollars were pumped into research aimed at mapping the human genome and individual genes, a race that is being waged by private companies and the governments of the Western world.

Without getting too technical, I'll provide the crude basics of what one needs to know about genetic research to understand the following discussion. First, dioxyribonucleic acid, or *DNA,* is the blueprint of all living creatures, and its double-helix structure is a long chain that links together molecules whose arrangement determines the essential information for life. It is the arrangement of the molecular sequence that scientists are trying to decode in their race to map the human genome. A *genome* is comprised of all the DNA contained in an organism. *Genes* are DNA chains made up of hundreds or thousands of molecules. Genes also contain information for proteins, which are molecules crucial to the production of hormones and enzymes, among other things.[20] There are roughly 6 billion different human genomes on the planet (one for each living individual), but because there are marked similarities common to all of those in the human species, the concept of "the" human genome refers to the "average" genome, the "average" person.

On June 26, 2000, the two rival forces (a governmental organization, the National Human Genome Project, and a private company, Celera) that have been working to map the human genome jointly announced that they both had completed a map of the human genome.[21] While it is understood that no one can patent the entirety of the human genome, or the code of life, the race to identify and patent individual genes for future use in drug products is only intensifying. "The race at this point is not for the DNA," stated Steven Holtzman, chief business officer of Millennium Pharmaceuticals. "That race is over. The race is in assigning to genes and to variations in genes a role in disease initiation and progression and drug response."[22]

The point of the research on the human genome was to create a "generic" map, one that represents, crudely, every living person on the planet.

But research on genetic variations found in individuals, indigenous groups, disease-prone populations and ethnically distinct communities is moving ahead full speed because of the commercial potential that exists in these populations.[23] The value of such data is demonstrated by the fact that Iceland—a country with a relatively unmixed, valuable gene pool—sold its genetic heritage to the genomics company deCODE, which in turn sold that information for $200 million to the Swiss company Hoffman LaRoche.

Dale Pfost, President and CEO of Orchid, stated: "The next three years are perhaps most crucial in the genetics revolution. Orchid will capture the high ground, finding medically important associations that create a whole new range of intellectual property rights." Pfost continued, "The genetic diversity market is now over $1 billion and will continue to increase through the natural outpouring of information from all the sequencing efforts around the world."[24]

Funded by the U.S. National Institutes of Health (NIH), the National Human Genome Project (NHGP) began in the early 1990s as an effort to produce a full map of the human genome by the end of 2005.[25] The NHGP joined forces with international organizations that, unlike private companies engaged in this practice, also want this scientific information to remain in the public domain.[26] Dr. J. Craig Venter—whose gene sequencing methods helped change the terms of gene science in the late 1980s—was once involved in the NHGP, but he broke away from it, building on what had already been mapped by the government's project to do private research that was funded by the Perkin-Elmer Corporation.[27] Tony White, CEO of Perkin-Elmer, very candidly stated:

> We are not a philanthropic organization, we have a revenue model for this. We are sure people will want to buy the information. . . . We will of course have first access to the data and be able to evaluate it. If necessary we will patent 100 to 300 of the very significant genes, but we do not know yet. We will license those genes. We do not want to hold them hostage. We want to contract people for research.[28]

It should be pointed out, of course, that the definitions of licensing and hostage-taking *are* quite similar in that both usually require a sum of money in exchange for the release of a thing or person.

Genetic Patenting and Medical Monopolies
In early 2000 U.S. President Bill Clinton and British Prime Minister Tony Blair made a joint announcement that caused the stock of companies heavily invested in gene patenting to plummet. In discussing the human

genome, they claimed that the map of the human genome should be the common property of humanity and should not be patented. The public read this statement as "gene research should not be patented." Far from being a call for a radical reevaluation of the patent system, rather, these two heads of state were discussing the raw DNA sequence as mapped by the public National Human Genome Project. Data on the DNA sequence are not patentable in the first place. The next day in a released statement, Clinton and Blair made explicit that they support the patenting of individual genes.[29]

The isolation and patenting of genes that may be associated with disease is of extreme importance to biotech and pharmaceutical companies, and the rate at which the number of genes being patented continues to explode. An illustration of the medical importance of gene patenting is the case of the U.S.-based Myriad Genetics, which successfully patented the genes BRCA1 and BRCA2.[30] These genes are significant because 85% of women who have a mutated version of the BRCA1 gene are predisposed to developing breast cancer. From this gene patent, Myriad developed a diagnostic test that costs approximately $1,000, giving a monopoly over tests and potential cures derived from this gene.[31] Moreover, any treatment based on research of the BRCA1 and BRCA2 genes that might be developed in the future must be licensed from Myriad Genetics or it cannot be legally distributed.

The private company Human Genome Sciences (HGS) received sharp criticism from some when it applied for a patent on a bacterium that causes meningitis, though, of course, that criticism did not cause the application to be pulled.[32] This company also acquired a large number of patents on genes, including genes that are connected to arthritis and to bone degradation diseases such as osteoporosis, as well as genes that play a role in regulating the immune system.[33] By early 1999, HGS announced in a press release that it had "discovered 95% of all human genes, sequenced 9,000 out of more than 12,000 novel secreted proteins, filed patents on 3,000 of them describing potential medical uses, and taken three new drugs to clinical trials."[34] In total, by early 2000, Human Genome Sciences had filed for patents on 6,700 human genes.[35]

One of HGS's most important patent holdings—a gene called CCR5, which is thought to give the AIDS virus a key to enter human cells—is quite controversial because the company had already owned the patent on the gene, but it was other researchers who later demonstrated the virus's connection to the gene.[36] CEO and Chairman of Human Genome Sciences, William A. Haseltine, bragged, "We believe that these patents affirm our leadership in converting our early lead in the isolations and characterization of a virtually complete set of human genes to proprietary product opportunities."[37]

Calydon has a number of patents related to the treatment of cancer, and many of these treatments are directly linked to research done on genes the company patented.[38] Similarly, in 1999 UroCor was issued a patent, and a notice for an allowance of another, for processes derived from genes that relate to the treatment of prostate cancer.[39] The Mayo Foundation for Medical Education and Research has patented a number of applications derived from gene related discoveries that are connected to a variety of ailments, from infections that AIDS patients are afflicted with to Lyme disease and asthma.[40]

Biocyte, a U.S. company, secured a patent on the cells from a human infant umbilical cord, cells that have been found to be important in marrow transplants, making it both a valuable commercial asset and beneficial to humankind. What makes the issuance of this patent particularly disturbing is the fact that it awarded ownership of *all* cells contained in the umbilical cord, a patent so broad it gives the company the right to license and/or deny permission for *any* applied research on those blood cells. Even though Biocyte merely deep-froze the umbilical cord sample and made no change to the blood itself, it still possesses commercial control over this area of the human body.[41] Another quite broad patent was issued to the U.S. firm Systemix, giving the company ownership of all bone marrow stem cells even though, as was the case with the Biocyte patent, the company did not alter the stem cells in any way whatsoever. The medical affairs vice chairman of the Leukemia Society of America, Dr. Peter Quesenberry, quipped, "Where do you draw the line? Can you patent a hand?"[42]

The list goes on. Genentech, a U.S. biotech company, patented the gene that regulates the hormone relaxin, something that is found in every pregnant woman (its action softens the cervix and helps reshape the birth canal).[43] The biotech company Progenitor and Vanderbilt University, in a collaboration that is typical of the current university-industrial complex, jointly filed for a patent in 1998 on the c18 gene, which could be used to flag heart problems before they arise. Similarly, Onyx Pharmaceuticals was granted a patent on the p53 tumor suppressor gene, which is linked to a certain form of viral cancer, and Cellmark patented the gene that is directly connected with the genetic disease cystic fibrosis.[44]

The London-based BTG, a buyer of intellectual property, holds a number of patents that give it control over a gene that produces the protein

Factor IX (as well as the protein itself), which is deficient in people who suffer from the blood disease hemophilia B. The company earns an annual 100 million British pounds by licensing its patent.[45] In 1998, Hyseq filed for patents that cover over 63,500 gene discoveries, one of the more audacious, though increasingly not unusual, attempts to gobble up what is left of the genetic commons.[46]

As of mid-2000, roughly 1,000 patents on human genes or gene fragments had been issued by the PTO and hundreds of thousands of applications were still pending. Incyte is by far the industry leader, with nearly 400 patents issued. Close behind is Human Genome Sciences (with about 100), and a variety of other companies and universities.[47] These companies have been involved in the widespread practice of applying for patents on genes for which the function is not entirely known. These patent applications are based simply on a reasonable guess about where the useful or remunerative genes lie in certain chromosomes. If these genes happen to be related to common inherited genetic diseases, this will create a large revenue stream for the companies by ensuring a monopoly over, and licensing revenues from, the research on those genes.[48] Rebecca S. Eisenberg, a law professor at the University of Michigan, stated, "You have people who haven't contributed to subsequent discovery being able to lay claim to these discoveries."[49]

The codes for the enzymes and hormones that regulate our bodies are being churned out of Venter's and other private companies' sequencing machines, allowing for them to sort through the important genetic information and patent it, giving them control of the practical applications of those genes.[50] For scientists to gain access to, for instance, Human Genome Sciences' database, they must sign a contract that assigns the patent rights on any genes that are discovered to HGS.[51] By law, other researchers will be allowed to work with the patented genetic material in "pure" research, but intellectual property owners will be able to dictate the terms of any applied research, such as clinical trials.[52]

Another rival company that makes money from licensing the contents of its genetic databases is Incyte, but Venter's company, Celera, is likely to dominate the field because of its claims to having the most complete database. The Vice President for biochemical sciences at Immunex said of Celera's database, "It's a more complete effort right now than what's available in the public domain."[53] Celera's proprietary gene sequence data was, the firm freely admits, combined with gene coding from the public database, a database that helped speed up the company's mapping of the genome.[54] Despite the fact that Celera jointly announced with the public

National Human Genome Project the mapping of the genome, Celera announced it would not release its sequence publicly until the company's subscribers had the chance to view it and search for patentable genes.[55]

Jeffrey Kahn, director of the University of Minnesota's Center for Bioethics, cautions that high licensing fees could hold medical progress hostage.[56] Dr. Gareth Evans, a consultant in medical genetics, claims that patents make research more secretive and restrictive and therefore lessens the chances of scientists finding cures.[57] NIH-affiliated University of Michigan law professor Rebecca Eisenberg states: "It's a really big problem if you have to sign lots of agreements. They might have inconsistent provisions. . . . licenses and material transfer agreements with companies are taking longer to negotiate, so it may take weeks or months to get a reagent or material, which would hold up the research."[58] Also, if researchers know that a person or company already holds the patent to a particular gene and will therefore reap the benefits of any research done on that gene, it most definitely can dissuade a nonowner from doing the research altogether.[59]

Haemochromatosis is a hereditary condition that can cause liver or heart failure. The gene is found in 1 in 10 people; nonetheless, in 1999 the patent for the gene was under dispute between two companies. The confusion over who owns the patent and to whom medical laboratories should pay licensing fees, essentially shut down research on DNA tests that can screen for the condition, with five labs halting testing for haemochromoatosis and 21 others deciding not to offer the test at all.[60] In addition, in the early to mid-1990s, British drug company Wellcome was prevented from marketing an improved version of a drug called tissue plasminogen activator (TPA), which is used to treat heart attacks, because the improved drug was derived from research on a gene patented by Genentech. This occurred despite the fact that Wellcome had independently isolated the gene and, further, vastly improved the product.[61]

As I mentioned earlier, Cellmark patented a gene that is thought to cause cystic fibrosis, and the firm has attempted to collect royalties from at least two institutes that developed diagnostic tests that identify the cystic fibrosis gene in people—even though, again, these tests were developed independently.[62] And if there is any doubt that these companies aren't out to gain a monopolistic control over medical research, one can heed the remark of Human Genome Sciences CEO William A. Haseltine, who explicitly stated: "Any company that wants to be in the business of using genes, proteins or antibodies as drugs has a very high probability of running afoul of our patents. From a commercial point of view, they are severely constrained—and far more than they realize."[63]

Resisting Gene Patenting

Just as was the case with the patenting of biological materials derived from plant matter, the wholesale patenting of human genes has met with opposition. The battle being waged at the beginning of the twenty-first century will decide which genes will be sorted out and placed in the public domain, and which will be placed in the hands of private corporations.

The moves made by Dr. Venter's companies and other similar corporations, nonetheless, prompted researchers at the federally funded National Human Genome Project to speed up plans by 2 years to complete the project and to take steps to ensure that a sizable number of genes will remain in the public domain.[64]

When protests are launched against the concept of patenting genes, cells, and organic materials, biotech and pharmaceutical companies counter that the cost of research and development is extremely high and that the only way to provide an incentive for research is through the monopoly that patenting gives. And, in a somewhat surprising move in 1999, 10 of the world's largest drug companies created an alliance with 5 of the leading gene laboratories to map and freely release to the public domain the many slight genetic differences among members of the human race.[65] The companies (including Bayer AG and Bristol-Myers) have specifically stated they are releasing their data into the public domain to ensure that genetic information can be freely accessed and used for research.

The alliance's goal counters the assertion that a public domain of gene resources would lead to commercial suicide and the end of research incentives.[66] These companies planned to spend $45 million on a 2-year plan to uncover 300,000 common genetic variations to "ensure that upstart biotechnology companies don't patent discoveries about important genetic differences and lock out competitors that want to create drugs based on that information."[67] This plan underscores the argument that the private ownership and careful guarding of scientific information hinders, rather than helps, research on medicine and other products. Research may be impeded by companies that patent genes in order to monopolize the drug market, charge other drug companies enormous licensing fees to develop research based on patented genes, or create large databases of genetic diversity with high access fees.[68]

The pharmaceutical company Merck is clearly in a minority with its policy of openly sharing information on the thousands of genes that company researchers have sequenced in its database, the Merck Gene Index. The company believes that allowing a large number of academic researchers the chance to work with the information is a more economical way of generating discoveries than what the company could do when left to its own resources. Merck claims that restricting the circulation of information having to do with structural and descriptive elements of genes does not ensure that the human genome will be maximally exploited for the public good.[69]

It is important to note that these moves did not sprout from a sense of altruism by big companies or a fundamental critique of the patent system. Rather, these moves are a reaction to the fear that the widespread granting of genetic patents would eventually lead to financial disaster for companies that have not acquired enough patents to stay competitive. The consortium mentioned above regularly publishes its research results on the Internet and in other public forums, ensuring that the information cannot be patented. (By law, once information has been released publicly, no patent can be assigned.) Dr. Venter, however, sees these efforts as posing no serious threats to his company. Venter has been unthreatened because the consortium's 2-year plan aimed to uncover only 300,000 common genetic variations, Venter expected by the end of 1999 he would have *several million* variations in his database.[70]

The Private Ownership of the Consumer's Image

In the 1990s, the average American appeared on roughly 100 mailing lists and in at least 50 databases.[71] Many of these databases (such as government databases) are in the public domain and are scoured by businesses to create mailing lists organized and stored in their own proprietary databases.[72] Personal information is collected from telephone books, marriage licenses, home sales records and birth certificates. This is one way companies that sell baby-related products, for instance, can send advertisements directly to parents days after a baby is born.[73] In addition, mail order, credit card and magazine publishing companies often sell their customers' names and information to other businesses.

Reader's Digest created a colossal database that exceeds 100 million names and addresses and is one of the largest consumer databases in the country (most other publications maintain similar lists).[74] By selling to other companies the valuable customer information in their own databases, record clubs and mail order companies often add to their profits. The personal information on product warranty cards is passed onto companies such as National Demographics & Lifestyles, a company that receives 25 million dossiers on individuals and their families a year, and similar companies like Polk has files on 90% of all U.S. households.[75]

Aside from these data collection methods, there are many other ways in which one's personal information is collected. When a consumer receives something without charge but divulges some sort of personal information—for instance, when a person participates in a free health screening—he or she may be placed on a variety of lists.[76] Local, state and federal government agencies also sell information in their own databases for profit and to offset operating costs.[77] But it is the U.S. Post Office that is the largest generator of personal information, selling to direct marketers and other businesses the information contained on the 40 million change of address forms Americans fill out every year.[78]

Some companies have found more surreptitious ways of collecting data on consumers. A commercial version of caller ID can be used in conjunction with computer-matching techniques to pull information together about mail order customers who call to place orders. Moreover, the Microsoft Windows 95 program contained a feature that repeatedly asked the consumer to register the program online rather than fill out a mail-in warranty card. The "Registration Wizard" automatically dials up Microsoft and downloads information on the user's hard drive, including information detailing what software the buyer has on his or her computer. This allows Microsoft to collect information on customers who own its competitor's software, including the names, addresses and lifestyle information pertaining to these particular consumers.[79]

Point-of-sale technology allows for companies to keep track of what customers buy, as well as where and when they buy it.[80] Frequent-shopper cards used by most major grocery store chains are not simply used to build customer loyalty by giving discounts; they are a way of tracking a consumer's purchases in the most precise manner possible.[81] For instance, Safeway has worked in partnership with food manufacturers to find out if a customer who has used a coupon will continue to purchase a product months after they made the purchase.[82] Business reporter Carrie Teegardin[83] enthusiastically wrote: "When the cashier runs the card across the scanner, members get check approval, automatic discounts and credit for coupons they didn't even have to clip. At the same time, a computer records every purchased product and adds it to the member's personal file in a massive database to be used in a marketing effort that Big Brother could only have dreamed about."[84] Grocery store consumption data may be combined with other information to create complex consumer profiles—or "data images."

The advances in computer-related technology facilitate the transfer of massive amounts of information about consumers that can create a comprehensive data image of a consumer.[85] Direct Marketing Association representative Richard Barton stated, "We have the capability to gather, store, analyze, segment and use for commercial (and many other) purposes more data about more people than was ever dreamed of and technology is providing us with even more ingenious ways to reach into the lives of every American."[86] ATM debit cards allow banks an unprecedented ability to track the behavior of their customers and, in conjunction with other databases, they can build layered information for the banks to target certain products to specific markets, something the U.S.'s largest credit card companies do as well.[87]

The information contained in these credit-card databases is proprietary; this allows these companies to sell information to retail outlets such as department stores, which have increasingly purchased the contents of these databases to more effectively target their customers.[88] Three of the largest consumer database operators—Donnelley, Metromail, and Polk—boast they can target specific individuals, right down to their lifestyle, hobbies, or food-consumption patterns. A sampling from their literature demonstrates how consumers are placed in hundreds of different categories—from cat owners, cellular-phone owners and homeowners to golfers, science fiction readers and scuba divers.[89]

The different sources of information used to construct profiles in consumer databases include birth certificates; drivers licenses; voter registration; school records; marriage certificates; ATM and credit cards; health, auto and home insurance; government assistance; telephone, electric, gas and cable companies; airplane and lodging reservations; court and attorney records; newspaper and magazine subscriptions; and real estate purchases.[90] From this abbreviated list, it is clear that it is almost impossible to exist within contemporary Western societies without having information about oneself collected and sold to marketers.

Effects of the Data Image on the Consumer

Individuals, as they are constructed as consumers, are affected in many ways by the collection of their personal characteristics and the subsequent commodification and use of their data image. People's data images become divorced and alienated from them because consumers generally have little control over how their image is constructed by database owners—often, consumers are unaware that this is taking place. The following story demonstrates in concrete terms how our data images affect us in very material ways:

When Rudine Pettus failed to secure the lease on a Los Angeles apartment she began to get suspicious, and inquired of one landlord why she was refused. She discovered that she was listed as "undesirable," and started to investigate how this conclusion had been reached. After considerable delay, she found that a certain "UD Registry" kept a computer file of her details, gleaned from public information such as court reports, combined with credit ratings, obtained from yet other sources. This, whether justified or not, explained her exclusion from that segment of the housing market.[91]

Our data image can come back to haunt us is if a database contains incorrect information which, in essence, distorts our actual self-image. Inaccuracies in our credit record have many negative consequences, from being flooded with pre approved credit-card applications to being prevented from getting an important loan, or worse. Piller[92] stated, "A 1988 survey of 1800 credit reports found that 43 percent contained errors. And a 1991 survey by Consumers Union found errors in 48 percent of reports requested from the Big Three [credit bureaus], including 19 percent with inaccuracies that could cause a denial of credit, such as delinquent debt."[93]

It is not uncommon for a simple mistake to cause undeserving people to be marked as credit risks; this happened to 1,400 residents of the small affluent Vermont town of Norwich, all of whom were "red-flagged" as high credit risks by TRW—a major credit bureau—because of a clerical error.[94] Even more importantly, the data images contained in credit reports are used to mark "undesirables" who come from lower economic backgrounds, ensuring that those people do not receive the same kinds of benefits afforded to wealthier individuals. While this sort of segregation is carried out in a more impersonal and subtle manner than overt, mean-spirited discrimination, it functions in much the same way.

Some of the effects of the data image appear to be not as insidious, though they are nevertheless significant in the way we carry out our daily lives. For instance, the Piggly Wiggly grocery chain discovered that the top 50% of its customer base accounted for 90% of its sales, so it began to consciously focus on directing significant marketing resources to that demographic. When the data on customers in the top tier was analyzed by food department, it allowed the store to create programs aimed at altering the buying habits of customers. The senior vice president and director of marketing and merchandising at Piggly Wiggly stated, "If they are not as good a produce customer, but they are a great customer overall, it gets down to creating incentives for them to buy produce from us."[95] As a result of these programs, the chain's top shoppers (who typically spent over $600 a month) purchased between 5% and 20% more each month than before.[96] These methods are similar to those that businesses use regularly to access information stored in databases—our data images, in effect—to affect our behavior as consumers.

Battles over the Intellectual Property Rights of Databases

At the turn of the century, the status of database contents is in a state of transition and is hotly contested. While this information has certainly been commodified and technology obviously allows for the collection, storage and dissemination of consumer data images, those data have not been granted full protection under copyright law. Database owners have sought to protect the expensive gathering, storage, analysis and marketing of information by fighting to develop a "sweat of the brow" theory of copyright in court battles, a move that was squashed by the 1991 *Feist Publications, Inc. v. Rural Telephone Service* U.S. Supreme Court decision.

In this case, Rural Telephone claimed that the information included in their telephone books was protected under copyright law, but the court rejected that claim, stating, "copyright protects originality not effort."[97] "To be sure, the requisite level of creativity is extremely low; even a slight amount will suffice. . . . The vast majority of works make the grade quite easily, as they possess some creative spark."[98] Justice O'Connor concludes: "There is nothing original in Rural's white pages. The raw data are uncopyrightable facts, and the way in which Rural selected, coordinated, and arranged these facts is not original in any way."[99] This ruling invokes the Enlightenment and Romantic notions of originality and creativity that have been discussed throughout this book.

Because of the absence of legal protection, companies have tried to defend their database contents from appropriation through licensing contracts with their customers.[100] In lieu of this lack of copyright protection, database owners worked hard to push for a *sui generis* property right (a kind of intellectual property right not prescribed by patent, copyright, and trademark laws) to be adopted in Europe and America.[101] In the mid-1990s, these owners succeeded in having their database protection proposal adopted by the European Union (EU). Moreover, during 1996, the Clinton administration and the EU supported the proposal for a very similar type of measure as an amendment to the Berne Copyright Convention, hosted by the World Intellectual Property Organization (WIPO) in Geneva.

The intricacies of that proposed treaty are too complex to detail here, but as an example of the powers this treaty would have granted to database owners, sports leagues would be granted the right to license the publication of sports statistics. Each league—the NFL, NBA, NHL, etc.—employs people to keep an official record of play-by-play statistics on the players and the game itself, which is then disseminated to the press and archived for historical purposes. The leagues' collection of sports statistics would most definitely qualify for protection under the treaty, which requires "substantial investment in the collection, assembly, verification, organization or presentation of the contents" of a database.[102]

This treaty met with opposition, drawing fire from American librarians, scientists and educators. Some Fortune 500 companies opposed it, fearing the treaty would create a barrier around the distribution of information and that this could cut into their profits.[103] This is similar to the situation described earlier in which some biotech and pharmaceutical companies instituted policies that released genetic information into the public domain. In all these cases, however, it is clear that those companies were motivated by the concern that the privatization of information would reduce their profits.

The database treaty met with such strong opposition, in fact, that negotiations on it were effectively dropped by the end of the Geneva conference. The Clinton Administration at first asked for quick approval of the database treaty but reversed its position in an effort to concentrate on pushing the remaining two copyright reformation treaties through.[104] It appears, in the end, that the database treaty failed to be accepted for a number of reasons, including poor wording, opposition by other countries, and—a major factor—the lobbying from very powerful corporations that claimed the measures contained in the treaty would hurt their business.[105] Despite the problems the treaty encountered, the issue has still not been dropped by many database owners, who continue to push for a *sui generis* intellectual property right.

The Private Ownership of the Celebrity's Image

Along with numerous other changes in the nature of fame in the twentieth century, a pivotal transformation in the way the celebrity is constructed was enabled by a new type of property law. The "right of publicity," essentially, has enabled celebrities to privately own and control the use of their image within the marketplace. I do not argue that the celebrity's image was never commodified in previous centuries—it certainly was. But commodification coupled with legal protection has altered fame in ways that have changed the nature of fame dramatically. Today, a celebrity's image generates economic value for industries that produce news, gossip, biographies and interviews that are highly sought after by the media and the public. There is a huge market for the merchandising of celebrity images, and celebrity appearances in advertisements enhance the marketability of the products with which they are associated.[106]

An entertainer makes a significant amount of income from appearing in advertisements and from licensing his or her image for T-shirts, posters, etc.[107] Obviously, this was not always so, something I will illustrate with an example. The Berkeley Pop Culture Project documents that "Mickey [Mouse]'s image is the number one most-reproduced in the world, with over 7,500 items bearing his cheerful little image. Jesus is number two, and Elvis is number three."[108] Disney aggressively guards against the appropriation of Mickey Mouse's image and protects its trademarks in court, as does the Presley estate on behalf of Elvis's image.[109] But no single corporate entity collects royalties from the reproduction of Jesus' image in the same manner Disney and the Presley estate do, even though Jesus' image, like Elvis's, has been commodified in many ways, such as in those mass-produced black velvet paintings.

As much as some televangelists may have desired it, Jesus Christ cannot be trademarked. Without any intellectual property protection for Jesus' image, churches cannot prevent the presentation of artist Andres Serrano's *Piss Christ*—the controversial photograph of a crucifix submerged in a glass of urine—in the same way that Disney can legally enjoin an offensive work of art that appropriates its trademarked characters. Just as it is impossible for churches to trademark the image of Jesus Christ, it is unthinkable that the Bible could be copyrighted. The Church of Scientology—a religion that emerged in the age of intellectual property law—copyrighted its religious writings, and it has filed numerous copyright infringement lawsuits throughout the past few decades to maintain control over the context in which those writings are presented.[110]

In recent years, the Internet has been a place where Scientology dissidents have organized and traded information, and many of the online critiques that have used Scientology's copyrighted and trademarked images have prompted intellectual property lawsuits.[111] For instance, in 1996 a judge ruled in favor of the Church of Scientology when a critic of the church published copyrighted Scientology writings on the Internet as part of an ongoing discussion among church dissidents. Citing the example of a person who wants to engage in a critique of Christian religious beliefs needing Bible text to work from, one defendant's lawyer unsuccessfully argued that the use of the copyrighted documents were necessary to engage with the Church of Scientology's ideas.[112]

The Church of Scientology has won numerous copyright cases against those who critique the church, and its court battles pertaining to the Internet helped set the first precedents concerning copyright and cyberspace.[113] The Internet is an increasingly significant venue for individuals to use celebrity images to help make meanings and build communities among people with common interests. It is also a site where celebrities have intervened to shut down uses of their image of which they do not approve. I will return to the way intellectual property law is used ideologically to manage celebrity images, but first I will give a brief history of the reproduction of celebrity images.

Early Stages of the Commodified Celebrity Image

The mass dissemination and sale of famous people's images are commonplace in capitalist societies, but before the twentieth century there was little to no litigation surrounding what is now considered unauthorized appropriation. Perhaps the earliest examples of the mass production of famous people's likenesses are coins. The likenesses of Roman emperors were common on coins and in sculptures throughout the empire—Caesar, Alexander, Augustus and others took advantage of the publicity value this gave them. For instance, Alexander the Great's image was featured in numerous public objects during his lifetime (sculptures and coins included) and after his death Alexander's image was appropriated by his successors in an attempt to suggest the late emperor's sanction of the current ruler's regime. Augustus took note of Caesar's program of publicity and made his likeness virtually omnipresent throughout the empire, something that later political rulers did as well, especially on coins.[114]

Images of famous people that appeared on various consumer-related items were common in centuries previous to the twentieth, especially in the years following the invention and proliferation of the printing press in the late fifteenth century. Elizabeth Eisenstein documents that sixteenth-century mass-produced portraits of Erasmus and Martin Luther were duplicated frequently. At the same time, she noted, "the drive for fame moved into high gear; the self-portrait acquired a new permanence, a heightened appreciation of individuality accompanied increased standardization, and there was a new deliberate promotion by publishers and print dealers of those authors and artists whose works they hoped to sell."[115]

During this period, the economic status of the artist and engraver was in the process of shifting from control by the patronage system funded by members of the aristocracy to the need for an audience of individual buyers in a marketplace system. Out of economic necessity, the printer now sought to please mass audiences, helping to develop new tastes in hero-worship that no longer solely belonged to people in traditional positions of power.[116]

The sale and distribution of the likenesses of celebrities had become big business by the second half of the eighteenth century in America—especially during and after the American Revolution.[117] For instance, in 1774 businessman Josiah Wedgwood began a line of portrait-medallions called "illustrious moderns" aimed at a more popular, less affluent audience, and by 1779 the medallions outsold the tea services that had been Wedgwood's primary business. His 1779 catalogue included numerous different heads for sale, including classical music composers, popes, monarchs, poets and artists, as well as Ben Franklin and George Washington.[118] In the nineteenth century, Madow writes:

> We can again find manufacturers making widespread use of the names and faces of famous and prominent persons. For example, after John Brown was hanged by the State of Virginia for his role in the raid on Harper's Ferry, entrepreneurs marketed lithographs, prints, busts, and photographs of him. During Sarah Bernhardt's 1880 American tour, manufacturers and merchants "cashed in with Sarah Bernhardt perfume, candy, cigars, and eyeglasses." Two years later, when Oscar Wilde visited the United States on a much-publicized and controversial lecture tour, advertisers put his image on trade cards for such products as Marie Fontaine's Moth and Freckle Cure.[119]

To use another comparative example, it would have been inconceivable for Martin Luther (the religious zealot who nailed his "Theses" to Wittenberg's church door back in 1517) to regulate the reproduction of his image in the same way that the estate of black leader Martin Luther *King Jr.* regulates his. Phillip Jones, president of the firm that manages the King estate and searches for possible infringements, stated: "King may belong to the public spiritually, but King's family is entitled to control the use of his image and words."[120]

The image of Ben Franklin, who promoted himself throughout Europe after the American Revolution, quickly appeared on fans, perfume bottles, and over a hundred other items of fashion. By the time Franklin was an old man, "his own face was displayed all over Europe in the shape of engravings, busts, statues, paintings, and even little statuettes and painted fans that looked like souvenir keepsakes."[121] Although Franklin could capitalize on his high visibility, he could not directly profit from the sale of his image on a perfume bottle in the same way that Elizabeth Taylor (who flatly acknowledged "I am my own commodity") does today with her line of perfumes.[122]

Nevertheless, Franklin's face *certainly was* a commodity that was exchanged in the marketplace, but without the extensive juridification of this sphere of cultural production it could not be privately owned and controlled by a single entity. It was perceived, instead, as being in the public domain. At this time, and even up until the early twentieth century, there was no conceptual framework to even conceive of one's own image as private property. The merchandising and commodification of the celebrity image continued through the twentieth century with little public outcry and virtually no litigation.[123] Harris writes:

> During previous centuries fads and manias had often swept large masses of people, caught up in enthusiasm for a cause, a hero, or a work of art. Actors, generals, opera singers, politicians, artists, ballerinas, novels, all had demonstrated a capacity to influence daily fashions, social customs, or habits of consumption. From Jenny Lind to Georges du Maurier's Trilbymania, from Louis Kossuth to Lillian Russell, celebrities stood at the center of temporary epidemics. Hats, dolls, canes, bicycles, theaters, toys, dinnerware, furniture, cigars, liquors bore the likenesses, names, or special symbols of various personalities. . . . Yet all this stimulated little litigation. Some unspoken assumption made famous people and literary characters a species of common property whose commodity exploitation required little control.[124]

It was during the last 2 decades of the nineteenth century that the assumption that the celebrity's image is common property was challenged in the courts and criticized in legal journal editorials. Around this time were the first reported lawsuits initiated by well-known people who were disturbed by the fact that their likenesses had been used in commercial products without their approval. Although it was increasingly considered wrong to appropriate these images, the courts were undecided and confused as to what legal right, if any, could protect a celebrity's image. Some courts believed that the use of a celebrity's likeness constituted an invasion of privacy, and some rejected that argument, while other courts couched these ideas in different legal concepts.[125]

A 1907 ruling on the unauthorized use of Thomas Edison's image on a medicine label framed the issue in terms of "property," and it represents what is likely the first such judicial recognition of a person's image. The court stated, "If a man's name be his own property, as no less an authority than the United States Supreme Court says it is, it is difficult to understand why the peculiar cast of one's features is not also one's property, and why its pecuniary value, if it has one, does not belong to its owner, rather than to the person seeking to make an unauthorized use of it."[126]

The Emergence of Celebrity Image Ownership

In the early twentieth century, protection from the commercial appropriation of one's image was far from a universally protected right, but contracts began to emerge that attempted to exclude others from freely appropriating a celebrity's likeness. Perhaps because the movie star emerged from a highly visual medium, it is logical that this was one of the first realms of fame that recognized the commercial value of the image. Contracts enabled movie studios to use a star's name, voice and likeness to promote the film, and more underhandedly, it allowed for the use of a star's image to be licensed for product endorsements, even in the most questionable and tangential circumstances.

Movie studios could use a star's image as it related to a particular film, and could license that image to businesses that produced greeting cards, toys and a myriad of other kinds of products in exchange for a royalty payment to the star image's owner, the studio. In fact, studios vehemently policed the unauthorized use of their property by outside businesses. By the 1940s a few stars who had the power to negotiate with the studios succeeded in contractually limiting the use of their image only to areas directly related to the promotion of a film, but these cases were extremely rare. Even Betty Davis's contract enabled a producer to use her image without any connection to the movies in which she appeared.[127]

At the height of her fame in the 1930s, Shirley Temple was able to secure merchandising arrangements that were disconnected from the studio she worked for in order to personally profit from the sale and distribution of her image.[128] Another exceptional early case was Roy Rogers—a pioneer in the licensing and merchandising of one's own image. His 1940 contract allowed him to create his own separate business completely independent of the production house that employed him. This laid the foundation for a merchandising empire in which Rogers appeared in advertisements endorsing Wheaties cereal and began promoting such items as electric ranges and dog food. Rogers licensed thousands of products—from records and comics to cowboy hats and harmonicas—that reaped millions of dollars in revenues during, and after, his lifetime.[129]

In 1953, the U.S. Court of Appeals for the Second Circuit handed down an opinion that defined a type of legal protection—the "right of publicity"—that celebrities could invoke in the face of unauthorized commercial appropriation. This court ruled on *Haelan Laboratories, Inc. v.*

Topps Chewing Gum, Inc., a breach-of-contract case involving two competing baseball card manufacturers that both printed a card with the same player's photograph. Haelan Laboratories argued that the right to privacy did not prevent their company from using that baseball player's image, regardless of any exclusive contract the player signed with another company.

The court's opinion stated that "a man has a right in the publicity value of his photograph, i.e., the right to grant the exclusive privilege of publishing his picture, and that such a grant may validly be made 'in gross,' i.e., without an accompanying transfer of a business or of anything else."[130] The court suggested "right of publicity," which grants "a person the exclusive right to control the commercial value and exploitation of his name, picture, likeness, or personality, and to prevent others from exploiting that value without permission, or from unfairly appropriating that value for their commercial benefit."[131]

The "right of publicity" has been enthusiastically embraced by the legal community; over half the U.S. states recognize the right of publicity, and that recognition has expanded to foreign jurisdictions as well.[132] Numerous court cases since the 1953 *Haelan Laboratories, Inc. v. Topps Chewing Gum, Inc.* decision have expanded what is considered to be legally protected—far beyond one's likeness. For instance, in the 1950s a U.S. appeals court ruled in a suit brought by Ed Sullivan that the name "Ed" could not be adjoined to "Sullivan" when the likelihood of confusion might occur.[133] The "right of publicity" case law has developed to include not just one's name but other characteristics unique to a particular person such as certain traits, characteristics, mannerisms or paraphernalia.[134] For instance, in 1996, basketball star Dennis Rodman sued the manufacturer of a long-sleeved T-shirt that bore replicas of his tattoos as they appear on his own body.[135]

There are many areas that fall under the domain of "right of publicity." Coombe writes, "It is no longer limited to the name or likeness of the individual, but now extends to a person's nickname, signature, physical pose, characterizations, singing style, vocal characteristics, body parts, frequently used phrases, car, performance style, and mannerisms and gestures, provided that these are distinctive and publicly identified with the person claiming the right."[136] For instance, Johnny Carson successfully sued a company that appropriated the famous opening phrase used to introduce Carson—"Here's Johnny"—in conjunction with the promotion of its portable toilets. In this case the court held that "Carson's identity may be exploited even if his name or his picture is not used."[137]

As far back as 1974, the U.S. Court of Appeals for the Ninth Circuit deemed actionable the use of a well-known race car driver's car in a cigarette advertisement. It was successfully argued that the use of the car was intended to associate that driver with the product—even though the driver was unseen.[138] More recently, in the *Vanna White v. Samsung Electronics America, Inc.* case, the U.S. Court of Appeals for the Ninth Circuit expanded publicity protection even further to include any commercial appropriation of the distinctive features of a celebrity. In that case, a Samsung commercial featured a robot wearing a blonde wig, jewelry, and an evening gown that stood in front of a display board that resembled the set of the game show—*Wheel of Fortune*—that featured Ms. White. The court decided that the commercial infringed on White's right of publicity, even though the commercial clearly employed parody.[139]

"Right of publicity" has expanded to protect a singer's voice from *imitation*. Previous to 1988, courts had rejected the notion that vocal style could be protected under a right of publicity theory, but today there are two significant precedents that have expanded that right.[140] In 1988, pop star Bette Midler brought suit against Ford Motor company and its advertising agency for the deliberate imitation of a Midler song by another singer for a television commercial. In *Midler v. Ford Motor Co.*, the California court held that "Midler had a legitimate claim under the common law right of publicity."[141]

This is quite different from the outcome of an earlier, similar case in which Nancy Sinatra's biggest hit, "These Boots Are Made for Walkin'," was performed by a female vocalist who was directed to imitate Sinatra in a Goodyear Tire commercial that also featured four women dressed in 1960s "mod" fashions (i.e., short skirts and high boots). In *Sinatra v. Goodyear Tire & Rubber Co.*, the U.S. Court of Appeals for the Ninth Circuit decided that "imitation alone does not give rise to a cause of action."[142] But when Midler's lawyers couched their arguments in terms of "property," she won.

After the Midler decision, Tom Waits successfully sued Frito-Lay for using a singer who imitated his raspy style for a radio commercial. The Ninth Circuit reaffirmed the Midler decision and awarded $2 million in punitive damages to the plaintiff. Stamets points out that this decision "represents a dramatic expansion of the publicity right defined in Midler. In the Midler case, Ford's advertising agency admitted trying to imitate Midler in a version of a song she made a hit. . . . Unlike Ford, however, Frito-Lay's sound-alike was given an original tune to sing, a tune never associated with the plaintiff."[143]

The Right of Publicity and Celebrity Image Management

Elvis Presley is a quintessential American celebrity who means many things to many people, and the history of the struggles over the use of his image is representative of the way a celebrity's image is managed today. Even though Elvis is no longer alive, his image remains tightly controlled by his estate, which went so far as trademarking "Elvis," "Elvis Presley," "Elvis in Concert" and "Graceland," among other things. Not only has the King's epitaph been copyrighted, but so has the inscription on Grandma Minnie Mae Presley's tombstone.[144] Since it was founded in 1979, Elvis Presley Enterprises (EPE) has filed hundreds of lawsuits pertaining to the unauthorized use of Elvis's image in a variety of contexts.

Recently, in 1998, a U.S. Circuit Court of Appeals barred a tavern from using the name "The Velvet Elvis." The establishment's owner argued that it parodied 1960s kitch, more generally, but the court rejected the argument, stating: "Without the necessity to use Elvis's name [to target the 1960s], parody does not weigh against a likelihood of confusion in relating to EPE's marks. It is simply irrelevant."[145] Despite this and many other successes, EPE has not been universally successful in court (it hasn't been able to stop Elvis impersonators). Nevertheless, it has won numerous court battles—enough to create the perception that, for Elvis's image to be used in any sort of commercially oriented artistic product, permission must be granted by EPE and the image must be licensed.[146]

To give a few examples, the 1980s television sitcom *Cheers* sought the permission of EPE for a planned episode in which a character had a dream about Elvis, and EPE made sure both the actor who portrayed Elvis and the script met with its approval. Similarly, before the ghost of Elvis was used in the movie *True Romance*, producers sought the permission of EPE. Elvis Presley Enterprises so emphatically protects the use of the King's image that it seriously considered suing the company that distributed the book *Elvis Alive?*, which came with an audiocassette that supposedly contained a conversation with the deceased Elvis Presley. As ludicrous as this sounds, because EPE owns Elvis's "performance rights," EPE lawyers felt justified in claiming that if this truly was a recording from *beyond the grave*, its reproduction infringed on the estate's proprietary rights. The idea was dropped after the book sold poorly.[147]

In addition, the threats contained in EPE's intimidating letters, combined with EPE's financial muscle, convinced the producers of a play, *Miracle at Graceland*, which was being staged at a small community arts center, to drop the word "Graceland" from the title and remove all images of Elvis from the set. While EPE's charges might not have held up in court, as is the case with many intellectual property lawsuits (or threats of suits), the producers complied because they lacked the resources to sustain a court battle.[148] As "right of publicity" has expanded to allow celebrities (and their families) more power to control the use of their images, it has at the same time affected the way everyday people appropriate celebrity images to generate meanings within their own lives and communities.

Celebrities and Audiences

Madow argues that, in their everyday lives, people "make active and creative use of celebrity images to construct themselves and their social relations, to identify themselves as individuals and as members of subcultural groups, and to express and communicate their sense of themselves and their particular experience of the world."[149] One of many examples of this use of celebrity images is Dyer's analysis of how 1950s urban gay culture reinterpreted the image of Judy Garland as a symbolic icon whose ambiguous masculine/feminine coding provided a way for gay men to engage in a dialogue about themselves and others.[150]

Because mass-media audiences are not lifeless sponges, it is no surprise that people draw on these images and texts to actively make sense of their own lives and the world that surrounds them. But "right of publicity" law centralizes the celebrity's decision-making power in determining what he or she "means" to an audience by allowing that celebrity the ability to decide what parts of his or her image to magnify, what parts to distort, and what parts to delete. This contemporary legal climate makes it more difficult for an audience to actively engage with star texts, let alone to produce and distribute alternative readings that generate effective, resistive cultural practices.

Before I examine the way the management of celebrity images affects the celebrity-fan relationship, I want to discuss the line of thinking that asserts audiences are not passive consumers who soak in media images without thinking. De Certeau,[151] Silverstone,[152] Jenkins,[153] and Fiske[154] argue that people actively "read" media texts using celebrity images, among other things, to actively create shared meanings within communities of fans.

De Certeau, who focuses on book-reading rather than other media, reminds us that we must not take people for fools. He attacks the perception that book-reading audiences are passive "sheep" who are content to graze in the pastures of a field they did not participate in creating. He finds this notion unacceptable, taking the stance that, far from being passive, reading is a productive act that is as creative as that of the novelist.

De Certeau positions the reader as a nomad who occupies and wanders into different territories, "poaching" meanings that are perhaps unintended by the author and the elite class who "police" preferred meanings through a variety of social mechanisms.[155]

Silverstone, in his fondness for militaristic metaphors, takes de Certeau's arguments as a call to arms. He claims that what is considered mundane, daily life is a kind of guerrilla war that is waged by the subjugated against oppressors in the field of everyday life, and he sees a revolutionary potential in the seemingly trivial practices of watching television. Rather than being a passive activity, television viewing, according to Silverstone, is the site of an enormous amount of cultural work on the part of both the producers and the receivers. He notes studies that demonstrate how television watchers integrate its texts within their own lives in a variety of ways, and he argues that even though the cultural power of institutions is deeply imbedded in the texts and the writer-reader relationship is unequal, there is still room for movement and some freedom.[156]

Similarly, Fiske argues that fans are extremely creative and active. He points out that the notion of a productive audience does not necessarily provide the basis for a movement that can change society; he conceptualizes resistance, instead, as producing a form of consciousness. Fiske argues that just in the act of listening to or watching a mass-media venue, fans are engaged in constant symbolic meaning formation. Audiences also talk about music or television shows with others, creating shared and constantly metamorphosizing communal meanings. Finally, fans engage in productive behavior when they create fanzines, videos, songs and other cultural products that are shared within their community.[157]

In one case, a fan video incorporated Jimmy Buffet's song "Leaving the Straight Life Behind" as the narrative that held together carefully selected clips of television cops Starsky and Hutch, edited to portray them humorously in a homoerotic relationship. The clips include images of the officers playing chess in their bathrobes, disco dancing together, embracing each other and jumping into bed together. Jenkins suggests that the activities of fans should be viewed as "poaching" rather than mindless consumption, and maintains that fandom is "a vehicle for marginalized subcultural groups (women, the young, gays, etc.) to pry open space for their cultural concerns within dominant representations."[158]

By generating alternate readings of mass-culture materials, Jenkins claims, these groups can transform the products of the media to serve their interests. His empirical study focuses on the participatory fan (re)writings of *Star Trek* storylines by largely female fans, which were written in a way that recognized and validated the authors' (and their audience's) experiences. He argues that resistance comes not from the original media texts themselves, but from the *practice* of writing new texts, distributing the fanzines and community building. Jenkins concludes:

> Nobody regards these fan activities as a magical cure for the social ills of postindustrial capitalism. They are no substitution for meaningful change, but they can be used effectively to build popular support for such changes, to challenge the power of the culture industry to construct the common sense of a mass society, and to restore a much-needed excitement to the struggle against subordination.[159]

The positions of de Certeau, Silverstone, Fiske and Jenkins are, to a certain extent, polemical—a reaction against Frankfurt School theorists such as Adorno who saw the products of mass culture as nothing but oppressive. Even if their arguments may be exaggerated, they were a necessary tactical move away from the deeply ingrained notion that everything is determined, that there is no opening that allows for social transformation. The above-mentioned authors were attempting to give agency back to social actors who had been stripped of it by critics of mass culture. But, as is often the case, polemics do not translate well into empirical research, and some of the more extreme claims made by the authors do not hold water.

I believe that in choosing to study the specific practice of *Star Trek* fanzine writing, Jenkins paints a much more optimistic picture of this type of cultural activity than actually exists because, as he acknowledges, Paramount (*Star Trek*'s copyright owner) tended to treat these unauthorized materials with "benign neglect" if they were nonprofit and relatively low profile. Most corporate owners of mass-distributed and highly profitable cultural texts *do not* react with "benign neglect" over the distribution of materials that use their privately owned property without permission.

There are many areas of mass culture (Disney and Lucasfilm are only the tip of the iceberg) in which this kind of fan activity is made very difficult and financially hazardous for the producers of texts who incorporate copyrighted and trademarked images. Because a large portion of the same type of cultural activity that fans engage in has moved from the medium of reproduced photocopies quietly mailed through the U.S. Postal Service (in the form of zines) to the very public forum of the Internet, this difficulty has intensified. The products of the fanzine-trading community were more difficult to detect by intellectual property-holding companies when they were distributed through the mail, simply because this community was more underground and difficult to keep track of.

While photocopied, hand-stapled fanzines certainly still exist, now much of the same kind of fan production has shifted to the Internet in the form of web sites, something that is easy to monitor with a simple keyword query on an Internet search engine (I will discuss this further in chapter 7). Again, I agree with the above-mentioned authors that receivers of media texts are productive and that people use these texts in meaningful ways. But it is difficult to use these texts to build support for social change and, in Jenkins' words, to "challenge the power of the culture industry" when owners religiously use intellectual property law to suppress the uses of texts that challenge dominant ideologies.[160]

The Ideological Management of Celebrity Images

When a T-shirt manufacturer began selling shirts that appropriated images of Mr. Rogers juxtaposed with the captions "Pervert" and "Serial Killer," Rogers sued the company, invoking "right of publicity" and trademark infringement. In addition, Rogers sued another company that allegedly sold a T-shirt of Rogers holding a gun. His lawyers stated, "It is antithetical to Rogers' and FCI's philosophy, image and business practice to be associated with the corrupted depiction of Rogers shown in defendant's shirt."[161] Similarly, Muhammad Ali successfully sued under "right of publicity" when *Playgirl* magazine published a drawing, subtitled "the greatest," of a nude black man seated in the corner of a boxing ring.[162]

Yet another case that highlights the way "right of publicity" is invoked in an ideological manner is the following. When the New York state legislature held hearings on a bill that would make the right of publicity something that can be passed on to one's descendents, John Wayne's children cited a greeting card sold primarily in gay bookstores that featured a picture of the late actor with the caption, "It's such a bitch being butch." While they objected to the card on the grounds that it siphoned off money that should go to the estate, more importantly, they saw the card as "tasteless" and believed it worked against their father's conservative image.[163]

John Wayne carries a lot of semiotic baggage; he is for many people the archetype of the ultimate American tough guy, representing a certain ideal of masculinity. But against this "preferred reading" can exist a resistive reading, such as what is embodied in the greeting card (which was considered so subversive by his family that they took their exception to it to the halls of New York state legislature). This resistive reading recodes popular conceptions of masculinity and heterosexuality in a way that many might find offensive, and is obviously something that Wayne Enterprises wanted to silence.[164]

The success of celebrity icons depends, in part, on their reworking of previous celebrity images and other resonanting signifiers. For instance, Coombe rhetorically asks how much Elvis Costello owes to Buddy Holly, or Prince to Jimi Hendrix. Madonna reconfigured many twentieth-century sex goddesses and ice queens, including (but not limited to) Marilyn Monroe, Jean Harlow, Greta Garbo and Marlene Dietrich.[165] But, Coombe argues:

> If the Madonna image appropriates the likenesses of earlier screen goddesses, religious symbolism, feminist rhetoric, and sadomasochistic fantasy to speak to sexual aspirations and anxieties in the 1980s and 1990s, then the value of her image derives as much, perhaps, from the collective cultural heritage on which she draws as from her individual efforts. But if we grant Madonna exclusive property rights in her image, we simultaneously make it difficult for others to appropriate those same resources for new ends, and we freeze the Madonna constellation itself. Future artists, writers and performers will be unable to creatively draw upon the cultural and historical significance of the Madonna montage without seeking the consent of the celebrity, her estate, her descendants or her assignees, who may well deny such consent or demand exorbitant royalties.[166]

"Right of publicity" law has opened up another area of culture to privatization, allowing for celebrities and their lawyers to police representations they do not approve. As cultural production and creative activity takes place more and more in the sphere of the marketplace, it becomes increasingly difficult to argue that the appropriation of celebrity images falls under "fair use," particularly because, like trademark law, it contains no developed "fair use" statute or exception. Moreover, "right of publicity" law is more ambiguous and inconsistent than trademark law, and it has even more potential to silence a number of different expressions having to do with celebrity images. When certain types of cultural production are engaged within the marketplace, the owners of privatized cultural texts—in this case, celebrities—have greater power to (if not win court cases) exert enough financial muscle to wipe out appropriations that are not to their liking.

Conclusion

The three primary examples of the private ownership of people in this chapter—via gene patenting, proprietary consumer databases, and "right of publicity law"—are extremely different. In each case, there are varied

articulations of labor relations, battles between large corporations, notions of authorship, and government policy, among other things. As we
have seen, the consequences of privatization vary quite a bit throughout
the above-mentioned contexts, and this illustrates that the privatization
of culture is not a highly determined, ahistorical process that generates
uniform actions.

One advantage of using articulation theory is that it allows us to make
connections across disparate areas of cultural production, such as the
ones discussed in this book. Perhaps most importantly, these connections all are articulated differently with intellectual property law because
there are conflicting operating notions of *what* is being authored, *how* it
is authored and *who* is doing the authoring. These distinct concepts,
which have arisen out of situated historical circumstances, have helped
construct who has control of the means of production, and control of the
means of production has worked to enforce a definition of authorship in
each particular area. Database owners most certainly define themselves
as authors because they own the software and hardware that can orga-
nize information relating to consumer behavior. To many, this fact makes
ascribing authorship and ownership of these data images to a corporation that has invested lots of money an obvious choice.

But, from another perspective, it was the labor of the consumers (i.e.,
in their trips to the shopping mall) that enabled the information to exist in
the first place. When individuals work 40 or more hours a week to be able
to consume the things they want or need, they also work as laborers for
the corporations that collect data on their purchasing behavior, data that
is in turn used to try to persuade them as consumers to buy more. The
companies merely trace and map the data trails that consumers leave,
organizing that information in particular ways that allow for the useful
and profitable manipulation of that data.

Consumers *don't* control the means of production of their data image,
nor are they considered the authors of their data image. Moreover, very
little legislation has been passed to empower American consumers in any
way, and for them certainly nothing like "right of publicity" law exists that
would allow consumers the right to similarly control their own electronically stored consumer profiles within the marketplace. The privacy laws
that do exist protect individuals from a variety of invasions of privacy, but
they do little to prohibit the collection of personal information—nor are
they intended to. Large corporations not only recognize the economic
power that access to consumer data images gives; they have successfully
secured their control of the means of production over the construction of

consumer data images, though they have yet to secure a type of intellectual property protection.

Because the methods of organization used by consumer database companies are not considered to be very inventive, database owners have not won full copyright protection for their property in recent court battles. In the 1991 *Feist Publications, Inc. v. Rural Telephone Service* U.S. Supreme Court decision, the court ruled: "There is nothing original in Rural's white pages. The raw data are uncopyrightable facts, and the way in which Rural selected, coordinated, and arranged these facts is not original in any way."[167] Because they lack originality, according to the court, the companies that own these databases do not qualify for authorship status and, therefore, the materials are not copyrightable. Another important reason for this lack of protection was the lobbying efforts of very powerful companies that would be negatively impacted by tighter database protection.

Just as noncelebrity individuals, as they exist as consumers, are alienated from the data image that they labored to produce, individuals are also deprived of the control of their own flesh as it is used by medical and scientific researchers. The case of John Moore—the man whose spleen provided the basis for a medicine that has generated over $3 billion in revenues—is instructive. As was discussed earlier, the California Supreme Court decided that John Moore had no right to claim any proprietary rights over his own body. Other exploited non-Western, noncelebrity people enjoy even fewer rights than a U.S. citizen like Moore because of Eurocentric intellectual property laws that perpetuate colonialist relations between the First and Third Worlds.

The precedent established by the successful patenting of plant and human genes has ensured that biological material is considered a legally protectable form of intellectual property. Because the notion of private property is hegemonic, groups who hold economic power have more control in defining *who* is considered an author, and, therefore, an owner. This particular definition of authorship and ownership has been employed by the U.S. court system and the Patent and Trademark Office, and that definition has increasingly shaped the content of the international trade treaties forced on foreign countries. Owning the means of production of scientific knowledge establishes author rights for companies that can afford the technology that isolates and analyzes genes. This provides a rather clear-cut example of how the balance of power is further shifted in favor of wealthy individuals, rich companies and the more powerful Western economies, all at the expense of powerless individuals and countries with few economic resources.

The battle between studios and film stars was first and foremost a labor struggle, one that actors won, in part, because of the leverage their relative economic privilege gave them. After movie stars and other celebrities successfully altered the contracts between themselves and their employers, they lobbied to expand the legal protection of their images from commercial appropriation. "Right of publicity" developed to meet the celebrities' desire to control their own images within the marketplace in order to profit from it, and this law recognizes that celebrities own the means of production of their own image. Elizabeth Taylor acknowledged this to a certain extent when, in discussing the marketing of her own line of "Liz Taylor" perfume, she asserted, "I am my own commodity."[168]

The celebrity can be seen as the singular author of his or her image, but, as Dyer argues, the celebrity image is constructed from multiple discourses originating from a variety of sources.[169] In *Heavenly Bodies*, Dyer traces the intersections of ways of talking about a celebrity persona, and he reminds us that film stars' images are not simply created directly by them or by the films in which they appear. The star's image is also created from texts relating to the promotion of the films (press photos, pin-ups, public appearances), as well as interviews, biographies, and the press coverage of a star's "private" life. The star's image is also comprised of what critics and commentators write or say about him or her in the media, as well as the way a star's image is used in "advertisements, novels, pop songs, and finally the way the star can become part of the coinage of everyday speech."[170]

In other words, in a critical sense the celebrity is no more the author of his or her image as it is reconstructed within popular culture than is the fan, whose intertextual associations work to construct meaning for an individual and a community. But through the labor battles between actors and studios that occurred in the first half of the twentieth century, and then through numerous lawsuits that created a strong body of case law, celebrities were able to gain control of the means of production of their own image. This form of ownership legitimizes the argument that the celebrity is the sole author of his or her image and, in turn, the establishment of the celebrity's authorship justifies his or her complete control over the valuable cultural product that is his or her image. Personal economic power allowed celebrities to gain control, through a long series of court battles, of the means of production. The same is true of the fields of genetics and consumer data collection.

The economic power of large corporations gave them the power to influence the way TRIPS was written, therefore helping to define authorship in ways that privilege corporate owners. But given the hegemony of the idea of private property in our culture, it is hard to argue against the logic that underpins the notion that database owners, scientists and celebrities should enjoy the fruits of their labor. As the president of the Sequana stated: "Gene discovery is just the first step in a 1,000-mile journey to find a therapy. It's a process that costs us millions and takes years of work. So how much does somebody who gets his arm pricked deserve?"[171] My intention here, more generally, is to complicate this common sense, ideologically charged notion of authorship and ownership by showing how power and access to capital have been key factors in the way various spheres of cultural production have become differently (and similarly) articulated with intellectual property law.

Celebrities, consumers and individuals whose genetic materials have been appropriated are all differently articulated with intellectual property law in a fundamental way. As I have argued in regard to the copyrighting of world music, and with plant and human genetic patenting, intellectual property law only recognizes certain types of authorship. So, for instance, under Western intellectual property laws, indigenous peoples who have their music or their blood "sampled" do not have the right to claim ownership over what they produce (be it their songs or their own genetic material). But those who have the capital to purchase a recording device or piece of scientific equipment—but who merely press the record button or run genetic data analysis programs—are recognized as authors and therefore as owners of these cultural products. Intellectual property law, like any property law, handicaps those who have few material resources and no access to the means of production, and it works to maintain unequal power relations.

Notes

1   Lyon, D. (1994). *The electronic eye: The rise of surveillance society.* Minneapolis: University of Minnesota Press.

2   Salopek, P. (1997, June 22). Gene hunters taking hits the global scramble for genetic cures in the DNA of small ethnic groups has provoked cries of protest—and they are getting louder. *Toronto Star*, p. F8.

3   Riordan, T. (1995, November 27). A recent patent on a Papua New Guinea tribe's cell line prompts outrage and charges of "biopiracy." *New York Times*, p. D2.

4   RAFI. (1997, January/February). The human tissue trade. *RAFI Communique* [Online]. Available: http://www.rafi.org/communique/19971.html

5   Salopek, P. (1997, June 22). Gene hunters taking hits the global scramble for genetic cures in the DNA of small ethnic groups has provoked cries of protest—and they are getting louder. *Toronto Star*, p. F8.

6   de Stefano, P. (1996, December). Genomics 101: The Xs and Ys of legal rights to genetic material. *Intellectual Property Magazine* [Online]. Available: Lexis-Nexis.

7   Lin, M. (1996). Conferring a federal property right in genetic material: Stepping into the future with the genetic privacy act. *American Journal of Law & Medicine, 22,* 109–134.

8   Rigden, P. (1997, June 22). Companies covet genes: Ethics and profits compete in the patenting of human genetic materials. *Alternatives Journal, 3, 23,* 8.

9   de Stefano, P. (1996, December). Genomics 101: The Xs and Ys of legal rights to genetic material. *Intellectual Property Magazine* [Online]. Available: Lexis-Nexis.

10 Rifkin, J. (1998b). *The Biotech century: Harnessing the gene and remaking the world.* New York: Putnam, p. 61.

11 de Stefano, P. (1996, December). Genomics 101: The Xs and Ys of legal rights to genetic material. *Intellectual Property Magazine* [Online]. Available: Lexis-Nexis.

12 Lean, G. & Wilkie, T. (1995, November 19). US slaps patent on tribesman's DNA. *Independent* [Online]. Available: Lexis-Nexis.

13 Hay, K. (1994, July). Patenting of human material postponed: Patent on cell from Guaymi Indian woman withdrawn. *Alternatives, 20, 3,* 11.

14 Bright, C. (1995, January). Who owns indigenous peoples' DNA? *Humanist, 55, 1,* 44.

15 Brown, R. (1994). Secretary Ron Brown to Ambassador Rex Horoi, March 3, 1994. *Rural Advancement Fund International* [Online]. Available: http://www.rafi.org/pp/brtoho.html

16　Rhein, R. (1995, December 4). Canadian group is "mouse that roared" on gene patents. *Biotechnology Newswatch,* 1.

17　RAFI. (1995, May/June). Gene hunters in search of "disease genes" collect human DNA from remote island populations. *RAFI Communique* [Online]. Available: http://www.rafi.org/communique/19953.html

18　Rigden, P. (1997, June 22). Companies covet genes: Ethics and profits compete in the patenting of human genetic materials. *Alternatives Journal, 3, 23,* p. 8.

19　Salopek, P. (1997, June 22). Gene hunters taking hits the global scramble for genetic cures in the DNA of small ethnic groups has provoked cries of protest—and they are getting louder. *Toronto Star,* p. F8.

20　Ben-Ami, L. (1999, March 15). Incomplete DNA sequences patented: Action under new guidelines raises questions, concerns. *New York Law Journal,* S1.

21　Mishra, R. (2000, June 27). The quest to map the human genome ends with a truce. *Boston Globe,* p. C5.

22　Pollack, A. (2000, June 28). Finding gold in scientific pay dirt. *New York Times,* C1.

23　RAFI. (2000, May). Terminator two years late. *RAFI Communiqué* [Online]. Available: http://www.rafi.org

24　RAFI. (2000, January/February). Phase II for human genome research. *RAFI Communiqué,* 3.

25　Johnson, G. (1999b, June 28). Secrets worth the price　　ain Dealer, p. 7B.

26　Government researchers escalate genome research. (1998, September 16). *Medical Industry Today* [Online]. Available: Lexis-Nexis.

27　Irwin, A. (1998, May 14). The gene genie racing to grab a fast billion. *Daily Telegraph,* p. 6; Shapley, D. (1994, June 14). Gene genie—A look at one scientist's potentially revolutionary effect on genetic-related business. *Financial Times,* p. 17.

28　Brown, P. & Walker, M. (1998, May 13). US company plans to patent key gene codes. *Guardian,* p. 3.

29　Sherrid, P. (2000, March 27). Patent woes will keep biotech stocks bouncing. *U.S. News & World Report,* 60.

30　Marshall, E. (1996, May 24). Rifkin's latest target: Genetic testing. *Science, 272,* 1094.

31　Solomon, E. (1996, May 23). Wars of the genes. *The Guardian,* p. 19; Walker, M. (1996, May 22). US groups to stop company patenting "breast cancer" gene. *Guardian,* p. 2.

32　Coghlan, A. (1998, May 16). Biotech companies are gobbling up patents on everything from DNA sequences to altered animals. *New Scientist,* 20.

33   Human gene patents issued to human genome sciences. (1996, April 17). *Medical Industry Today* [Online]. Available: Lexis-Nexis.

34   Over 95% of human genes identified. (1999, March). *Applied Genetics News* [Online]. Available: Lexis-Nexis.

35   RAFI. (2000, January/February). Phase II for human genome research. *RAFI Communique*, 1–16.

36   Denholm, A. (2000, June 27). Battle starts to exploit the commercial potential. *Scotsman*, p. 6.

37   Human Genome Sciences reports twenty-seven U. S. patent issues. (1998, May 18). *PR Newswire* [Online]. Available: Lexis-Nexis.

38   Calydon announces issuance of two patents for technologies that destroy cancer tumors, including prostate cancer. (1999, June 10). *PR Newswire* [Online]. Available: Lexis-Nexis.

39   Prostate cancer genes patented. (1999, May). *Applied Genetics News* [Online]. Available: Lexis-Nexis.

40   Schmickle, S. (1998, July 22). Genetic engineers are getting patents on code of life. *Star Tribune*, p. 1A.

41   Rifkin, J. (1998). *The Biotech century: Harnessing the gene and remaking the world*. New York: Putnam.

42   Ibid., p. 62.

43   Wilkie, T. (1995, March 23). Patent rights "slowing medical progress." *Independent*, p. 4.

44   Onyx gains U.S. patent for viral cancer therapy. (1997, October 15). *Medical Industry Today* [Online]. Available: Lexis-Nexis; Watts, S. (1994, April 27). The genetic gold rush. *Independent*, p. 21.

45   Meek, J. (2000, June 26). The story of life: Who owns the genome? *Guardian*, p. 8.

46   Hyseq's patent filings now cover over 63,500 discoveries. (1998, April 23). *PR Newswire* [Online]. Available: Lexis-Nexis.

47   Pollack, A. (2000, June 28). Is everything for sale? *New York Times*, p. C1.

48   Porter, H. (1999, April 20). The joker. *Guardian*, p. 10.

49   Pollack, A. (2000, June 28). Is everything for sale? *New York Times*, p. C1.

50   Irwin, A. (1998, May 15). Gene scientist races to grab a quick billion. *Gazette*, p. B6.

51   Wilkie, T. (1995, March 23). Patent rights "slowing medical progress." *Independent*, p. 4.

52   Irwin, A. (1998, May 15). Gene scientist races to grab a quick billion. *Gazette,* p. B6.

53   Pollack, A. (2000, June 28). Is everything for sale? *New York Times,* p. C1.

54   Friend, T. (2000, April 7). Investors rejoice in Celera promise. *USA Today,* p. 1B.

55   Saltus, R. (2000, June 27). Decoding of genome. *Boston Globe,* p. A1.

56   Kluger, J. (1999, January 11). Who owns our genes? *Time,* 51.

57   Bower, H. (1997, November 9). Whose genes are they anyway? *Independent,* p. 52.

58   Coghlan, A. (1998, May 16). Biotech companies are gobbling up patents on everything from DNA sequences to altered animals. *New Scientist,* 20.

59   To own the human genome. (1998, May 15). *Washington Post,* p. A26.

60   Cohen, P. (1999, December 25). A liver disorder may have gone unnoticed because of confusion over patents. *New Scientist,* 10.

61   Wilkie, T. (1995, March 23). Patent rights "slowing medical progress." *Independent,* p. 4.

62   Watts, S. (1994, April 27). The genetic gold rush. *Independent,* p. 21.

63   RAFI. (2000, January/February). Phase II for human genome research. *RAFI Communique,* 3.

64   Government researchers escalate genome research. (1998, September 16). *Medical Industry Today* [Online]. Available: Lexis-Nexis.

65   Gillis, J. (1999, April 15). 10 big drug firms launch genetics project. *Milwaukee Journal Sentinel,* p. 13.

66   Gillis, J. (1999, April 15). Drug companies, gene labs to join forces: Collaboration aims to probe genetic differences—without proprietary interests. *Washington Post,* p. E1.

67   Gillis, J. (1999, April 15). 10 big drug firms launch genetics project. *Milwaukee Journal Sentinel,* p. 13; Gillis, J. (1999, April 15). Drug companies, gene labs to join forces: Collaboration aims to probe genetic differences—without proprietary interests. *Washington Post,* p. E1.

68   Gillis, J. (1999, April 15). 10 big drug firms launch genetics project. *Milwaukee Journal Sentinel,* p. 13.

69   Caplan, A. & Merz, J. (1996, April 13). Patenting gene sequences: Not in the best interests of science society. *British Medical Journal, 312,* 926–.

70   Marshall, E. (1997, December 19). "Playing chicken" over gene markers. *Science, 278,* 2046; Gillis, J. (1999, April 15). 10 big drug firms launch genetics project. *Milwaukee Journal Sentinel,* p. 13.

71   Branscomb, A. W. (1994). *Who owns information?: From privacy to public access.* New York: Basic Books.

72   Privacy. (1988, November 7). *Business Week,* p. 49.

73   Ibid.

74   Horovitz, B. (1995, December 19). How to safeguard your privacy: Large corporations know your profile. *USA Today,* p. 4B.

75   Ross, C. (1995, July 10). Take steps to guard financial privacy: Information explosion raising concerns. *Atlanta Journal and Constitution,* p. 5E; Hatch, D. (1994, February). Privacy: How much data do we really need? *Target Marketing,* 35–40; Martin, E. (1996, October 16). Direct mail gets a lot smarter. *Business Journal-Charlotte,* p. A23.

76   Privacy. (1988, November 7). *Business Week,* p. 49.

77   Hillbery, R. (1993, July 30). An invasion of private information. *Minneapolis-St. Paul City Business,* p. A13.

78   Branscomb, A. W. (1994). *Who owns information?: From privacy to public access.* New York: Basic Books.

79   Nader, R. & Love, J. (1995). Ralph Nader on WINDOWS 95 problems. *Consumer Project on Technology* [Online]. Available: http://www.essential.org/listproc/tap-info/0168.html

80   Culnan, M. J. (1991). The lessons of the Lotus MarketPlace: Implications for consumer privacy in the 1990's. *Consumer Project on Technology* [Online]. Available: http://www.cpsr.org/dox/conferences/cfp91/culnan.html

81   Stores strike gold in the data mines. (1998, February 11). *Times* [Online]. Available: Lexis-Nexis.

82   Boyd, M. (1994, November). New directions in supermarkets. *Incentive,* 41–45.

83   Teegardin, C. (1994, July 2). Keeping tabs on shoppers: A&P membership card records each purchase in a database. *Atlanta Journal and Constitution,* p. B1.

84   Ibid.

85   Himelstein, L. (1994, June 6). Attack of the cyber snoopers. *Business Week,* 134.

86   Hatch, D. (1994, February). Privacy: How much data do we really need? *Target Marketing,* 35.

87   Shermach, K. (1999, January). Database tools bring consumers into view. *Card Marketing, 3, 1,* 21–23.

88   Customer management. (1998, August). *Chain Store Age State of the Industry Supplement,* 20–23.

89   *Donnelley Marketing Inc. Consumer Lists*. (1996). Greenwich, CT: Donnelley Marketing; *Metromail Mailing List Catalog*. (1996). Lincoln, NE: Metromail; *Polk TotaList Fall 1996 Rate Card*. (1996). Southfield: Polk.

90   Gandy, O. H. (1996). Coming to terms with the panoptic sort. In D. Lyon & E. Zureik (Eds.), *Computers, surveillance & privacy* (pp. 132–155). Minneapolis: University of Minnesota Press.

91   Lyon, D. (1994). *The electronic eye: The rise of surveillance society*. Minneapolis: University of Minnesota Press, p. 137.

92   Piller, C. (1993, July). Privacy in peril. *MacWorld, 124–130*.

93   Ibid., pp. 125–126.

94   Hatch, D. (1994, February). Privacy: How much data do we really need? *Target Marketing, 35–40*.

95   Yovovich, B. G. (1998, October). Loyalty cards invite companies to usher in database marketing. *Card Marketing* [Online]. Available: Lexis-Nexis.

96   Ibid.

97   Branscomb, A. W. (1994). *Who owns information?: From privacy to public access*. New York: Basic Books, pp. 38–39.

98   Rose, M. (1993). *Authors and owners: The invention of copyright*. Cambridge, MA: Harvard University Press, p. 135.

99   Branscomb, A. W. (1994). *Who owns information?: From privacy to public access*. New York: Basic Books, pp. 38–39.

100 Love, J. (1996). A primer on the proposed WIPO treaty on database extraction right that will be considered in December 1996. *Consumer Project on Technology* [Online]. Available: http://www.essential.org/cpt/ip/cpt-dbcom.html

101 Lash, A. (1996, December 13). U.S. backs off database treaty." *Net* [Online]. Available: http://www.news.com/News/Item/0,4,6188,00.htm

102 Love, J. (1996). Government proposes new regulation of sports statistics and other 'facts'. *Consumer Project on Technology*. [Online] Available: http://www.essential.org/cpt/ip/ wipo-sports.html. [December 20, 1999]

103 Lash, A. (1996, December 13). U.S. backs off database treaty." *Net* [Online]. Available: http://www.news.com/News/Item/0,4,6188,00.htm; Caruso, D. (1996, December 16). Proposed treaty on copyright spurs debate. *New York Times CyberTimes*. [Online] Available: http://search.nytimes.com/web/docsroot/library/cyber/digicom/1216digicom.htm. [December 20, 1996]; Schiesel, S. (1996, December 21). Global agreement reached to widen copyright law. *New York Times CyberTimes* [Online]. Available: http://search.nytimes.com/web/docsroot/library/cyber/week/1221wipo.html.

104   Lash, A. (1996, December 13). U.S. backs off database treaty." *Net* [Online]. Available: http://www.news.com/News/Item/0,4,6188,00.htm; Caruso, D. (1996, December 16). Proposed treaty on copyright spurs debate. *New York Times CyberTimes.* [Online] Available: http://search.nytimes.com/web/ docsroot/library /cyber/digicom/1216digicom.htm

105   Friedman, T. (1996, December). Global copyright treaties slammed by US lobby. *AFP*, p. 5.

106   Madow, M. (1993). Private ownership of public image: Popular culture and publicity rights. *California Law Review, 81*, 125–; Fowles, J. (1992). *Starstruck: Celebrity performers and the American public.* Washington: Smithsonian Institution Press.

107   Madow, M. (1993). Private ownership of public image: Popular culture and publicity rights. *California Law Review, 81*, 125–.

108   Ibid., p. 208.

109   Stern, J. & Stern, M. (1992). *The encyclopedia of pop culture.* New York: HarperPerennial.

110   Mallia, J. (1998, March 4). Inside the Church of Scientology. *Boston Herald*, p. 25.

111   Global struggle over truth and eternal life. (1995, August 20). *South China Morning Post*, p. 4.

112   Copyright law applies to internet; Judge rules Scientologists win U. S. lawsuit. (1996, January 21). *Toronto Star*, p. A13.

113   Church satisfied with copyright judgement. (1996, October 16). *Phoenix Gazette*, p. A5.

114   Braudy, L. (1986). *The frenzy of renown: Fame and its history.* New York: Oxford University Press.

115   Eisenstein, E. L. (1983). *The printing revolution in early modern Europe.* Cambridge: Cambridge University Press, p. 131.

116   Braudy, L. (1986). *The frenzy of renown: Fame and its history.* New York: Oxford University Press.

117   Madow, M. (1993). Private ownership of public image: Popular culture and publicity rights. *California Law Review, 81*, 125–.

118   Braudy, L. (1986). *The frenzy of renown: Fame and its history.* New York: Oxford University Press.

119   Madow, M. (1993). Private ownership of public image: Popular culture and publicity rights. *California Law Review, 81*, 125–, 151–152.

120   Ibid.

121   Braudy, L. (1986). *The frenzy of renown: Fame and its history.* New York: Oxford University Press, p. 377.

122   Wolmuth, R. (1987). Liz Taylor leaps into a vial business with passion. *People Weekly, 28, 14,* 38.

123   Madow, M. (1993). Private ownership of public image: Popular culture and publicity rights. *California Law Review, 81,* 125–.

124   Harris, N. (1985, Summer). Who owns our myths? Heroism and copyright in an age of mass culture. *Social Research,* 241–267, 251.

125   Gaines, J. (1991). *Contested culture: The image, the voice, and the law.* Chapel Hill: University of North Carolina Press; Madow, M. (1993). Private ownership of public image: Popular culture and publicity rights. *California Law Review, 81,* 125–.

126   Madow, M. (1993). Private ownership of public image: Popular culture and publicity rights. *California Law Review, 81,* 125–, 153.

127   Gaines, J. (1991). *Contested culture: The image, the voice, and the law.* Chapel Hill: University of North Carolina Press.

128   Ibid.

129   Phillips, R. W. (1995). *Roy Rogers: A biography, radio history, television career chronicle, discography, filmography, comicography, merchandising and advertising history, collectibles description, bibliography and index.* Jefferson: McFarland & Company, Inc.

130   Hetherington, L. H. (1993). Direct commercial exploitation of identity: A new age for the right of publicity. *Columbia-VLA Journal of Law and the Arts, 17,* 1–49.

131   Right to privacy and publicity. (1996). In *Corpus Juris Secundum (Vol. 77)* (pp. 481–544). St. Paul: West Publishing, pp. 539–540.

132   Ferri, L. M. & Gibbons, R. G. (1999, April). The growing right of publicity. *The Intellectual Property Strategist, 5, 7,* 7.

133   Schwartz, H. (1996). *The culture of the copy: Striking likenesses, unreasonable facsimiles.* New York: Zone Books.

134   Halpern, S. W. (1996). The right to publicity: Maturation of an independent right protecting the associative value of personality. *Hastings Law Journal, 46,* 853–873.

135   Rodman sues manufacturer, distributors over shirts depicting his tattoos. (1996, July 31). *Entertainment Litigation Reporter* [Online]. Available: Lexis-Nexus.

136   Coombe, R. J. (1998). *The cultural life of intellectual properties: Authorship, appropriation, and the law.* Durham, NC: Duke University Press, p. 90.

137 Rahimi, T. J. (1995). The power to control identity: Limiting a celebrity's right to publicity. *Santa Clara Law Review, 35,* 725–753.

138 Halpern, S. W. (1996). The right to publicity: Maturation of an independent right protecting the associative value of personality. *Hastings Law Journal, 46,* 853–873.

139 Giftos, A. C. (1994). The common law right of publicity and commercial appropriation of celebrity identity: A whole new wardrobe for Vanna. *Saint Louis University Law Review, 38,* 983–1008.

140 Stamets, R. A. (1994). Ain't nothin' like the real thing, baby: The right of publicity and the singing voice. *Federal Communications Law Journal, 14,* 347–373.

141 Giftos, A. C. (1994). The common law right of publicity and commercial appropriation of celebrity identity: A whole new wardrobe for Vanna. *Saint Louis University Law Review, 38,* 997.

142 Gaines, J. (1991). *Contested culture: The image, the voice, and the law.* Chapel Hill: University of North Carolina Press, pp. 108–109.

143 Stamets, R. A. (1994). Ain't nothin' like the real thing, baby: The right of publicity and the singing voice. *Federal Communications Law Journal, 14,* 347–373, 349–350.

144 O'Neal, S. (1996). *Elvis Inc.: The fall and rise of the Presley empire.* Rocklin, CA: Prima Publications.

145 Soocher, S. (1998, May). Blue Velvet. *Entertainment Law & Finance, 14, 2,* p. 5.

146 O'Neal, S. (1996). *Elvis Inc.: The fall and rise of the Presley empire.* Rocklin, CA: Prima Publications.

147 Ibid.

148 Ibid.

149 Madow, M. (1993). Private ownership of public image: Popular culture and publicity rights. *California Law Review, 81,* pp. 125–, 143.

150 Dyer, R. (1986). *Heavenly bodies: Film stars and society.* New York: St. Martin's Press.

151 de Certeau, M. (1986). *Heterologies* (B. Massumi, Trans.). Minneapolis: University of Minnesota Press.

152 Silverstone, R. (1989). Let us then return to the murmuring of everyday practices: A note on Michel de Certeau, television and everyday life. *Theory, Culture and Society, 6, 1,* 77–94.

153 Jenkins, H. (1988). Star Trek rerun, reread, rewritten: Fan writing as textual poaching. *Critical Studies in Mass Communication, 5,* 85–107; Jenkins, H. (1992). *Textual poachers: Television fans and participatory culture.* London: Routledge.

154   Fiske, J. (1987). *Television culture.* New York: Routledge; Fiske, J. (1992). The cultural economy of fandom. In L Lewis (Ed.), *The adoring audience: Fan culture and the popular media* (pp. 30–49). London: Constable.

155   de Certeau, M. (1984). *The Practice of Everyday Life.* (S. Rendall, Trans.). Berkeley: University of California Press.

156   Silverstone, R. (1989). Let us then return to the murmuring of everyday practices: A note on Michel de Certeau, television and everyday life. *Theory, Culture and Society, 6, 1,* 77–94.

157   Fiske, J. (1987). *Television culture.* New York: Routledge; Fiske, J. (1992). The cultural economy of fandom. In L Lewis (Ed.), *The adoring audience: Fan culture and the popular media* (pp. 30–49). London: Constable.

158   Jenkins, H. (1988). Star Trek rerun, reread, rewritten: Fan writing as textual poaching. *Critical Studies in Mass Communication, 5,* 85–107, 87.

159   Ibid., p. 104.

160   Ibid.

161   Mr. Rogers seeks beautiful day in court in trademark suits. (1999, February). *Sports & Entertainment Litigation Reporter, 10, 10,* 6.

162   Grossman, M. (1998, April 17). Right of publicity tested on the net. *Broward Daily Business Review,* p. B1.

163   Madow, M. (1993). Private ownership of public image: Popular culture and publicity rights. *California Law Review, 81,* 125–.

164   Ibid.

165   Coombe, R. J. (1998). *The cultural life of intellectual properties: Authorship, appropriation, and the law.* Durham, NC: Duke University Press.

166   Ibid., p. 98.

167   Branscomb, A. W. (1994). *Who owns information?: From privacy to public access.* New York: Basic Books, pp. 38–39.

168   Wolmuth, R. (1987). Liz Taylor leaps into a vial business with passion. *People Weekly, 28, 14,* 38.

169   Dyer, R. (1986). *Heavenly bodies: Film stars and society.* New York: St. Martin's Press.

170   Ibid, p. 3.

171   Salopek, P. (1997, June 22). Gene hunters taking hits the global scramble for genetic cures in the DNA of small ethnic groups has provoked cries of protest—and they are getting louder. *Toronto Star,* p. F8.

Chapter 7

Intertextuality, the Internet and Intellectual Property Law

This book covers an absurdly diverse array of subjects, from celebrities to seeds, with folk music, visual collage and hip-hop thrown in for good measure. It's a safe bet that no other book has discussed Dr. Dre, Mr. Rogers, Martin Luther King Jr., Tom Waits, Elizabeth Taylor, Pablo Picasso, Vanna White, Jesus Christ, Kraft Real Cheese, Mickey Mouse, Andy Warhol and Willie Dixon, as well as Scientology, Sony, Bristol-Myers and Monsanto (it seems the only things missing are *Beverly Hills 90210*, Will Smith, circus clowns and whipped cream). Articulation theory, however, has allowed me to identify and explore the links between these varied areas of cultural production, while at the same time making sense of the ways in which they become integrated into the logic(s) of intellectual property law. Articulation theory lends coherence to my project by demonstrating *how* various areas of cultural production are connected with each other. Without articulation theory to guide my analysis, the variety of examples I give would be, at best, eclectic, and, at worst, unfocused.

Hall discusses religion as an example of articulation in a way that is relatively analogous to how I have been thinking about the connections between intellectual property law and cultural production. He points out that religion has no necessary political connotation, but it continues to be a significant cultural force that has a long history, which predates the contemporary, rational systems of social organization. Across a range of societies, at different points in history, religion has been bound up with various cultures in particular ways, "wired up very directly as the cultural and ideological underpinning of a particular structure of power."[1]

There are what Hall calls "lines of tendential force," which articulate a religious formation to the political, ideological and economic formations within particular societies throughout history.[2] In discussing religion, Hall states:

Its meaning—political and ideological—comes precisely from its position within a formation. It comes with what else it is articulated to. Since those articulations are not inevitable, not necessary, they can potentially be transformed, so that religion can be articulated in more than one way. I insist that, historically, it has been inserted into particular cultures in a particular way over a long period of time, and this constitutes the magnetic lines of tendency which are very difficult to disrupt.[3]

Turning his attention to religion's role across the world, Hall points out that there is an enormous diversity in the way it has been integrated—articulated—into certain popular social movements. He argues that in social formations where religion is very significant, "no political movement in that society can become popular without negotiating the religious terrain. Social movements have to transform it, buy into it, inflect it, develop it, clarify it—but they must engage with it."[4] He uses the case of Rastafarianism, the Jamaican religion that served as the foundation for a very important and popular social movement. As a religion, Rastafarianism is very much the articulation of traditional African forms of worship, the Christian religion the colonists brought, and the contemporary social and political situation within Jamaica in the mid-twentieth century.

To make sense of the Bible, Rastafarians had to invert it, turn the text upside down, and reread it in such a way that they could understand its writings as saying something about them and their social struggle with the colonists who came to their island. In so doing, they reconstituted themselves as new political subjects who could speak in a voice of liberation, and, as Hall states, "they spoke it with a vengeance."[5] This voice was quite new, as Rastafarians did not solely reach back into the past to recover a "pure" cultural identity but also to engage with a variety of cultural resources, learning to speak through reggae music as a form of mass media.

Hall argues: "This is a cultural transformation. It is not something totally new. It is not something which has a straight, unbroken line of continuity from the past. It is transformation through a reorganization of the elements of cultural practice, elements which do not in themselves have any necessary political connotations."[6] Intellectual property law also has no necessary political or ideological connotations, and as it encounters differing areas of cultural life it has potentially differing consequences. But, because intellectual property law is rooted in a particular notion of authorship and ownership that has been carved out within the development of capitalism, it is most often employed to strengthen the hegemony of those who are economically and politically advantaged.

It is no small matter that the notion of articulation began where it did, with Laclau originally theorizing articulation around the question of how two different modes of production coexist, with one eventually subsuming the other.[7] Marx's writings provide an early treatment of the way in which different modes of production come to be articulated, and his essay, "Results of the Immediate Process of Production," addresses the question of how capitalism takes over other more archaic modes of production. Marx engages in a detailed discussion of this process, which he conceives not as an instantaneous event, but, rather, as a multistaged process.[8]

For Marx, there is a shift from an older mode of production to the continued existence of that mode in conjunction with a capitalist mode of production, then to the total subsumption of the older mode when the logic of capitalism completely takes over. He argued that the transition to a new mode of production does not occur instantaneously, an argument that was revisited in the "modes of production" debates that emerged in the late 1960s and 1970s, which further spurred the development of articulation as a theory.

Slack provides an abstract description of what I have tried to emphasize throughout the book when she states: "This is what a cultural study does: map the context. . . . To put it another way, the context is not something out there, within which practices occur or which influence the development of practices. Rather, identities, practices, and effects generally, constitute the very context within which they are practices, identities or effects."[9] The phrase "map the context" is not just simply a fancy, jargonistic piece of cultural studies detritus; it is a useful way of describing the way in which a cultural studies analysis can be engaged. I mapped the connections between numerous historically situated contexts, demonstrating how a body of law that evolved out of Enlightenment and Romantic notions of authorship and ownership—and out of capitalism—works to shape the framework within which certain culturally productive practices are engaged.

This book is *more* than simply an illustration of how intellectual property law strengthens the hegemony of wealthy individuals, powerful corporations and Western countries. I have also used articulation theory in a way that can provide a tool for later analyses that similarly focus on the intersections of two or more areas of cultural life. In essence, I've attempted to recover a way of thinking about articulation that has remained underdeveloped for 20 years and, in addition, I've expanded upon the theoretical and applied possibilities articulation theory holds.

Intertextuality and Cultural Production

Throughout this book, I examined how differing, culturally specific conceptions of what constitutes authorship, ownership and originality negotiate each other, and how power comes into play in those articulations. The concept of intertextuality has provided a useful way of framing the types of sampling, collaging, referencing, voice-merging and other modes of cultural production that have been analyzed. But the value of using intertextuality does not simply lie in its ability to contextualize the widespread and varied forms of appropriation that take place across the different areas of cultural production. As something that has been central to cultural production not just in oral cultures but to contemporary literate cultures as well, the existence of intertextual practices undermines the situated notions of authorship and ownership that lie at the heart of various intellectual property laws.

Intertextuality is a grounding principle of the folk music-making process, and it dominated societies long before the time of Homer (whose *Iliad* and *Odyssey*, it was discussed in chapter 2, were most likely the product of oral, rather than written, methods of transmission). As something that grounds communicative practices across cultures, intertextuality is so powerful that it continued through the development of manuscript and print culture. Intertextuality has survived the entrenchment of print culture, something that is anecdotally indicated by the fact that—in the course of writing chapter 2—I happened across six early country songs that used exactly the same vocal melody. None of these borrowings, which came from what was considered a cultural commons, resulted in copyright lawsuits, but by the second half of the twentieth century this mode of cultural production had run afoul of intellectual property law, which defines these borrowings as, essentially, plagiarism.

The ways in which many of the famous classical music composers borrowed from themselves, each other, and traditional European folksongs trace their direct roots within the folk mode of cultural production. But while many composers appropriated, Handel's extensive borrowings have landed his legacy in hot musicological waters. As has been discussed, many critics have accused him of unoriginality and outright theft, two concepts that make absolutely no sense within cultures that ground their basic modes of cultural production in intertextual practices. During the time Handel lived and wrote his music, there were two competing conceptions of what constitutes authorship—one that places a great amount of importance on individuality and originality, in the modern sense, and one that emphasizes intertextual borrowing practices.

The African-American form of oral folk preaching arose directly out of an oral culture of people (slaves and ex-slaves) who were denied the right to learn how to read and write. Intertextuality—for orators (the preachers) and the audience (the congregation)—was, and remains, a key aspect of African-American religious culture. For instance, two sermons that were heard by Martin Luther King Jr. when he was a child—"The Eagle Stirs Her Nest" and "Dry Bones in the Valley"—date back to the end of slavery and continue to be heard in black churches today.[10]

In the context of oral folk preaching, radical originality and a departure from the way cultural texts are traditionally produced in this community are often looked on with suspicion, and the imitation of particular sermons and preaching styles was a fully accepted method of apprenticeship among the black folk preachers from whom King learned. (As I argued early on, accusations of unoriginality and plagiarism are revealed to be culturally bound concepts, ones that devalue other ways of understanding cultural practice.) King, whose father and grandfather were African-American oral folk preachers, grew up surrounded by these particular intertextual cultural practices, so it comes as no surprise that he applied what he had learned to his graduate school studies, engaging in the "straddling" of cultures that Reagon discussed.[11] The controversy surrounding plagiarism in his dissertation stemmed from the radically different notions of authorship that ground these two articulated areas of cultural production.

Another form of African-American culture, hip-hop music, evolved out of an entirely different context. Whereas Martin Luther King Jr. and others who came from the oral folk preaching tradition referred to the past through the practice of "voice merging," hip-hop artists help recover and renew old recordings by black artists, many of which might have faded from the popular cultural landscape. This intertextual practice of merging one's "voice" with textual elements of the past is not just unique to hip-hop, but exists in other genres of African-American music, such as jazz. This form of quoting is not uncommon in African-American culture and it is central to many other areas of cultural production as well.

Sound-collage artists share some compositional techniques with hip-hop artists, though both forms evolved out of very different traditions. Rather than using primarily musical texts as the basis for building new tracks, contemporary sound collage artists look to the mass media, broadly defined, as the source material for their collages. Negativland wrote: "Appropriation sees media, itself, as a telling source and subject, to be captured, rearranged, even mutilated, and injected back into the barrage by those who are subjected to it. Appropriators claim the right to create with mirrors."[12] Intertextual practices are used by Negativland as a method of actively producing cultural texts and reinserting them back into the system of distribution. This attempt to turn consumption into an act of production has established roots in the avant-garde sound-collage tradition. For instance, the phonograph was reconceived and written about as an instrument of creation rather than reception by Dadaist Kurt Schwitters in the early part of the twentieth century.[13]

Although the Dadaists did not invent the tradition of visual collage discussed in chapter 4, they played an important role in the development of this technique after it was first introduced to the art world by Picasso. Dadaists engaged in the act of creating collages and also theorized it in their many manifestos. This aesthetic was also embraced by artists associated with the Pop Art movement, who, by the mid-twentieth century, were among the first to wholly embrace the products from an increasingly immense mass media and integrate them into their own works. Robert Rauschenberg, Jasper Johns and Andy Warhol, among others, incorporated mass-media imagery into their pieces by cutting and pasting or by painting images taken from advertising, cartoons and newspapers, thus using these texts as a kind of vocabulary through which these artists could interpret their world.

This tradition of appropriating from the mass media continued through Situationism and contemporary Appropriation Art, broadly defined, but it was not until relatively recently that artists began to be the target of copyright infringement lawsuits. These lawsuits are an illustration of the way that a print culture works to close down intertextuality.[14] To this end, Rose states, "Copyright depends on drawing lines between works, on saying where one text ends and another begins."[15] Such restrictions that surround the act of producing culture in all of the areas described above might lead one to be more sympathetic toward a position that argues that people should have the unrestricted right to borrow from whatever sources they wish. But this argument is complicated when the issue of unequal power relations is added to the equation.

When producers exist in different relations to power, "free appropriation" is a problematic concept because this type of borrowing can potentially have a detrimental effect on certain groups of people. Take the example of African-American music, which has provided a wellspring of inspiration for twentieth-century American popular music. There are negative consequences when the music of minority groups is freely appropriated by musicians from more privileged groups and who are supported by powerful record companies. Cultural and musical appropriation can take the form of imitation or mimicry—such as the case with Pat Boone, who sold millions more records than the black artists whose songs he covered in the 1950s, and the same is true today with white pop acts that perform R&B-derived songs.

Discussing the difference between the black artist Joe and the white group the Backstreet Boys, Jive Records executive Dave McPherson states: "Joe sings his ass off. His last album sold more than a million copies. Now compare Joe vocally to the Backstreet Boys, who sold over 30 million records. White artists that do Black music sell a lot of records."[16] Nevertheless, cultures *do* influence other cultures, and it is unrealistic and simpleminded to believe that some members of a culture should never take up the practices and styles of a different culture. On the other hand, the reason this kind of cultural borrowing creates such discomfort within certain parts of the black community, for instance, is because of the very real power differentials and the history of racial exploitation within the music industry and in the United States.

By its very name, copyright requires literacy and a familiarity with print culture, which puts those who have emerged from an oral culture at a distinct disadvantage (in the case of blues artists Willie Dixon, he had to rely on his daughter to transcribe his songs and register copyrights). Similarly, when contesting patent claims that involve uses of plant extracts, communities have to provide *written* evidence of "prior art"—which is an unfair burden for many different oral-based cultures who might be affected by the appropriation of their collectively cultivated knowledge of plants. Similarly, this is true of so-called world music artists.

Artists like Deep Forest and Enigma do not procure entire songs, but they sometimes take recognizable chunks from the traditional music they sample. With their cut-and-paste of found sounds captured with samplers, the mostly dance-oriented artists who sample the music of indigenous peoples from around the world most closely resemble the previously mentioned sound-collage artists, despite obvious differences.

For some cultures, music is extremely important and bound up in daily life, with songs having the power to bring life or death, rain or drought, food or starvation. Therefore, keeping their songs tightly controlled is vital to many people in a particular culture, something that Western intellectual property laws do not recognize as legitimate because these songs generally were not created by a single "original" individual. The same logic operates in the way that Western copyright and patent law, respectively, facilitate the appropriation of both "world music" and the indigenous knowledge of plants because these are considered "common heritage." The tenet of "free appropriation"—despite the fact that it subverts the Lockean notion of personal property that informed copyright law—nevertheless is a Western-based concept that positions the motivations of the individual artist over the needs of a community.

In these contradictions, there is no simple solution that can fairly balance, for instance, the needs of African-American hip-hop producers and the rights of similarly oppressed people in developing countries. By loosening the legislative restrictions on the appropriation of intellectual property, one is potentially creating a more fair system for one marginalized group while putting at a disadvantage another marginalized group. But this is often what happens when cultures encounter and negotiate one another, and sometimes the differences in varying cultural systems simply cannot be resolved in a way that is not problematic for one, or more, cultures.

Intellectual Property Law, the Internet and the Future

Having established throughout this book the fact that intertextuality is a key component of cultural production, I want to begin thinking about how intellectual property law may affect our communicative practices in the future—how it will further attempt to close off intertextuality. In the past quarter-century, the sphere of intellectual property law has expanded to encompass areas of cultural production in ways that previously were inconceivable, and there is no doubt that this sphere will continue to enlarge.

To ground a discussion of the future, I cite the Internet as a model for the way in which much of our communication and information exchange will be based in the coming years. The Internet represents a model for important future sites of communicative activity because, while interpersonal interaction will never come close to disappearing, most long-distance and wide-scale forms of communication and information transfer are taking place increasingly on these sorts of commercially mediated terrains.

I acknowledge that there are fundamental differences between the forms of electronic information transfer prior to the Internet's spread and the ones now in use. Nevertheless, online forms of information transfer were important to the business world before the Internet was used by individuals for more recreational reasons, and today this way of transferring information has become even more important to the economic sector. Although commerce is a central feature of the Internet, it is also a site where a significant amount of cultural activity has shifted, and continues to shift.

In distinguishing between culture and the economy, however, it is important to note how cultural activity and commerce are also bound up together.

In chapter 6 I made the point that much of the fan activities associated with fanzine communities have moved from the relatively underground distribution of photocopied zines to Internet fan sites. This shift is extremely important, because within the more surreptitious distribution system associated with the zine world, it was more difficult for intellectual property owners to police un*authorized* uses. But on the Internet, a simple keyword search can help keep track of the ways in which copyrighted and trademarked goods are incorporated into web sites. I'll now discuss the way in which intellectual property laws have been used to monitor meaning-making and the distribution of cultural texts on the Internet.

World War MP3

MP3 ("Motion Picture Experts Group, audio layer 3") technology digitally compresses sound files in a way that facilitates the relatively quick transferral of songs to one's computer, even over phone lines. This digital music format caught the music industry completely off guard, and by the time the music industry began to pay attention, in 1998, the free distribution of copyrighted songs on the Internet had become extremely commonplace.

To put the extent of the distribution of MP3s in perspective, in 1998, roughly 846 million CDs were sold, but by 1999, at least 17 million MP3 files were downloaded *each day* onto personal computers.[17] Also, by 1999, the term "MP3" had outpaced what had previously been the most used web search term, "sex."[18] Though the music industry, feeling as though its back was to the wall, had as far back as 1997 sued sites for freely distributing copyrighted songs, it began to fight back with a number of lawsuits aimed at various players in this new digital domain.[19]

The MP3 format, and other similar digital compression formats that will surely follow, scare the hell out of the music industry because it holds the potential of wresting control of the means of production from the hands of the companies to the hands of others, including the artists themselves. According to *Rolling Stone*, some have characterized it as "a protest movement against record companies, which many artists hate because they control access to the music market."[20] Ironically, the current situation is the direct result of actions record companies took throughout the 1980s to push the digital compact disc format on the public, a public that was largely happy with the cassettes and LPs that were popular at the time.[21]

Despite millions of dollars spent trying to convince the public of the merits of CD technology, by the mid to late 1980s, the format still had not taken off. This prompted all of the major labels to meet in a quasi-conspiratorial fashion and institute an industrywide record-return policy that essentially forced retailers to stop carrying LPs. Because the vast majority of records released in a given year fail commercially, a liberal return policy has been an industry norm since its beginnings, and because record stores could no longer sell LPs without financial risk (caused by being unable to return them), the sales ratio of LPs to CDs dramatically reversed.

> Costs are now both *higher* for consumers and *lower* for record labels. CD prices have continued to rise to a now unbelievable $16.98 list price (soon to be $17.98!) while manufacturing costs have now dropped to *less* than it costs to manufacture a $9.98 vinyl release. A CD, with its plastic jewel box, printed booklet and tray card now costs a major label about 80 cents each to make (or less) and a small independent label between $1.50 and $2.50. CDs should now cost the consumer *less* than their original prices over a decade ago, not more. But apparently consumers got so used to the idea of paying the higher price (and the labels got used to their higher profit margin) that nobody ever complained. And the musicians? Why, they're still paid royalties to this day that are based on the list price of vinyl. That extra 4 or 5 or 6 bucks goes right into the pockets of the record labels. It is not shared with musicians.[22]

The shift in the sales of CDs had little to do with the demands of consumers. It was orchestrated by the record companies that wanted to increase their profits by having music fans first, purchase music at a higher price per unit, and second, buy new copies of albums they already owned on this new digital format. The irony is that this digital format set the stage for the MP3 controversy that would arise a decade later because, by selling music in a digitized form, it became easy for fans with CD-ROM drives to "rip" (record) music onto their computers and upload music onto the Internet. Jim Guerinot, manager of The Offspring (a group whose music is heavily traded in MP3 form on the Internet), believes that the current situation was clearly prompted by the earlier actions of the industry. He stated: "When [record companies] complain about all the free music that's out there, I say to them, 'Hey, I'm not the one who went out and had sex without a rubber. This is your problem, not mine.'"[23]

The dramatic fights in the late 1990s that centered on the duplication of music are even more fevered than the fights over home taping in the 1980s. With the record companies' control over the music they distribute growing more slippery, digital distribution will continue to be a crucial area of contention in the future. These battles, to a certain extent, are battles over ownership of the means of production, though the music industry has a significant advantage because, through the enforcement of intellectual property laws, record companies have the ability to bring the policing power of the state to bear upon infringers.

Fan and Foe Web Sites

Another area of contention is web sites which, because of the medium, necessarily must reproduce trademarked and copyrighted images in order to comment on, critique or fawn over the subject of their site. Numerous fan sites exist, and many of them haven't run into legal trouble. But those sites that go beyond simply promoting a television show, movie or fictional character by using those privately owned images in ways not approved by the parent company often raise the ire of the property-owning company.[24] Among the first sites to be threatened with copyright and trademark infringement lawsuits were *X-Files* fan sites, whose presence Fox disliked despite the fact that it was word of mouth on the Internet that helped catapult to popularity the fledgling Chris Carter-created sci-fi show.

In one case, Fox lawyers sent a registered letter to 17-year-old Dennis Wilson, warning him that he must remove from his personal homepage all Fox-owned copyrighted and trademarked images (i.e., photos, logos, sound bites) or they "may be forced to take legal action to have them removed."[25] Fearing lawsuit, Wilson removed the copyrighted materials, though, interestingly, one of the aspects of the site the lawyers did not have a problem with was the link to the official Twentieth Century Fox *X-Files* merchandise site. In a weak sign of protest (though perhaps the only one available to this teen), Wilson posted a copy of the letter from Fox lawyers with a graphic that read "Just because you're paranoid doesn't mean Chris Carter isn't out to get you" next to a copyright symbol.[26]

Such heavy-handed tactics are relatively common for Fox and other companies that have been vigilant in policing the use of their copyrighted and trademarked images on the Web. In 1995 and 1996 alone, when the Internet was relatively young, Fox sent out 25 to 35 warning letters to web sites that infringed on everything from its *X-Files* to its *Simpsons* intellectual properties.[27] Another series also created by Chris Carter, *Millennium*, prompted unauthorized, unofficial fan sites to crop up before the show's debut.[28] For example, Fox sent a warning from its lawyers ordering college student Gil Trevizo to take the site down, in part because the studio itself had spent $100,000 on its own *Millennium* site, which it planned to unveil during the first airing of the show.[29]

The student, forced to comply with Fox's demands, stated, "They don't understand an active medium where you have to interact with people as a community, rather than purely as customers."[30] This prompted an e-mail "flame war" against the studio, with one perceptive fan, Lori Bloomer, arguing, "If you look at the official sites, they tell you exactly what they want you to know."[31] She continued, "It is becoming clear that this is not just a matter of either copyright or trademark . . . but that Fox execs want complete and total control over how every facet of their company is portrayed on the Internet."[32] With the numerous site closings, some site operators satirized Fox's actions by playing on instantly recognizable lines from the *X-Files*: "They're shutting us down, Scully" and "Free speech is out there."[33]

As Jenkins[34] has documented, fan communities centering on science-fiction shows are extremely active, with many members having participated in the creation of fanzines. Today, while traditional, paper fanzines still exist, the Web is now the primary locus of this kind of cultural activity, with *Star Trek* sites proliferating on the Internet.[35] The significance of this shift is highlighted by the fact that, when Jenkins first began studying "poaching" in sci-fi fan communities, *Star Trek* intellectual property-holder Paramount (now owned by Viacom) was much less restrictive in the company's control of its property.

But today, Viacom regularly patrols the Internet looking for unauthorized and disapproved uses of its property. It has sent numerous letters to *Star Trek* web-site managers whose pages threaten either the wholesome image of its characters or its online revenues (especially after the company began a subscriber-only "official" *Star Trek* page on the Microsoft Network service).[36] Star Trek sites still do exist, but under the watchful eye of Viacom.

Star Wars property owner Lucasfilm has been well-known for monitoring the contexts under which its trademarks and copyrights appear, and they are extremely careful to maintain its "family" image. While ideological reasons play a large part in Lucasfilm's (and Viacom's) desire to control the context in which its copyrights and trademarks appear, there are also economic motives, particularly with such a lucrative property like *Star Wars*. For instance, the fourth installment of *Star Wars* (*The Phantom Menace*) did not need to sell a single ticket to recoup its $115 million budget because its initial merchandizing licensing agreements brought in revenues far exceeding the film's production costs.[37] Therefore, protecting its property is of the utmost importance if the company is to maximize profits.

Not surprisingly, around the time when the hype machinery surrounding *The Phantom Menace* began, Lucasfilm kept a close eye on *Star Wars* web sites, and the company began to control the contexts in which its copyrighted materials appeared on fan sites.[38] One of the Internet's most prominent *Star Wars* web sites felt the force of Lucasfilm's power when it was coerced into removing copyrighted material pertaining to the upcoming film, with Lucasfilm warning the site not to engage in moves that would prompt "further action that neither of us want."[39] Scott Chitwood, a man who helps run TheForce.net, stated: "Basically, we've had free rein for as long as anyone can remember. . . . Now there's more of a definite line that you can't cross."[40] Jill Alofs—the founder of Total Clearance, a firm that specializes in multimedia and web site clearances—stated:

> An individual fan may create a site and not think that they are doing anything bad, but that is not necessarily the case in the eyes of all entertainment companies. . . . The entertainment companies want to have a sense of control over their properties, and often these Web sites do not fit in with the marketing and imaging that companies want to present.[41]

Of course, fan sites are not the only targets of corporations; even more troublesome is the proliferation of sites that criticize intellectual property-owning companies. Increasingly, companies are using trademark law to silence criticism because trademark law contains no formally defined "fair use" provisions. For instance, in chapter 1, I discussed how Safeway successfully enjoined its union workers from handing out literature that contained the Safeway logo. In trademark law, in which the unauthorized use of a trademark is simply considered theft, free speech is a nonissue, allowing, for instance, computer company Gateway 2000 to have a restraining order served to the home of Jeff Blackmon, a disgruntled former employee who ran an anti-Gateway 2000 homepage.[42]

Freedom of expression® in cyberspace has certainly been curtailed in the wake of the ruling in which the Church of Scientology won an intellectual property infringement case against church dissidents who used its copyrighted and trademarked texts and images to critique Scientology online. Blackmon started his "Gateway 2000 Sucks" page after he quit the company because of the way he was treated as a computer technician. The page initially included "Top Ten Reasons Not to Buy a Gateway 2000 Computer," but after he got a number of hits and e-mails, he expanded the page to include a "Gateway 2000 Sucks Message Board," as well as the confidential e-mail address of Gateway cofounder Ted Wiatt.

Gateway obtained a temporary restraining order against Blackmon, arguing that his use of Gateway's black and white cow pattern logo constituted trademark infringement. Blackmon complied by taking the site down in exchange for Gateway 2000 not pursuing hundreds of thousands of dollars in damages against him, with the 25-year-old stating that he "learned a lot." Blackmon said, "I was just praying that I wouldn't lose my house over all this."[43] In these and many other cases, intellectual property law is clearly used in this area to restrict free speech and maintain the hegemony of corporations' worldview.

Yet another example of trademark rights successfully being used to stamp out criticisms include the case of Michael Lissack, a Wall Street whistle-blower and former managing director of the brokerage firm Smith Barney. The main page of Lissacks's web site (devoted to documenting municipal bond scandals) greeted visitors with a spoof of his former employer's advertising slogan, "Smith Barney making money the old-fashioned way," which was illustrated by the image of a thief picking a man's pocket. Lissack was forced to alter the site's content. After the firm threatened him with a trademark infringement lawsuit, a Smith Barney representative stated: "To adopt our trademark over what he calls the municipal bond scandals is on the face of it a misuse of our property."[44] Corporations can impose their will on others because trademark law does not make room for any conception of culturally rich trademarked signs as being anything *but* property.

Similarly, a former employee of Kmart, Jim Yagmin, began a "Kmart sucks" site in 1995, where the teenager painted an unflattering portrait of his former employer.[45] Yagmin then received a threatening letter from Kmart's lawyers ordering him to: "(1) Remove the icon 'K' and any appearances of 'K' with the likeness of that used by Kmart, including the red Kmart and the blue and gray Kmart sucks. (2) Remove the name Kmart from the 'title' of any page. (3) At the bottom of 'The Eternal Fear' page remove the lines 'Go steal something from Kmart today, and tell em Punk God sent ya'."[46] Kmart spokeswoman Mary Lorencz stated: "We monitor the use of our trademark everywhere, including cyberspace. . . . We've spent a great deal of time and money creating a positive image for it, and it's obviously important to us."[47] Despite the fact that Yagmin replaced the Ks with Xs, the modification was not enough for his nervous Internet service provider, which told him the site would have to be removed completely.

In another example of the way in which intellectual property law is used ideologically, Zack Exley, a University of Massachusetts, Amherst graduate student, registered the unclaimed domain names "gwbush.com," "gwbush.org," and "gbush.org." In 1999, he set up a satirical web site, a sort of "parallel universe" Bush campaign site. The same year the Bush campaign sent Exley a letter threatening to sue him if he continued to use their copyrighted and trademarked images on his site. He promptly removed the images, though the content of the site still remained critical of the Bush campaign. Bush could do nothing about Exley's ownership of those domain names, but Exley's actions pushed the campaign to buy 260 other domain names, including the hilariously paranoid registering of such addresses as "bushsux.com" and "bushblows.com."[48]

While Bush could do nothing about Exley's registering of these domain names, a number of courts have found in favor of trademark-owning companies in "cyber-squatting cases." "Cyber-squatters" are those who have registered domain names that echo the trademarks owned by a company, such as the name "HomoeroticGIJoe.com." By 1999, trademark law had expanded to protect this previously untouched aspect of the Internet.[49] Sally M. Abel, International Trademark Association board of directors member, stated: "Courts as a whole are bending over backward to respect trademark rights. . . . [The courts] appear to have accepted that this is a commercial medium."[50] That is, because the Internet is a site of commercial activity, the concept of trademarks purely as property should win out over the idea that they are important signifiers that can be used to engage in discourse about contemporary life.

In yet another example, the domain name "ringlingbrothers.com" was registered by the animal rights organization People for the Ethical Treatment of Animals (PETA), and the organization linked the name to a web site that was critical of the company Ringling Brothers and Barnum & Bailey Circus. PETA loaded its site (which included a disclaimer that it was not affiliated with the company) with information about a federal investigation into the death of a Ringling Brothers elephant, general mistreatment of animals, and the message, "It's up to you to make a difference. Choose only circuses that do not use animals."[51] Ringling Brothers and Barnum & Bailey Circus then sued PETA for trademark infringement and, in light of the current case law that has built up around trademarks and domain names, the animal rights organization eventually capitulated and handed over the web-site address to the circus. PETA's official position was that it simply could not afford a court battle.[52]

In a unique case, the artist formerly known as Prince (to whom I will refer as the Artist) changed his name in 1993 to a unpronounceable symbol that merged the traditional symbols for the male and female into one ambiguously gender-coded squiggle, which he trademarked. In 1999 he began to sue fan web sites that reprinted his lyrics, reprinted photographs of him, traded digital audio files of rare recordings and, most interestingly, reprinted his trademarked identifying symbol.[53] In his suit filed in 1999, one of the strongest aspects of the Artist's case was the fact that the web sites and fanzines had been using his squiggle trademark without permission.[54]

Alex Hahn, a lawyer that represented one of the defendants, said, "The notion that a person can change his name to a symbol, ask everyone to use that symbol and then sue them for using it is legally absurd."[55] The irony of the Artist suing fan web sites is that, as a musician, he has acquired one of the largest and most devoted fan bases on the Internet, enough so that he was able to sell over 100,000 copies of his expensive four CD *Crystal Ball* box set exclusively online.[56]

The case of the Artist is extremely interesting, more because it exists as a kind of metaphor. The Artist is now referred to as a legally trademarked symbol, and through trademark law he has the power to control many of the contexts in which it appears—in much the same way that corporations can restrict the use of their trademarks. I mention corporations because this is where the metaphor comes into play: today, corporations essentially *are* individuals. First, in their day-to-day activities, people often refer to (or are reminded of) companies as much as they might mention or think about their friends or family, demonstrating how much corporations have been integrated into people's lives.

Second, not only do corporations enjoy all the benefits of their economic power, they also receive many of the legal protections individuals do. In a typical example of the twisted logic of U.S. jurisprudence, the U.S. Supreme Court reinterpreted the Fourteenth Amendment—written to safeguard freed slaves—to protect corporations by defining them as "individuals" in the late nineteenth century. (Howard Zinn documents that, between 1890 and 1910, of the Fourteenth Amendment cases brought before the Supreme Court, 19 of them dealt with black Americans and 288 dealt with corporations.[57])

The current rulings that treat domain names as trademarks have strengthened the cases of, for instance, Mattel (the maker of the Barbie doll line) in its efforts to prevent the use of Barbie-derived addresses such as "badbarbies.com." Mattel stated in the suit, "Defendants have adopted and used the Barbie trademarks with the intent to trade on the enormous goodwill that Mattel has earned in the Barbie products and to extort a payment from Mattel for the transfer of domain names."[58] And in 1999,

Porsche Cars North America, using a new legal strategy, filed an umbrella lawsuit against 138 online addresses that used the Porsche name, or any variation of it (such as "porsch"). By suing the domain names and not the individual registrants, companies can avoid the hassle of physically tracking down the people or groups that use the Internet to maintain their anonymity.

In the Porsche case, Gregory Phillips, a lawyer representing the company, derisively stated: "A guy in Libya, in just five minutes, can register for $70 a site called CokeSucks that is filled with offensive material. . . . It is the functional equivalent of constructing misleading road signs on a highway to divert people. You'll see a Chevron sign but when you turn off the exit, you pull into a Podunk gas station."[59] But even a cursory look at the inflammatory example ("a guy in Libya"?) he gave with "CokeSucks.com" reveals that his argument does not hold water because, rather than acting as a billboard, "CokeSucks.com" is more akin to a handwritten or spray-painted sign made by an activist.

For Porsche, it is clear that the use of "Porsche" in domain names is less about consumer confusion (can you imagine pulling off the road for gas based on a "Chevron Sucks" road sign?) and more about a desire to monopolize the market and control everything that is said about them. Though the case has not yet reached the verdict stage, Porsche's strategy was successful, with roughly half of the 138 sites that incorporate "Porsche" in their address surrendering the domain name to the company. In the wake of this success, Bell Atlantic filed a similar suit, and companies such as Chanel and Nissan are considering this course of action as well.

On November 29, 1999, corporations such as Porsche won a major lobbying victory when the U.S. Congress passed the Anti-Cyber Squatting Consumer Protection Act, which ensures penalties of up to $100,000 for people who use trademarked names in domain names (such as "CokeSucks.com," etc.).[60] In the wake of the passage of this bill, companies have been particularly aggressive in pursuing legal action against those who incorporate their trademarks into domain names. For instance, Ford Motors filed a lawsuit against 95 companies and individuals who violated this law, a law that only conceives of these culturally loaded signifiers as private property and the use of such trademarks as trespassing.[61] At the same time that companies have been able to invoke trademark law to gain control of existing, registered domain names, the number of remaining domain names are being gobbled up, not so much by "cyber-squatters" but by the corporations that can purchase thousands of domain names at an annual fee of $70 apiece.

Perhaps of most importance, the very nature of the way the Internet is structured technologically and economically allows companies to own the manner in which information is transferred within this communicative terrain. The U.S.-based Priceline.com company, a spin-off of Walker Digital, was granted a patent so broad that it protects "not just the virtual nuts and bolts of its electronic commerce system, but also its entire business model for buying and selling goods and services on the Internet."[62] The patent grants a monopoly over both the method and use of "buyer-driven commerce" (for instance, allowing consumers to name their own price in Internet airline ticket auctions), making this patent over an *entire mode of doing business* akin to the EPO soybean patent, now owned by Monsanto, that covers *all future genetically altered soybeans*.[63] Walker Digital applied for 71 patents in 1999, most of which were business-method patents, with the hopes of turning the company into a commercial powerhouse by staking down claims on the fundamentals of communication online.[64]

The patenting of business practices is quickly becoming the norm, and the patents being granted are extremely broad. Another example is U.S. Patent No. 5,960,411, which is the "method and system for placing a purchase order via a communications network."[65] Put more simply, this patent gives Amazon.com, for instance, a monopoly over "one-click" ordering in which a customer can buy an item by pressing a single icon (the customer's stored credit card and shipping information is then automatically accessed). During the 1999 Christmas shopping season, Amazon.com won an injunction against Barnesandnoble.com, which was using a similar system, forcing their rival to add deliberate complication to its ordering process.[66]

Litigation over these kinds of patents spread quickly. Multi-Tech Systems sued three PC makers (Compaq, Dell and Gateway) who supposedly were in violation of their patents on transmitting voice and data. Priceline.com sued a number of different companies (including Microsoft's Expedia.com), another company sued Ebay.com over database technology, and a St. Louis patent broker sued Yahoo over a "method of effecting commerce in a networked computer environment in a computerized form"—in other words, shopping online.

The New York Times Magazine reports that "companies have gotten patents for keeping calendars on the World Wide Web, for downloading Web pages at regular intervals, for storing documents in databases, for 'real-time shopping,' for auctioning cars, for creating profiles of users, for search engines, for payment systems and for variations of *every other* fundamental gear and lever in the theoretical machinery of online business."[67] While absurd patents can be overturned, the cost of challenging a patent averages $1 million, making this a battleground that can only be occupied by large corporations with deep pockets and the best patent lawyers. Even though patenting has been traditionally spun as a law that protects the lone "genius" inventor in the proverbial garage (just as copyright supposedly protects the "genius" author), historically, patent law essentially has protected the monopolies of big companies.[68]

In the past 2 decades, we have seen a dramatic expansion in the scope of what intellectual property law protects, with copyright owners staking their claims on an increasing number of things that once belonged in the cultural commons. Trademark law, which doesn't contain any formally written "fair use" protection, is used by corporate owners to fence off their very recognizable and commonly shared signs (McDonalds®, Barbie®, etc.). Further, patent law has expanded to cover previously unimaginable aspects of our lives: how we communicate (e-commerce patents), what we eat (food patents) and—with human gene patents—*who we are*. Defending the breadth of these types of patents, U.S. Patent and Trademark Office commissioner Todd Dickinson dismissed the terminology that describes patents as allowing for a "government sponsored monopoly." Instead, Dickinson said candidly, cheerfully and without irony, "We like to say right to exploit."[69]

Notes

1   Hall, S. (1996). On postmodernism and articulation: An interview with Stuart Hall. In D. Morley and K. Chen (Eds.), *Stuart Hall: Critical dialogues in cultural studies* (pp. 131–151). New York: Routledge, p. 142.

2   Ibid.

3   Ibid., p. 142.

4   Ibid., p. 143.

5   Ibid.

6   Ibid.

7   Laclau, E. (1971, May/June). Feudalism and capitalism in Latin America. *New Left Review, 67,* 19–38.

8   Marx, K. (1976). Results of the immediate process of production. In *Capital: A critique of political economy* (Vol. 1) (pp. 993–1084). New York: Penguin Books.

9   Ibid., p. 124.

10 Miller, K. D. (1991, June). Martin Luther King, Jr. and the black folk pulpit. *Journal of American History, 78,* 120–123.

11 Reagon, B. J. (1991, June). "Nobody knows the trouble I see"; or, "by and by I'm gonna lay down my heavy load." *Journal of American History, 78, 1,* 111–119.

12 Negativland (1995). Fair use. In R. Sakolsky and F. Wei-Han Ho (Eds.), *Sounding off! Music as subversion/resistance/revolution* (pp. 91–96). Brooklyn: Autonomedia, p. 92.

13 Korn, A. (1995). Renaming that tune: Audio collage, parody and fair use. In Negativland (Ed.), *Fair use: The story of the letter u and the numeral 2* (pp. 221–234). Concord, CA: Seeland.

14 Ong, W. (1982). *Orality and literacy.* New York: Routledge.

15 Rose, M. (1993). *Authors and owners: The invention of copyright.* Cambridge, MA: Harvard University Press.

16 Kenner, R. (1999, September). Black magic. *Vibe,* 184–188.

17 Peraino, V. (1999, August). The Law of Increasing Returns. *Wired,* 144–145.

18 Atwood, B. (1999, May 15). Sorting out myths and facts about MP3. *Billboard,* 71.

19 Sorkin, A. R. (1997, June 16). Internet song use spurs recording industry suits. *New York Times,* p. D6.

20   The big five hit the web. (1999, May 8). *Economist,* 63.

21   Goodell, F. (1999, July 8–22). World War MP3: It's labels vs. artists in the fight for control of the record business. *Rolling Stone, 816/817,* 43–46.

22   Negativland. (1996). Shiny digital plastic and aluminum. *Baffler, 8,* 30.

23   Goodell, F. (1999, July 8–22). World War MP3: It's labels vs. artists in the fight for control of the record business. *Rolling Stone,* 43.

24   Schwadron, T. (1996, December 16). Postcard from cyberspace. *Los Angeles Times,* p. D1.

25   Eldredge, R. L. (1997, April 6). N. C. boy's home page joins "X-Files" ex-sites. *Atlanta Journal and Constitution,* M2.

26   Ibid.

27   Belsie, L. (1996, December 17). Web war: Hollywood tangles with fans' on-line sites. *Christian Science Monitor,* p. 1; Microfile. (1997, August 14). *Guardian,* p. 11.

28   Belsie, L. (1996, December 17). Web war: Hollywood tangles with fans' on-line sites. *Christian Science Monitor,* p. 1.

29   Harmon, A. (1996, November 12). Web wars: Companies get tough on rogues. *Los Angeles Times,* p. 1A.

30   Belsie, L. (1996, December 17). Web war: Hollywood tangles with fans' on-line sites. *Christian Science Monitor,* p. 1.

31   Harmon, A. (1996, November 12). Web wars: Companies get tough on rogues. *Los Angeles Times,* p. 1A.

32   Belsie, L. (1996, December 17). Web war: Hollywood tangles with fans' on-line sites. *Christian Science Monitor,* p. 1.

33   Harmon, A. (1996, November 12). Web wars: Companies get tough on rogues. *Los Angeles Times,* p. 1A.

34   Jenkins, H. (1992). *Textual poachers: Television fans and participatory culture.* London: Routledge.

35   Viacom aims phaser at "trek" web sites. (1997, January 3). *Arizona Republic,* p. E2.

36   Gamboa, G. (1997, February 3). Star Trek owners, citing copyrights, target "the resistance." *Miami Herald,* p. BM16; Kramer, A. (1997, January 3). Netwatch. *Atlanta Journal and Constitution,* p. 35.

37   Fost, D. (1999, May 18). The force of licensing; Galaxy of players cash in on "Star Wars" merchandise. *San Francisco Chronicle,* p. D1.

38   Orwall, B. & Lippman, J. (1999, March 14). "Star Wars" sites could feel darker side of Lucas' force. *Houston Chronicle,* Business, p. 2; Ward, C. (1999, May 12). Mr. Lucas, may the farce be with you. *Times* [Online]. Available: Lexis-Nexis.

39   Orwall, B. & Lippman, J. (1999, March 14). "Star Wars" sites could feel darker side of Lucas' force. *Houston Chronicle,* Business, p. 2.

40   Ibid.

41   Atwood, B. (1997, May 24). Oasis in c'right dispute with fans' web sites. *Billboard,* 3.

42   Harmon, A. (1996, November 12). Web wars: Companies get tough on rogues. *Los Angeles Times,* p. 1A.

43   Jackman, T. (1996, October 8). Computer firm ex-employee takes his anger online. *Kansas City Star,* p. B2.

44   Harmon, A. (1996, November 12). Web wars: Companies get tough on rogues. *Los Angeles Times,* p. 1A.

45   Neuborne, E. (1996, February 28). Vigilantes stir firms' ire with cyber-antics. *USA Today,* p. 1A.

46   Harmon, A. (1996, November 12). Web wars: Companies get tough on rogues. *Los Angeles Times,* p. 1A.

47   Ibid.

48   Anderson, M. (1999, July 1). Bush-whacker, meet Zack Exley: Computer consultant, online satirist, pain in the ass. *Valley Advocate,* pp. 12, 19.

49   Friedman, M. (1999, May 28). Lawyers 1, Domain pirates 0. *Canadian Business,* 74.

50   Richtel, M. (1998, May 28). You can't always judge a domain by its name. *New York Times,* p. G6.

51   Masters, B. A. (1998, April 25). Circus is serious about trademark; Ringling sues animal rights group over Internet. *Washington Post,* p. B4.

52   Richtel, M. (1998, May 28). You can't always judge a domain by its name. *New York Times,* p. G6.

53   Furman, P. (1999, March 3). Artist in princely court battle. *Daily News,* p. 30.

54   "The artist" sues web site run by fans, claims piracy. (1999, March 4). *Wall Street Journal,* p. B5; Newsmakers. (1999, April 19). *Detriot News,* p. A2.

55   Ellin, A. (1999, March 21). They're king-size issues, whatever you call him. *New York Times,* p. C2.

56   Nelson, C. (1999, March 23). Ex-Prince rules net postings must end. *SonicNet* [Online]. Available: http://www.sonicnet.com

57   Zinn, H. (1995). *A people's history of the United States: 1492—present.* New York: HarperPerennial.

58   Feeley, J. (1999, February 5). Suit filed to save Barbie's good name. *Chicago Sun-Times*, Financial, p. 59.

59   Swartz, J. (1999, May 27). Court case could stop cybersquatters. *San Francisco Chronicle*, p. D3.

60   Cyber-piracy bill passes. (1999, December 11). *San Diego Union-Tribune*, Auto, p. 8.

61   Truby, M. (2000, May 30). Automakers fight cyberpirates. *Detroit News*, p. 1.

62   Lewis, P. H. (1998, August 10). Web concern gets patent for its model of business. *New York Times*, p. D1.

63   Ibid.; Tackling home mortages. (1999, July 7). *Financial Times*, 10.

64   Ratliff, E. (2000, May). Patent upending. *Wired*, 208–224.

65   Gleick, J. (2000, March 12). Patently absurd. *New York Times Magazine*, p. 44.

66   Gleick, J. (2000, March 12). Patently absurd. *New York Times Magazine*, pp. 44–49.

67   Gleick, J. (2000, March 12). Patently absurd. *New York Times Magazine*, p. 46.

68   Gleick, J. (2000, March 12). Patently absurd. *New York Times Magazine*, pp. 44–49.

69   Gleick, J. (2000, March 12). Patently absurd. *New York Times Magazine*, p. 46.

Epilogue

During the summer of 1999, when I was in the middle of writing this book, I went on a camping trip with Eric Morgan, Lisa Rudnick and Susan Ericsson—three friends and colleagues. After we loaded up the car with camping supplies and a grocery bag full of Pop-Tarts®, Tostitos®, and Pete's Wicked Ale®, among other things, the four of us set out for the small Western Massachusetts town of Goshen, which contained a camping ground and a large lake that is jokingly referred to as "Goshen's Ocean." For the most part, the camping trip was pretty typical—filled with a mixture of serious conversations and goofy small talk that is typical of academics who like to unwind, kick back, and have a good time. It was also a night peppered with references to media texts, something that was not unusual but that was more noticeable in light of the fact that we were about as far away as we could get from our television sets.

As with most camping excursions, it was necessary to build a campfire and, once we had nurtured a healthy flame, someone began shouting in a staccato manner, "Fire! Fire! Fire!" (a reference to *Beavis and Butthead*, those symbols of moronic irony MTV churned out during the 1990s). Later, as someone emerged from the tent, zipping up its entrance, Eric shouted, "Zip it! Zip it good!"—a reference to the then-current *Spy Who Shagged Me* Austin Powers sequel, which was itself an allusion to the 1980 Devo song, "Whip It." Then, as we cooked dinner and Lisa stuck the fork in the sausages that lay directly in the flame, Susan said that it looked like they had blackened, prompting Eric to launch into a spirited rendition of the 1988 Metallica song "Blackened."

"Blackened is the end!" Eric growled, "Winter it will send/throwing all you see/into obscuriteeeeeee!" Susan and Lisa stood dumbstruck at Eric's unknown-to-us Metallica fandom, their bemusement enhanced by the fact that he and I had taken them aback earlier during a spontaneous a capella rendition of the Beastie Boys' 1986 classic story rap, "Paul Revere." Our repertoire was not limited to metal and rap; we also sang age-old campfire songs in the round, but despite the fact that Susan, Eric and Lisa could hardly be called "media whores" (they collectively watch less television than the average American), our conversations were often laced with media references.

For instance, the next morning, when someone tried to express what a good time we were having in away that seemed hokey, we lampooned the cliché of "good friends and good times" by employing a particular signifier known to us all. After one person began to sing, we all joined in on the opening lines of a Lowenbrau beer commercial that was a staple in America during the 1970s and 1980s: "Here's to good friends, tonight is kind of special . . ."

As the camping trip wound down, somebody suggested that "we should pour some water on the fire," after which Lisa and I looked at each other, knowing exactly what the other was thinking, and launched into the chorus of a so-bad-it's-good song by 1980s hair-metal cheeseballs Def Leppard: "POUR some sugar on me!" After that I shook my head and asked, "Is everything a reference to media on this trip?" Lisa sarcastically shot back, "Isn't it usually?" After cooking a tasty potato-and-sausage breakfast and soaking in the warmth of the small fire, this idyllic early morning scene was shattered by the sight of a Coca-Cola® truck driving through the campground. We knew it was time to go.

Though for some reason that trip was much more packed with allusions to media texts than most nights spent with friends, Lisa's comment highlighted something that only resonated with me in the abstract. Researchers have demonstrated that media texts play an important part of people's lived experiences; they can provide the grist for talk, identity formation and the building and maintaining of communities.[1] That night, we did not act like hapless sponges that soaked in media messages only to turn around and regurgitate what we heard and saw in a mindless manner. For instance, we used the Lowenbrau® commercial as a spontaneous way of subverting the disconcerting feeling that we were living a sentimentalized cliché, a reference that everyone understood as such and which provided a semiotic shorthand that everyone shared.

People don't incorporate media texts into their own lives thoughtlessly; they interact with those texts within communicative situations in ways that illustrate that they are integral parts of our culture. But though these texts are meaningful to us, it doesn't mean we aren't pulled into the commodity system through the way we use them interpersonally on a day-to-day basis. Such references can be fun and funny, and the more knowledge we gain through consumption of these media texts, and the more consumption we engage in more generally, the greater pleasure we get—which isn't to deny the pleasure or the realness of the experience. Nevertheless, while making references simultaneously allows us to connect and make meanings with other people, it also reinforces our existence as consumers.

There we were, in a national forest, away from television, movie theaters and radio, and we still found ourselves referring to those cultural texts. This is a demonstration of the significant role that intertextuality (manifested not just as an allusion to specific texts, but as a cultural practice more generally) plays in our lives. Moreover, this example shows how tied up our communicative experiences are with cultural texts that are privately owned. Susan, Eric, Lisa and I borrowed things—pulling them out of our collective memory—in much the same way that people from oral folk cultures stitched together cultural texts from a commonly shared pool of signifiers in order to make sense of their experiences.

In these small group, face-to-face interactions we can still, and most likely we will continue to, refer to these trademarked and copyrighted songs, commercials and phrases without fear of the "intellectual property police" jumping out of the woods to arrest us in the act of singing an ASCAP-controlled song (like Metallica's "Blackened") around the campfire. And, in these particular social situations, we can continue to make sense of these media texts in ways that may or may not contradict the ideological intentions of the producers.

But as an increasing amount of our communicative practices take place outside of the proverbial campfire circle, we expose ourselves to the watchful eye of intellectual property holders and the enforcement of those laws. We could verbally cut-and-paste trademarked and copyrighted phrases, songs, and commercials at the campground in ways that are ironic, sincere, satirical or critical, but to interact in the same manner with cultural texts on, say, a web site opens one up to potential (and very real) legal problems. Because of the nature of the medium, web sites (and future electronically mediated forms) facilitate communication by using more literal representations—pictures, sound files, etc.—and, further, they exist within a terrain that is clearly defined as commercial and can be therefore easily policed. It is this terrain that we will increasingly have to navigate in the coming years—a land of high fences, information "stupor-highways" and expensive, exclusionary tollbooths.

Note

1   Ang, I. (1985). *Watching Dallas*. London: Methuen; Hobson, D. (1982). *Cross-roads: The drama of a soap opera*. London: Methuen; Hodge, R. & Tripp, D. (1986). *Children and television*. Cambridge: Polity Press, UK; Katz, E. & Liebes, T. (1984). Once upon a time in Dallas. *Intermedia, 12, 3*, pp. 28–32.

INDEX

('n' indicates a note)

Toby Miller
General Editor

Popular Culture and Everyday Life is the new place for critical books in cultural studies. The series stresses multiple theoretical, political, and methodological approaches to commodity culture and lived experience by borrowing from sociological, anthropological, and textual disciplines. Each volume develops a critical understanding of a key topic in the area through a combination of thorough literature review, original research, and a student-reader orientation. The series consists of three types of books: single-authored monographs, readers of existing classic essays, and new companion volumes of papers on central topics. Fields to be covered include: fashion, sport, shopping, therapy, religion, food and drink, youth, music, cultural policy, popular literature, performance, education, queer theory, race, gender, and class.

For additional information about this series or for the submission of manuscripts, please contact:

Toby Miller
Department of Cinema Studies
New York University
721 Broadway, Room 600
New York, New York 10003

To order other books in this series, please contact our Customer Service Department:

(800) 770-LANG (within the U.S.)
(212) 647-7706 (outside the U.S.)
(212) 647-7707 FAX

Or browse online by series:

www.peterlangusa.com